IN ANY EVENT

INSIGHTS INTO MANAGING ANY CORPORATE EVENT

Simon Maier

BLOOMSBURY
LONDON · BERLIN · NEW YORK · SYDNEY

First published in United Kingdom in 2012 by

Bloomsbury Publishing Plc
50 Bedford Square
London
WC1B 3DP
www.bloomsbury.com

A CIP record for this book is available from the British Library.

ISBN: 9-781-4081-6833-2

This book is produced using paper that is made from wood grown in managed, sustainable forests. It is natural, renewable and recyclable. The logging and manufacturing processes conform to the environmental regulations of the country of origin.

Design by Fiona Pike, Pike Design, Winchester
Typeset by Saxon Graphics, Derby
Printed and bound by CPI Group (UK) Ltd, Croydon, CR0 4YY

For Jane

'Speak the speech I pray you as I pronounced it to you, trippingly on the tongue; but if you mouth it as many of your players do, I had as lief the town-crier spoke my lines. Nor do not saw the air too much with your hand thus, but use all gently; for in the very torrent, tempest, and, as I may say, whirlwind of your passion, you must acquire and beget a temperance that may give it smoothness.'

William Shakespeare, *Hamlet* III.ii

CONTENTS

ACKNOWLEDGEMENTS

I have a huge number of people to thank and far too many to mention here. Suffice it to say I'm enormously grateful to all the people in the events industry, junior and senior, friend and foe, who gave so freely of their time. On the whole, each was patient beyond the call of duty. To the people of whom I asked questions from outside the events industry, a very heartfelt thank you for your kindness, help, cake, coffee and occasional alcohol. For all insights I am so grateful. For all the people I've worked with who've added vim and vigour to my work and, hopefully mine to theirs, yet another big thank you. And, of course, this book wouldn't have been remotely possible without the help and encouragement of my wife and my dear cousin who travelled the Atlantic many times to help me in my endeavours (as I did to help him in his but he still owes me $373.67.)

The biggest thanks must go to my sons who constantly remind me of the theatre, of the wonder of stagecraft and the music, magic and sparkle of great performances. When my eldest son, Ben, was small, I took him to see the set-up and rehearsals of a big event I was producing. He stayed for three days and sat with the crew, ate with the crew and, maybe because he was my son, the crew treated him well and explained everything, although I like to think that it was because he was and is an interested, interesting person and one who listens well. He watched things unfold and his face, in turn, was brilliant to watch. Years later he gave me a poem in which he wrote that an event producer is someone who 'winds up a world and sets it in motion' and that any show, before the curtain goes up, was 'full of glittering potential'. On both counts he's perceptive and right.

ABOUT THE AUTHOR

SIMON MAIER has been involved in delivering events for 25 years throughout the world – and for every imaginable purpose. He's been responsible for many corporate, public and televisual events and he's held a number of very senior posts with international events agencies and communication consultancies, including his own. He's now a board director of the TFI Group and is still passionate about great events (large and small) and great communications.

Simon has published a number of books including *The 100: Insights and Lessons from 100 of the Greatest Speakers and Speeches Ever Delivered*, co-authored with Jeremy Kourdi (Marshall Cavendish); *Speak Like a President: How to Inspire and Engage People with Your Words* (A&C Black); *Inspire! Insights and Lessons from 100 of the Greatest Speeches from Film and Theatre* (Marshall Cavendish); *The Diary: 100 Days and Lessons in Corporate Communications* (Marshall Cavendish). Simon is also mid-way through writing a novel – a thriller. He regularly writes articles for management journals, newspapers and magazines and is published around the world. He is an accomplished keynote speaker on event delivery and the future of communications. 'There are very few people I know with more insight than Simon Maier,' says author and TV writer Anthony Horowitz. Many clients for whom he's worked regard him as an event quarterback. Despite that, he can't play American football, but he can be reached on simonmaier@btinternet.com

INTRODUCTION

Way back in the day, as my dear American cousin is fond of saying, I was visiting a British venue with some colleagues. It was a wet day and the reception staff were unhelpful, the hotel's duty manager was unhelpful, the advertising agency account director with whom we were working was unhelpful, his lady friend was sulking and the venue was horrible. The carpets held ghastly secrets and the conference room ceiling held strange stains. As we came out, a lady wearing a beautifully cut suit and brilliant red shoes was addressing a short, fat man with greasy hair, a lip piercing and jeans that showed the world not only his underwear (grey) but also his upper buttocks (pink). The two were arguing about a gala dinner that had taken place the night before. Apparently, everything that could have gone wrong with someone's corporate conference had gone wrong – from the flowers (dead) to the videos (wrong format) to the bedrooms (not enough) to the meals (bad on every count) to the guest speakers (both of whom didn't show up). The conversation escalated into a full-scale and very loud argument where violence was at least threatened if not practised. My colleagues and I (along with a nervous advertising agency account director and his pouty friend) scuttled away and breathed the damp Bradford air. It was then, and this was long ago when I was knee high to a grasshopper (in event years anyway), that I thought that a book on corporate event management and delivery might be useful to someone like me who knew little and wanted to know a lot.

Many years later, when I had written several other books, but not yet this one, I was standing at the back of an auditorium watching the start of a corporate event for a major bank. The opening motivational video, which I'd written and produced, had just finished and people were applauding, some even whistling and cheering. The chief executive appeared on stage as if by magic and began a powerful presentation, which I'd written. His presentation was moving and, at its end, people applauded once more. The lighting, sound, set, staging, venue, accommodation, food and beverage – all planned brilliantly by a brilliant team – worked superbly well and I thought, now I'll write this book. More years later, when I still hadn't written it, but was jotting down some insights on a plane following my involvement in producing an international awards ceremony, a colleague asked about what I was writing and, when I explained my notes to her, she said that I was stupid not to have put them into a book. When I got home I relayed the tale to my wife, Jane, and she agreed that I was indeed stupid. That was last year and here's the book.

I've produced or managed thousands of events around the world and, barring a very few, I've loved being involved with each one. I lecture on event management and delivery. From time to time, I facilitate events. I still produce events and frequently write about them. I've been CEO of some brilliant event businesses and I've met a lot of people who want to deliver great events. I know the ingredients and the very hard work that should go into a perfect event, no matter how small or modest. This book of insights is primarily for people who have a responsibility for delivering the perfect corporate event – mostly within production companies and agencies, but it's also for people on the client side who are faced (and sometimes *suddenly* faced) with managing and delivering a perfect event.

Events, as a word, covers a multitude of occasions where there is a (usually large) gathering of individuals or members of one or several organisations, to discuss or better understand matters of common interest. It's where there's an interaction between the givers of information and receivers (sometimes middle management in the hunt for better and hotter coffee and croissants). An event can involve an audience of ten or ten thousand people, or indeed a television audience of millions. It can be an AGM (Annual General Meeting in case you don't know), an EGM (Extraordinary General Meeting where the delivery lead-time might be two days), a party political conference, a televised occasion, a TV song contest beamed around the world, a business or sales presentation, part of an incentive programme, the opening and closing of a major sporting ceremony, a convention, an association conference, a press or media gathering, a training seminar, a trade exhibition, a motor show, a boat show, an IT show, a product launch, a marketing or management conference, an awards ceremony…the list goes on, but I won't. You get the idea. And each is important. While the result may be fun, the effort and hard work that must go into a great event is a serious and highly skilled business.

The notion of events and meetings for the dissemination of information has been around for a very long time. People get great hope and consolation from events. They receive information. That information is then disseminated and sometimes understood; sometimes misunderstood. Events can be reassuring, comforting or frightening. They can enthuse, enthral or terrify. They can unite people and tear people apart. They can unite a business or tear companies and political parties apart. There is huge power invested in the executives who come up with the idea of holding an event in the first place, as there is in the managers who have the task of delivering the event and the agencies whose job it is to support those managers. With that power should come responsibility but that, as we'll see, isn't always forthcoming. I take (and always have taken) that responsibility very seriously indeed. To be given the opportunity to deliver something excellent, no matter how modest, on any stage anywhere in the world – in a small hotel, in a huge convention centre or in an Olympic park – is an honour and often a privilege. The results of event delivery can be brilliant, fabulous, magical or they can be dull, lifeless, lacklustre and damaging. There are levels in-between, of course, but the point is that we humans like face-to-face contact, whether it's rock, whether it's theatre, whether it's religion, whether it's politics or whether it's corporate. Whether for personal, business, entertainment or political purposes, an event is multifaceted and the abuses that go on in the name of their delivery are legend. Equally, there are and have been some extraordinary and simply wonderful events around the world. And I have indeed been very privileged to have driven the design, management and delivery of some of those. There are some amazing people delivering events and indeed there are some great clients (the folk who want and commission the event in the first place and who pay the bills) regularly taking creative risks and huge leaps of faith.

This book will focus on business events and, while there are some (possibly vague) similarities with occasions like country fêtes, weddings, bar mitzvahs, retirement parties or other family and office gatherings, please forgive me if I don't dwell on them, apart from the occasional vague nod in their direction. It's not that there's anything wrong with those kinds of occasions and their accompanying celebrations, but their delivery would make up another book.

The corporate events industry has changed dramatically since I started out – fervently advising a client's senior executives that their audience could of course see the stage through a conference room pillar, or suggesting that there was nothing wrong with tomato soup for their gala dinner in aid of 700 Middle Eastern tractor and motor traders. I've been in the events and communications industry for a long time and I certainly don't know it all. I don't know many people who *do* know it all. Technology changes, ideas move on, fashion for design alters. Clients are considerably savvier now when it comes to ideas, communications, costs, venues and creativity and that's a very good thing. New technology allows for creative people and producers to present information in charismatic, entertaining and engaging ways. Audience engagement is key, something that true rhetoricians always recognised, but these days something that clients and, yes, agencies often ignore.

There are so many tools and effects at our disposal now that we can make a corporate event much like a West End production if we want although that won't work if we miss out on engaging our audience. But we have fabulous and exciting toys with which to play. For example, lighting techniques have shot ahead in leaps and bounds over the last five years or so. Same with sound and staging ideas. These days (this makes me sound ancient and I assure you that I'm not), there is a vast array and variety of guest speakers from which to choose to populate events. There are brilliant videos and films being produced to use at events and there are devices which aid interaction and engagement which, when used properly, are superb. Indeed, the interaction between the 'stage' and the audience is now multi-faceted and, occasionally, gives one that tingle at the back of the neck – when you hold your breath and exhale with a 'wow'.

However, on both sides of the business fence I'm always amazed at how less than little people know about some of the most obvious aspects of corporate event planning, design and delivery. I'm amazed at how the production companies and communications agencies waste client money. I'm amazed at how client businesses waste their *own* money. I'm amazed at what some clients expect for very little money or at how little agencies deliver sometimes for a lot of money. I'm amazed at how committees will save large amounts of money on one really important thing that will make a huge difference to the event's success and then spend an absolute fortune on another that really doesn't matter at all. I'm amazed at the way client managers want what *they* want in an event's content, but not necessarily what the audience members will need. And I'm amazed that an agency's creative people often want what *they* want and not what the audience needs or wants and then wonder why the event doesn't do the job it was meant to do. I'm amazed at the way that (some) client businesses or event suppliers have little interest in measurement and I'm absolutely gobsmacked that (often very senior) people who make presentations don't rehearse or practice, sometimes at all. Then – suddenly – I'm amazed at the sheer creative verve and vigour when I see (and still get a huge buzz and frisson from watching) a story unfold on a stage.

Of course, events *are* all about storytelling, whether it's the activities of the past versus plans for the future, or the launch of a new product, or an awards ceremony, or the beginning of an international sporting event. Storytelling is paramount in all of these scenarios and many people who should know better are sometimes very bad at it, sometimes extraordinarily good.

It's interesting that the 'good' and 'bad' are evenly split, because people in the events industry round the world have come from a variety of backgrounds and some have transferred and translated brilliantly, some not. It's the kind of industry for which there are no established qualifications despite the growth in Event Management and Media Studies degrees and diplomas, some of which, perhaps most of which, just don't focus at all or much on event production, management or delivery. There are very few in-house training courses at agencies or production companies. Client companies too will have had very little, if any, training provision in event design, management or delivery. So, frequently, clients and suppliers learn on the back of each other. But the thing is this: there *are* experts who understand venues without selling you something that is wrong or you don't need; there *are* experts in set design, staging, lighting, sound, mechanics, choreography, talent management, transport, equipment, food and beverage, facilitators, exhibition design and so on. The key is to find these good people. Normally, we find some bad ones on the way to discovering what good looks like. Unfortunately, there are people in and around the industry who don't advise well or who are full of hot air, there are some who are after the money, and there are some, a precious few, who are really at the top of their game.

Corporate events used to consist of low rent exhibitions, a works outing, or maybe an AGM with accompanying green baize-covered tables – and that's about all. And, truly, not that long ago either. My first career was in lecturing (Shakespeare) and I've always had a passion about acting and a love of the theatre since I was aged about three. I joined the events industry in 1984 and, while I don't have to use a Zimmer frame just yet, much of that industry is still mostly an unregulated discipline and, as event professionals, we can be working 'blind' on many initiatives because they're not part of a legal or ethical code of practice. Certainly there are tighter health and safety dos and don'ts, tighter controls on venue use and better processes for managing teams – but the overall whole is vague.

However, with a tough economic climate and much focus on the true value of conferences, exhibitions and other media, the events industry has become a bit of a battleground. Events companies and agencies vary from the very small (two people in a tiny office in Pimlico) to the large (say, thousands of people spread across every continent worldwide). Some event businesses are part of vast marketing or advertising conglomerates. Others are focused on only a very few clients and consist of a handful of staff, with the owner being a practitioner who still gets his or her hands dirty (not a bad thing by the way). Some event businesses are run by individuals who have become very wealthy on the back of a number of huge successes. Some event businesses are run by decent people; a few are managed by industry experts who really understand corporate communications strategies and the role of events within them. The industry has an opportunity to equip itself now with the knowledge, standards, frameworks and tools to create events that are part of a larger client programme in a way of our own devising. That means understanding much more about the return on investment in communications – specifically events.

It's astonishing how many clients aren't interested in event results, by which I mean what the event achieved. The key to producing an event with a tangible return on investment (ROI) is to share the issues and challenges at the heart of the client business with the event supplier. It's absolutely critical (more than ever when money is tight) to determine how the client wants to, or should, measure success at the outset, and whether the proposed event is the most effective use of budget to convey the business or other messages. Clients need to focus on how the event will resolve a need, a strategic objective, an entertainment plan, a business issue or a crisis. You'd be amazed at how many clients don't know, or don't care. And it's surprising how many agencies haven't a clue either, or think that an exit poll given to delegates when they just want to leave the venue as fast as possible, because the event's been dreadful, is a good thing.

We often see clients getting carried away by the glamorous aspects of an event while the serious, mundane and, sometimes, critical elements take a back seat. The message can (and often does) become lost mid-way through the planning process, which equates to an enjoyable experience in its own right and is, to some, much more satisfying than the end result. Freud would have a field day. In this scenario the event itself shouldn't be blamed, but it's the planning process that needs to be put in the dock.

Many organisations have cut back on their events, exhibitions and incentive programmes and, while that's understandable, it's often for the wrong reasons. It is definitely the case that face-to-face events can have a mercurial power in rewarding (and keeping) staff, changing their minds, reinforcing opinion and informing audiences about new ideas, services, products – not just in times of plenty, but in times of trouble too. But very often (and sadly) the opportunity to change minds, to reinforce opinion and so on, is missed. I wish that agency leaders and client managers would take some note of the great speeches and presentations of history – the rhetoric, the oratory, the power to persuade. Face-to-face communication is powerful and does work. And it doesn't need lashings of wretched PowerPoint. What it does need is a single-minded proposition beautifully and artfully positioned and a story well told.

For the cynical amongst the corporate event attenders, conferences are a good way to rack up some frequent flyer miles, get out of the office, perhaps see a new city and get some free food and drink. Unfortunately, there is a heavy price to pay for this. The cynic may be forced to sit in a darkened auditorium that smells a little of the gala dinner held in it the night before. Then some important people tell our cynic how important he/she is and how important his/her important ideas are. After a few hours of Garamond font size 14 PowerPoint (containing lots of red, pale yellow or purple arrows) and breathless speeches from self-important people who've not prepared properly and who either a) grip the lectern for fear of falling over or b) wander the stage aimlessly in and out of light, our cynic will be sent into a smaller room with squeaky chairs to discuss any important ideas with a few colleagues. This is called a breakout session. Back in another plenary session, our delegate will be obliged to feedback the (important) answers from the breakout session held to be vital 'going forward', and all the flipchart notes will have been gathered in, summarised and completely ignored or lost en route, and if they're not lost en route they'll be lost or binned when they're taken back to someone's office.

By the end of this exercise, the important people will be satisfied that our cynic and various colleagues will have now been fully informed, consulted, rejuvenated, motivated and mobilised. But just to make sure of complete 'engagement', there will be a guest speaker, brought in at vast expense and who makes a long and circuitous case that climbing Everest is just like good management. (This normally serves to show why people who climb high mountains should never be allowed to manage a business.) The audience members at large laugh at the jokes about frostbite on the chap's extremities and accord him due respect although, when shaking his hand afterwards, our cynic is embarrassed to discover that the Everest climber has no fingertips at all and so confusion reigns as to what part of the arm or shoulder should be clutched in a show of comradeship.

There has to be a better way of making use of conferences. In truth, the plenary and syndicate/breakout sessions are often a waste of time because the plenary is all 'stand up and talk' material that (only) the CEO deems important – and he or she doesn't really want to know what the audience members think anyway. The breakout sessions are often there to fill an empty bit of the afternoon and it gives the bosses a chance to have a private meeting.

The real action happens in the unscheduled time. This is when all the delegates mingle around looking and feeling vaguely lost while at the same time desperately trying to exude an air of importance and urgency. Here inebriation sets in and much corporate sucking up is done. There is desperation in the air and most delegates completely miss any opportunity to network properly. They mix mainly with people they already know. In a global conference our cynic will find New York office delegates speaking to folks from Manhattan and Paris office delegates speaking to Parisians. On the plane back home, anything and everything to do with the event is forgotten. The cascade and legacy materials have been mislaid, the memory stick has gone AWOL, but the goody bag is safe. The emails that the cynic will receive as a result of the event will be binned and no blogs or Tweets will be answered. Not all conferences and events are like this but, oh my, many are.

The provision of events is worth billions of any currency around the world to a huge variety of support industries – from hotel chains to sustainability experts – and it's still all growing rapidly, with small events and mega shows, management seminars and worldwide road shows, training events, massive political gatherings, incentive programmes for twenty people and streamed meetings targeting millions of viewers. So that's the focus here – corporate events of all sizes for organisations and their stakeholders, shareholders, suppliers, partners, staff, the media and customers. I absolutely (repeat absolutely) didn't want this book to be a 'how to' and 'how to jolly well not to' tome. It's surprising how many 'how to' books speak of situations that nobody I know of in the events industry has ever come across. The stories that are told and the instances that are given in those books often remind me of one of my favourite children's authors, Enid Blyton, where the sun was always shining and where the picnics comprised of packages of sliced egg sandwiches (on hand cut, home-baked white bread), lashings of ginger beer and home-made lemon drizzle cake. Oh, and bicycles, swarthy villains, nice cousins, nasty cousins and comely aunts with hefty bosoms. I am perfectly aware that my experiences are by and large British but, and it is a very big but, everything I've written about here encompasses my experience of producing and creating events in almost every continent in the world – and working with people in and from all parts of the globe.

I did (and of course do) want this book to entertain as well as to inform. The events business can be on occasion very funny indeed and actually very emotional and moving. But, I was concerned that I could only present my viewpoint and maybe, I thought, that would be a) a bit boring and b) not sufficiently fair or rounded. I've met so many different people on the agency side and the 'other' side that is the client world, and I wanted to bring in some other voices as well as my own. In my mind's eye, as I recollected situations to reinforce each of the points herein contained, I thought of certain people I'd met or with whom I've worked and could hear what they said. I have also made vast quantities of notes over the years and have a pretty good record of verbatim comments. I also interviewed a wide variety of people in the industry and outside it, to get their often professional opinion of certain things on which I held a strong view (for balance) or on which I knew little (for sense). In so doing, most decreed that they didn't want to be quoted, so I thought that perhaps I would usefully ascribe comments, considerations and theories to unnamed third parties. So that's what I've done. The book incorporates a wide selection of real people (and, honestly, they are *all* real as are their transcribed comments), but to whom I've attributed no name.

I've managed large international agencies and been involved in producing some of the world's biggest events and, indeed, many that were much smaller and no less important or successful. I've taken part in seminars, road shows, AGMs, emergency events, sales conferences, management conferences, training programmes, televisual events and some of the world's biggest sporting extravaganzas. It's been a roller coaster ride and it's not finished by any means. I love it. There have been moments of breath-taking excitement, terrible ennui and despair – in fairly equal measure too – and moments of hilarity. I still remember well the time early in my career when, during an AGM, a company chairman went to the washroom and gave vent not only to his bladder, but also to his views on his deputy. His microphone, attached to his tie, was still switched on and his booming voice, along with the sounds of the washroom, could be heard throughout the Albert Hall, London.

So, I leave you to some of the points, thoughts and insights that I think you, as a deliverer of events, might find interesting and might want to remember or to roll around your head and ponder. Some are so blindingly obvious that they will make you squirm or shout out loud in anger (good for you) and others will hopefully make you think. I trust that the thinking will outweigh the squirming or the anger. Others may induce you to sling a shoe at that chap on the other side of the aircraft, not only because of this book, but also because his snoring is really too loud. You may also disagree with many of the points I make and, of course, that's fine. You should. Your experience won't be the same as mine and mine isn't, I'm sure, any better or any more correct than yours. But my points are a collection of concerns and light-bulb moments over which I've considered long and hard while managing events and communications agencies or while in the throes of producing something that can be termed an event. In the course of that process, I've met some amazing people and that, in itself, has been a privilege.

Suffolk, 2012

CHAPTER ONE
COMMUNICATION AND OTHER HEADACHES

COMMUNICATION

Communication: it's a terrible word really because it means everything and, because it means everything a business *should* do, it means nothing. It's a word behind which client businesses hide and it's a word in front of which production companies and agencies pose. A central aspect of any business is communication and ensuring that high levels of contact are maintained is a key concern for any organisation, or it should be. Recently I heard a very senior someone, a so-called captain of industry, who should know better, say, 'Communication is just so easy these days.' Well, of course it isn't. Talking is easy (albeit not always with sense), but communication, an exchange with another party or other parties, requires greater skill. An exchange that is *properly* two-way demands that we listen and speak skilfully, not just talk mindlessly. Similarly with events – they should ensure that after they're done, the participants (or whoever comprises the audience) are better informed, entertained or clearer in their thinking than they were before.

'Events are considered one of the strategic marketing and communication tools by companies of all sizes,' says a writer colleague of mine. He grins partly because he's just been asked to write a communications strategy for a soft drinks company and he likes doing that kind of thing. He's also just told me a story about his traffic experiences the previous day. He was apparently yelling obscenities at a Ferrari in front of him which was burbling along throatily but only at 15mph. My writer colleague was so demented with the need to reunite himself with his family after touring with a road show for two months that when he and the aforementioned Ferrari stopped at some traffic lights, he wound his window down, quickly checked the stature of the driver and then, satisfied that the driver couldn't ever rip his head off, screamed something at the Ferrari driver about the dimensions of his intimate parts. The Ferrari then moved off in front of him and stuck at 5mph after that.

'From product launches to press conferences,' my writer friend asserts, 'events are created to help organisations to communicate. The problem is that, very often, clients – or potential clients – don't really tell a supplier agency or production company what that communication *is* or what it's really there to achieve. The suppliers have to guess and invariably they guess wrong. It also makes it very hard for them to brief people like me and that can end up being something of a waste of time and money.' He grins again, takes the last biscuit (a Bourbon as I recall) and steps out of the café into the slushy snow of London's deep midwinter.

Another writer colleague also has views on the matter. As I wait for him to make coffee, I look around his study in the large Edwardian house that he inhabits in Highgate, North London. His library is vast and intricate. I become absorbed in a treatise on Shakespeare's sonnets beautifully bound. 'That was a gift from a minor royal after I'd helped prepare a speech for her,' says the colleague, having completed his coffee preparations. I think for a moment about the fact that the event industry is full of such a wide variety of people and from an equally wide variety of backgrounds. Back in the day (the 'day' in this case being the 1980s) most people in the industry came from the theatre or 'rock n' roll'. Maybe a few from the world of design, but that was it.

My pink-cheeked, apple-faced writer friend and I get back to the topic of events and communications. 'The delivery of an event,' says he, getting into his enthusiastic stride, 'involves studying the intricacies of a client's brand, identifying the target audience, devising the event concept, planning the logistics and coordinating the technical aspects before actually executing the detail of the proposed conference. Post-event analysis and ensuring a return on investment have also (rightly) become significant drivers for the event industry. Of all these, the communication objectives are the most important. I can't stress "the most" enough. But, invariably, client companies skate over the communication issues and event objectives. That's either because nobody has explained them internally (extraordinary, but often perfectly true) or because the brief is coming via Purchasing or Procurement where those folks have, by and large, no real interest in the body of the brief, just the numbers.' I nod and tend to agree. We'll discuss the gods of Procurement a little later, but understanding the communication needs of the client (and the project at hand in particular) is absolutely key to delivering anything in the name of an event.

Another contact I have, this time on the client side, who works in London's Canary Wharf within the communications and event management team for a major international bank, sits down in her office's Charles Eames chair (whereupon I wonder at the bank's profits.) 'I would agree,' she says. 'Communication *is* vital. Obviously. As far as we're concerned, if our conference suppliers don't understand what we want, then they've failed. A bit harsh you think? Well they need to get under the skin of our culture and our overall strategic messages – and fast.'

And, in a way, that's quite right, although one might argue that my bank buddy and her colleagues should maybe spend more time helping (and ensuring that) their event agencies *really* understand their company's plans and strategies although, on the other hand, it's most definitely an agency's job to find out what it needs to know in order to respond accurately to a brief. Some agencies complain that they are not allowed to discuss the brief (at all or face-to-face), but I've never experienced that (although face-to-face or a video conference can require persuasion) and certainly clients in my experience will always give an agency the time it needs, within reason obviously, to get the information it must have. However, a big problem is that some agency people have no idea what to ask. Or they turn out someone with little communications experience and with little idea as to how a brief should be tackled, questioned or perhaps challenged.

An agency or production company trying to win business from a potential client has to understand the potential client's *mores* and something of its culture, its market positioning and its operation, its weaknesses and strengths and, most of all, its brand. But, even more than all of that, the agency needs to know how the client or potential client communicates and connects with its audiences. It doesn't have anything to do with what one luminary from a small production company said to me, I think in jest but I'm really not certain: 'Well, the best thing is to get the punters in and give 'em a skip-sized bucket of popcorn along with a two-gallon vat of Pepsi Max. Job done.'

Says a very large communications agency's creative director with a taste for garish socks and, sometimes, odd ones: 'We all understand this. Or we all should. Corporate communication helps companies to shape and mould corporate presence, identity and reputation in the minds of customers and other important stakeholders.' I agree with him and he goes on, perhaps encouraged: 'It's important for an organisation to invest in corporate and marketing communication initiatives to perpetuate its long-term image and brand identity to internal and external audiences. And events are a terrific way of doing or reinforcing that.'

I ponder what he says. Events, under the banner of corporate and marketing communication, must indeed be part of the process by which brands are built and the objectives of an organisation espoused inside and out. Events (and of course other media) should be part of a series of well-coordinated and planned programmes to highlight that organisation's products, services, annual achievements, philanthropy, sustainability practices, social development efforts, change, development, sales, marketing initiatives, process change, highs and lows – and so on. The emphasis is on promoting a consistent and coherent corporate identity, message and image – even if the specific propositions are different. I once had a potential client who was extraordinarily cultured and absolutely charming. Whenever he handed out a brief, invariably not written by his fair hand, he would avoid any question about the brief or its contents. His pet subject was British art of the 18th century. 'Best-known for his portraits,' he said once when I had asked a specific question about a management conference's messaging, 'Suffolk-born Thomas Gainsborough, 1727 to 1788 if you didn't know, but I'm sure you did, would have preferred to spend his time painting landscapes, but couldn't make a living at that. He stuck to "face-painting" as he called it, with increasing ill humour. Now, what was it you wanted to know? More coffee?'

The creative director nods when I relate this, examines a fingernail, then looks at his now empty glass.

CORPORATE COMMUNICATION

Corporate communication is often a key strategic enabler in today's highly competitive and information-driven business environment. It's vital that a supplier agency or production company understands the potential client's overall strategy and specific corporate message or messages. It's pretty important that the person with whom you're dealing at the potential client end understands his/her own organisation's strategy and the event's proposition. A corporate strategy can show a great deal – if there is one. Some businesses, quite large ones at that, simply don't manage strategically. They thump around and *react* to circumstances or communicate in ways that they have done for eons because, well, that's more or less what they always have done. They change processes and opinion on things only if they absolutely must. I admit that this is a generalisation and, of course, there are fewer and fewer of these businesses, not least because many go bust, merge with other more modern businesses or become managed differently, but be aware that when you say, 'I wonder if we might hear a bit about the strategy concerning the launch of your new "xyz",' you might not always get much back. Or, and it's a big 'or', the person with whom you're dealing may not have the information you seek or need. 'Sometimes,' says a producer from an American event company, 'clients or potential clients put their brains on standby, park their true selves in limbo and abandon their sense of what someone like me might need in order to respond effectively to a brief. They can become quite aggressive when you ask them a question to which they simply don't know the answer or they might give you a totally inappropriate or inaccurate response.' Clients must get more focused on what agencies need so that they, the agencies, can react properly and respond with a quality proposal for an event or other communication. Very often we find out at the pitch stage more than we knew beforehand – and that's just a waste of time and effort.

THE IMPORTANCE OF MESSAGE AND THE COMMUNICATIONS STRATEGY IN WHICH THE MESSAGE SITS

Whatever the corporate event, by which I mean whatever the purpose, you're going to need to know and totally understand the message from a potential client (or even a current client with a new project) that will provide the mainstay and will drive the content for that event. The message will become the proposition. And you want to hear both sensibly, thoughtfully and consistently expressed in a well-articulated way. You want to know how the proposition is being reinforced by other communication activities. You, as an event deliverer, producer, manager, account director, agency boss or whatever position you hold, will benefit enormously from a clear understanding of the overall strategy in which an event sits. Such a strategy focuses everything.

An international events project manager at a North American bank once said, 'The corporate communication department in a client company like ours is in charge of devising and crafting a workable and flexible communication plan for most of the bank's initiatives. The marketing, HR or finance departments, for example, will establish the objectives with our help – but we input into how the initiative, whatever it is, will be communicated. It's our job to make sure that the agency understands what we mean by our communication plans and our overall strategy. If *we* don't understand our strategies, then obviously we can't communicate them to our agencies and other suppliers. And we really do need to communicate the bigger picture. If we don't then we really can't expect gold from our suppliers.'

An experienced professional from the industry, who has been involved in more events than anyone I know, says, 'One of the lessons that anyone at any level within the events industry must keep learning is the importance of driving through an overriding message, the proposition – and then the communication points within that message. Another absolute is that we have to be crystal clear as to what the client wants to accomplish and what therefore *we* want to accomplish in delivering that. We have to check our assumptions about our audience's current reality. And we have to craft and deploy a message that bridges any gap.' I agree.

WHAT AN AGENCY/PRODUCTION COMPANY SHOULD DELIVER

Let's be clear (if it isn't already) that there are a plethora of organisations supplying some aspect of event management or delivery. There are the big communications agencies that will have the ability and resources to offer up huge events. But, sometimes, small production companies get a chance to do those too and then buy in the requisite expertise on a needs basis. There are the small businesses that specialise in, say, video production but, as an adjunct, do some event production as well, and vice versa. There are event management agencies that specialise in getting client delegates from A to B and looking after them when they reach B. There are agencies that focus only on finding flights or hotel rooms. There are DMCs (Destination Management Companies) that provide knowledge about local entertainment, venues, transport and accommodation and can book the same. There are PCOs (Professional Conference or Congress Organisers) that work as conference consultants for academic and professional associations. There are specialists in all aspects of the event delivery process and there are some who say that they can do everything within the event cycle. The problem is – few companies or agencies *can* indeed do it all. They may *say* that they can and, even if they buy in the services they don't have in house, they still need experts on hand to manage those third party elements.

Every agency could never employ sufficient full-time specialists to deal with all event angles, so they all use more or less the same freelance experts. Some of the latter are (much) better than others. Some have been in the industry for what seems like an eternity, while others are simply brilliant, reliable and absolutely up to date with their expertise and knowledge. But most of these people are rarely directly in contact with the client apart from a little on-site during the event set-up. Others are indeed put in the front line and then agencies are troubled when they discover that the client likes the freelancers better than the agency itself. And sometimes that freelancers will go solo and the client flies with them.

I discuss this with a senior producer who specialises in financial road-shows. He nods and says, 'Well, in an agency or production company, there are key people who should, day in and day out, be the agency face to the client or, to begin with, the prospective client. This is the producer, account manager, account director or project manager. They all do slightly different things, depending on the agency and its size or scope, but basically they are responsible for end delivery and client relationships. The agency's account manager or producer is the person who plans and often executes the event once it's been sold in.' A senior colleague of his joins us at the bar, orders a pint of cider, and says, 'My frontline job is to make sure that what the client is expecting is what the supplier delivers or, if there are changes, then that person ensures that everyone knows what's what. Communication is key. And, just as important, is the agency's understanding of the event's messages and its proposition – as well as ensuring that the delivery is superb. But the client-facing representative might also be involved in more than just the direction, planning and execution of the event. There might also be brand building, marketing and communication strategy. Obviously I get input and support from our in-house or freelance creatives and designers, but the main responsibility is mine.' So, responsibility is an important word because, as a famous Australian scriptwriter acquaintance says over mineral water (we're both driving) and pretzels in a New York hotel bar, 'The project manager ... or producer ... should have expert knowledge of the creative, technical and logistical elements that help an event succeed. They have to understand set design, print, video production, PowerPoint layout and delivery, scriptwriting, logistics, budgeting, negotiation and, of course, client service. It's a multi-dimensional profession.'

Most producers or project managers work very hard and have a great number of tasks to understand and perform. They are often expected to know something about everything to do with events: site surveying, client service, brief-taking (and, very importantly, brief clarification), budgeting, cash flow management, supply chain identification, procurement, scheduling, technical design and supply – including rigging, sound, sets and lighting – plus health and safety, scheduling, rehearsals, logistics and transport, hotel and venue management, entertainment, menus, design, print and security. A small supplier company will expect their people to do the lot and that can't always be a good thing. But the more you do know the better you will be able to advise a client.

An internal communication director at a major international bank with its head office in New York, once said to me, 'I expect that the agency team, with which my people and I deal, should have the necessary expertise to cover *every* angle. I don't want to have to worry that they may not have the right skills – either before or during the event when it's too late. I expect them to have the experience necessary and I certainly don't want to be the guinea pig for anything new. Some clients are happy with that. I'm not. I have a team that will take risks, but not with communication.'

ORGANISATIONAL CHANGE

Events usually tend to be connected with some aspect of organisational change. That can be a good thing of course – new product launch, information about market-place success (or failure), an update on sales performance or maybe an introduction to new products, a celebration, an opening, a closing, an awards ceremony, a new incentive programme for senior management – and so on. It's worth making sure that you, as a budding or experienced event specialist, understand what such change implies for your client or potential client. An account director (at a large agency, itself part of a huge marketing conglomerate) points to a hefty document on her desk at least eight inches thick, and states, 'There's no one perfect way to communicate change – but that,' she says pointing at the small forest worth of paper, 'probably isn't it. Print may not be the answer and neither might be an event. An event is but one method of communicating and, on its own, it doesn't necessarily do the whole job. Some corporate change, particularly where there are staff cutbacks or individuals need to do things differently, is uncomfortable and adapting to change is usually messy and can't be fixed quickly. Behaviour and long-held habits are not easy to alter. While events won't be the answer on their own, they are useful arrows in the communications' quiver.'

The account director and I stroll through the agency's atrium that has, at its centre, a pool with a tinkling fountain. She continues as we watch the afternoon sun dapple on gin clear water: 'Too many change programmes are heavy on the jargon and light on the substance. Well-planned events can make the process a great deal easier, particularly if worries are cleared and confidence built. Sometimes the news is bad and that takes skill, real learned skill, to communicate well – giving people dignity and clarity. Part of my job is to help clients to do that. That's a communications job, *not* event specific. Many client people don't understand the need to communicate well, really well. Some think that it's just about set design and great lighting. It's also about rhetoric and oratory, great copywriting, measurement and attention to detail.' We're back in her office by now. She looks at the neat stack of paper on her desk which seems to have grown in our absence. 'If I put this in my desk drawer, it'll never see the light of day again.'

Client clarity is important, otherwise no medium (let alone a conference) is going to work properly and the result might be useless or, worse, damaging. Also, with any exercise in communication, let alone one dealing with organisational change, you *must* know what results the client wants – an obvious point perhaps, but – and I'm really not trying to be unpleasant here – some clients and agencies don't have a clue. Says one experienced account manager from a London based agency, 'You have to ask some pointed questions. What's the call to action for the communication programme? What systemic or operational changes are under way that will provide the framework for the desired results and behaviours? Invariably when a conference dealing with change is being briefed, not all the communication experts within a client company have been involved – sometimes none of them. They are only included after a backlash is in full force, when the leaks, external rumour mills and internal water cooler conversations are rampant. Then, in a way, it's too late and it'll be very messy.'

Organisational change is hard, really hard. Keep in mind that quantity is fine, but the quality and consistency of a communication plan and strategy are crucial. Many senior executives, including the CEO of an international bank, have said to me that organisations can't communicate too much, but that they *can* communicate too much insignificant, irrelevant or insensitive information. It's perfectly true – you can't communicate too much significant, substantial information. And that's the big problem – people at the top don't always decide what gets communicated or how – and they should. They're the architects, the communication blueprint owners. The biggest problem, according to one ever cheerful industry journalist, is that agencies and clients alike sometimes confuse process – vision statements, planning, endless (oh, endless) PowerPoint presentations – with communication. Communication is all about a simple message and, usually, a single-minded proposition; that's it. Everything else is concerned with making that single message clear and remembered long after the plane's landed back at Heathrow. Why do I beat the drum for this? Because it's the single most important point that is often forgotten in communicating anything, and it's frequently the most ignored aspect of an event brief.

"'OH LORD, WON'T YOU BUY ME A MERCEDES BENZ?" WELL YES, OF COURSE I WILL, BUT ONLY IF YOU GET RID OF THE PHRASE "GOING FORWARD"'

Anyway, this neighbour of mine is a politician. I enjoy his company but he is prone to use acronyms and general jargon to the point where I have to excuse myself and kick a brick very hard. I was once on a trip to Venice, producing an event for a bank, and my family joined me afterwards (at my expense, thank-you) for a few days in that magical city that hasn't changed much since Shakespeare wrote about the quality of mercy. My eldest son, Ben, then aged about six, was fascinated by the pigeons in the Piazza San Marco while my wife and I were enjoying a coffee for which we had paid the equivalent of the national debt of a South American state. It happened that a delegate from the conference I'd just completed came by and he joined us (without actually being invited so to do). Within minutes he was jabbering away using language infested with jargon and phraseology that I'd never before witnessed. If my memory serves me right, my attention wandered while I sat there nodding in a hopefully sincere way at the nonsense that poured forth from this banker, and nothing irritated me more than the phrase 'going forward'.

Politicians, business leaders, middle managers, agency and production company staff, rock and roll stars and (some) broadcasters all use the superfluous, meaningless, ubiquitous phrase 'going forward' in speech, in writing and at events. If event delivery is about anything at all, it is indeed about informing, entertaining and persuading and, like any medium, it has to follow some rules. One of those rules should be the management of language. I've been in many meetings, planning gatherings, briefing sessions, dinners, lunches, high level summits and pitches where the language that people use (very important people too) is misleading and wrong. That means that briefs are misinterpreted or that understanding is diminished.

It's impossible to get through a meeting today without being verbally assaulted by this 'going forward' inanity. And it nearly always is verbal; you have to be truly unthinking to commit it to paper. When I hear those two words, 'going forward', I switch off and think about something more interesting, such as why I have a headache intense enough to take precedence over all enquiry about language, or why the facilitator at the management conference is wearing odd socks, or why the HR director is wearing none. Things like, 'We have to consider the campaign's prospects going forward' or similar ghastly phraseology genuinely makes me feel queasy and I have to crunch my teeth – which can have expensive results. Well you may not care a whole heap about the phrase 'going forward', but to me it's like someone scraping long fingernails down an old-fashioned blackboard.

The phrase, and indeed others, is sometimes deployed as a sneer, as an add-on – a kind of smug addition – 'I'm far, far cleverer than you' – at a sentence's end; sometimes, it seems to serve as punctuation much like the (mostly) teenage use of 'like' or 'you know'. But it's especially infuriating when used with the word 'plan'. I heard a member in the current British government use the phrase twice in the same presentation a few days ago: 'Going forward, the plan is …' How can a plan be about anything *but* the future? Planning the past would be a remarkable skill yet to be enjoyed by the 21st century, or indeed any other, let alone a smirking politician.

Why *do* people speak like this? I'm at a buffet dinner hosted by someone close to the seat of power in London, there to discuss aspects of London as a conference city. The décor is great. It's one of the London Guild buildings, beautifully restored with a tangible feel of history, something I love. A huge table is laid with buffet dishes from which people begin to grab. Cherubs on the ceiling, pink and chubby, gaze down at the throng, seemingly pleased with what they survey. Gargoyles grimace; some look like ex-colleagues. I sit next to a professor of linguistics who tells me that he can only offer two possible explanations on the matter of 'going forward'. 'The first,' he says 'relates to "going forward" as a phrase that lazy people use to imply that someone messed up big time, but we don't want to dwell on whose fault it was. Instead, we must all just adopt an optimistic outlook and so, if you please, we'll start thinking about the future, not the total mess in which we currently wallow. So that's one definition. The other, less scatological definition might be that the phrase means "in the future" or "somewhere down the road" when in fact it is an attempt to dodge the use of these words, which generally indicate "I don't have a clue". This usage is, I'm sad to report, gaining momentum.' Am I alone in thinking about such a silly phrase, I wonder? I must have wondered aloud because people around me stare.

Of course you may be saying, 'Ok, I get it now about jargon, but kindly let's get back to events.' Well, tough luck, because I do want to pursue this, so bear with me – it is relevant. It's difficult to pinpoint the birth of 'going forward' but, despite the probable fact that the phrase emanated from the United States of America, its use has become prevalent in the UK and even sits comfortably amongst other Europeans when they address TV cameras or conferences in English. What would the greats from the world of oratory have said? Cicero wouldn't have used such broad meaningless phrases. Abraham Lincoln would never have perpetrated such a solecism: 'Fourscore and seven years ago our fathers brought forth on this continent a new nation, conceived in liberty and dedicated to the proposition that all men are created equal, going forward.'

JARGON

Even before you get anywhere with an event brief or discussing much of an event's content, there is the important matter of jargon to avoid – yours and your company's, if not the client's. Both sides of the event delivery fence all over the world use far too much jargon and meaningless phrases and it's both confusing and irritating. The rule has to be that we, who are supposed to uphold the value of good communications, should speak clearly and, if your client insists on using nonsensical jargon, then you have to ask for clarification and meaning. There is no value in sitting on your hands and pretending that you understand just because you don't want to seem stupid. But, to be fair, we on the supplier side of the wretched fence are as guilty – and suppliers can talk a load of meaningless jumble from time to time too.

One agency owner, normally reserved, puts this very well. 'We get jargon thrown at us all the time by clients. Phrases like "out of the box" for "think differently", "touch base" for "make contact", "incentivise" for "encourage", "downsizing" for "reduce", "ducks in a row" for "organised", "face time" for "meeting", and so many more. It's all of it just painful. Yesterday we had a meeting with one of our clients and the language their people used was full of terms like "synergy", "aha moment", "paradigm", "product evangelist", "platform atheists", "push back" and so nauseatingly on. When we don't understand what on earth someone is talking about, we're stuck and nobody likes to admit they don't know. Well, I tell my people to politely ask for an explanation if something's not clear. There should be no shame in that.'

So, business jargon – those nasty, trend-setting little phrases that are being kicked around countless conference rooms as you read this – has become epidemic. An experienced freelance speech and proposal writer states, 'Some phrases take root because they are initially an expressive use of imagery to get a point across, like the clichéd "think outside the box". Some phrases become entrenched in business communications because the writer or, more usually, the speaker, mistakenly believes that using jargon puts him or her squarely in the camp of "knowledgeable insider". In reality, most jargon use is simply an ego stroke for the user and gets in the way of the prime directive of good business writing and speaking – simplicity and clarity.'

You must agree surely. Excessive jargon or the use of tired phrases makes for a difficult and annoying reading or listening experience. Instead of providing a '30,000 mile high view', why not provide an overview or summary? Instead of 'operationalising' something, why not just do it? Instead of 'running it up the flagpole', why don't you just request feedback? People should also stop saying they're trying to 'nail jelly to the wall' just because they're trying to do something difficult. And please stop talking about 'human capital'. They're people for crying out loud! People use jargon because they want to sound smart and credible when in fact they sound slow-witted and complicated, which defeats the purpose of speaking in the first place. Now, forgive me if I just go and synchronise the incremental projections.

If you tend to sprinkle your writing, conversation or speeches liberally with jargon, you should root it out with all of the vigour that my neighbour applies to his weeds. And please get rid of phrases like 'low hanging fruit', 'pushing the envelope' and 'bandwidth' (unless you're actually talking about fruit, envelopes and … bandwidth, of course). 'Thought shower' doesn't float my boat, and neither does 'heads up' or '360 degree thinking'. You probably think I'm exaggerating, but here's a line or two from a blue chip CEO's speech for an event which took place a month ago: 'Our view of the high yield market remains constructive. However, interest rates appear to be a headwind. High yield has lower duration than most fixed income products, but it is being impacted, nevertheless. The current environment is negatively influenced by technicals more than fundamentals. We continue to see heads up default rates decline which is benefited by an improving economy going forward.' I haven't changed a word.

Speak clearly and eschew clichés and you'll set yourself apart. Clear and concise language makes you a better executive. The key to being a good speaker is being able to speak to everybody in the audience at once. American presidents, as my cousin is fond of telling me, often have this skill – and it really is a skill. Franklin Roosevelt and Ronald Reagan had that ability as does Barack Obama, whatever your political views. If your clients are using complicated vocabulary, odd imagery, acronyms that nobody truly understands and jargon that makes people's teeth ache, they are going to lose people's attention, and that defeats the object. If it's you who's doing it, then desist.

MORE ABOUT JARGON …

I'm having a quick chat with a lecturer who knows about the use and abuse of language. He's just been out for a brisk walk with his dog in the snow. 'Look,' he says when we're safely ensconced in front of a fire drinking very good coffee, 'jargon is the language of specialised terms used by all groups or professions. It's common shorthand among experts and, used sensibly, I suppose it can be a quick and efficient way of communicating. Most jargon consists of unfamiliar terms, abstract words, non-existent phrases, acronyms and abbreviations, with an occasional euphemism thrown in for good measure. It's the confidence or arrogance I detest – that everyone in one industry should assume that everyone in it and everyone else should know what they're talking about.'

I recall working with an international legal firm where I was producing a whole series of road shows, most of which were focused on human resources issues. It blew me away – or rather the jargon did. Human resources departments never sack or fire anyone. They 'refocus the company's skills-set'. Other tasty morsels included – and I can remember each one now, clear as a bell: 'career alternative enhancement programme', 'dehiring staff', 'derecruiting resources', 'employee reduction activities', 'implementing a skills mix adjustment', 'negative employee retention', 'optimising outplacement potential', 'rectification of a workforce imbalance', 'redundancy elimination', 'right-sizing employment', 'vocation relocation policy' – oh for goodness sake – that's enough.

If a human resources department uses one of these phrases to fire you, take heart, you're not unemployed. You're simply 'in an orderly transition between career changes while undergoing a period of non-waged involuntary leisure during your temporary outplacement.' Bet you'd feel much better knowing that. One of the best bits of jargon I've heard was from the British army and it's this: 'incontinent ordnance', which means bombing your own troops. Bet that makes them feel much better too.

An acquaintance of mine who's written excellent books on the vagaries of the English language says, 'We all hide behind a language that makes us feel that we belong. It creates a safe environment. Everyone does it, from teachers to bus drivers. It isn't healthy because anyone on the "outside" has no clue what's going on, and that's partly why people use jargon.'

SERIOUSLY, CONGRATULATIONS: YOU'VE GOT THE CHANCE TO PITCH

If organisations are going to justify the spending of precious money and time on an event (and if they're sure there's a good reason behind it all), then we must ensure that we respond well. Pitching or tendering for a new piece of business is what that's all about. So, congratulations! You've been given an opportunity to pitch along with other event companies for a decent slab of business. If, by the way, there are more than three other pitching companies (four maximum) in the frame, then you're nuts, or your company is. The odds are just too great unless you absolutely know that you have a better than good chance. Being the incumbent is that 'good chance' but not always, by any means, not least because your client might be looking for a change. That you're in the mix at all means that your client relationship is brilliant or your sales people, or maybe you, have done a good job. Or maybe it's because your company has a good reputation that has reached the ears of the folk who've put your company on their list. I have spent a lot of time with emerging event planners, producers, project managers and so on and many of them feel that their number one skill is that they can make sense of the chaos of the briefing and pitch process.

If the potential client is indeed brand new then, in advance of the first briefing meeting, learn everything you can about the organisation you're going to see. The chances are you'll know a little already. But you need to know a substantial amount. You also need to know about the *person* or key people you're going to see or, indeed, those who are coming to see you. Sounds obvious? Well, here's the thing – many event businesses just don't bother to do any or much homework. No, I don't know why either. So, for one thing, it's important to understand how the business you're after makes money. Read its website – especially the press or news release section. Google the company and the individuals involved. Use LinkedIn too and delve deep into the Internet to find out about any obstacles to the company's success. Try and establish what it is that keeps your prospective client up at night – broadly for the potential client company as a whole and specifically for what might be your direct contact's main concerns. At the end of your research, you should be conversant with (and have some views on) the prospective company's business and its industry. But never ever presume to know more about your prospect's business than they do.

If you are not familiar with this prospect's industry, go to some of the trade group or industry websites likely to feature the company or organisation. It's astonishing that some who pitch to clients or potential clients have no idea whatsoever where the client or potential client is in the marketplace. Sometimes agency people don't even know what their own agency is doing for other clients in exactly the same industry as their prospect. Some people I know don't even review their firm's website or walk down the corridor to find out the hot areas in which their firm is involved. Cross-selling and natural synergies with agencies or event companies seem alien to some – and that's just arrogant and/or lazy.

I'm in Los Angeles, and I'm not sure that I like it very much. I see the big LA moon, hanging over the Hollywood hills, pouring a cold light over California. It's freezing cold. That's one of the misconceptions about LA – that it's always hot and humid – that Beverly Hills, Mulholland Drive and Sunset Strip are always subject to white heat. 'Let us not forget,' I am reminded by my somewhat solemn host, 'that the LA climate is a desert one and the temperature plummets at night.' My hosts are the partners of a large American events agency, one that truly does offer every aspect of the event cycle.

Over dinner, I ask the team of three about pitching. One, the senior partner, says, 'Make sure you're prepared and don't leave anything to chance. If the potential client is visiting *you*, remember some obvious things. Obvious but often ignored. For instance, inspect where you will be meeting. If it's on home ground, sit where the client/potential client will sit. Make sure the meeting room walls are not scuffed, ensure that paintings or photographs are hung straight and there is no clutter – no old, fading artwork or the remains of someone's lunch in view. Remove the detritus. You may think that it adds character and indeed you may have the view that "they can take us as they find us," but that's mostly wishful thinking or just lazy. You're supposed to be in the business of delighting your clients. You're supposed to be in the business of "show".'

He's right of course. There are other things you can do. Let others in your firm know whom you are meeting, in case they have any connections or intelligence that might be helpful, or in case you want to introduce them. One of the other LA partners says, 'Some agencies like to do tours with potential clients. They're meant well, but are usually dreadful because there will have been little or no preparation – just some vague heads-up email to keep desks tidy.' The third partner, with whom I've worked on many events, says 'Those client tours are really silly. Tours are fine, sure, but they need preparation and then you have to keep it real. Clients aren't stupid and they recognise time wasting or irrelevancies. There was one occasion, way back when I was starting out, when the boss couldn't introduce me because he couldn't remember my name and neither did he know which accounts I worked on. I'd been there for two years.'

Make sure your appearance is good. 'I had my flies open for a whole pitch once,' says the commercial director of a marketing agency based in Frankfurt, but who's also visiting LA. I thank him for this invaluable contribution and am about to ask what happened, but his iPhone rang and that was that.

In a pitch scenario, think about all the angles. Demonstrate, for example, how you have helped other clients facing the same issues as the target client. State that you would very much like to help your new prospect to reach their objectives. Never say you are swamped with work and please don't keep on and on (as some agency people seem so pleased to do) about how tired you are. It sounds pathetic and is boring. Neither should you say that you're rushed off your feet and have no time to do anything. And don't then follow that up with an inane grin. Make the potential client feel like their event/programme/project would be the highest priority on your desk. Make them feel that having their business would be a privilege.

Once underway, make your pitch and then listen – properly. Listen carefully to questions and answer them, not the question you want to answer. People don't listen properly as a rule, mainly because they are preparing to say the next thing that's in their head, but if a potential client is saying something do the courtesy of listening, not just hearing. It may not all be fabulous philosophy or indeed anything else but, if you won't listen, you won't pick up possibly vital detail. Don't all speak at once or interrupt or, as one colleague of mine once did, repeat everyone's sentences, or *finish* people's sentences. Also don't forget to discuss and give examples of value-added services your firm provides – but only (I stress only) if relevant and *truthful*. Include in what you say something about how the account/project will be managed. Tell the potential client that the team they see before them is the team that'll be working on the business. 'Make sure,' says a production company director who meets me at London's Paddington Station, 'that this is true, otherwise the client won't be one for very long.' I do wonder, and not for the first time, at how terrific London's mainline railway termini look.

After the pitch meeting, follow up with an email, possibly even a handwritten note and/or a phone call. Obvious, yes, and most of you will do this, but some people don't. 'That's all well and good,' mutters the Paddington Station interviewee, 'but I've been in lots of pitches and they tend to follow the same pattern. For instance, people, particularly the most senior agency one there, will gush. There's always someone on the agency side who just goes on and on about him or herself or about how brilliant he or she is – and nobody is remotely interested. Sometimes this person will just talk endlessly about their company's sixteen offices dotted round the world and about the umpteen awards the agency has won. People just won't be interested unless that information is *absolutely* germane to the potential client or to the brief. Potential clients want partnerships and solutions. They want to know how the agency, their agency, is going to solve a problem. The harried, sleep-deprived marketing director sitting across the table wants help from people who understand his problem and, yes it is invariably a problem, not an opportunity. People are busy. And even those who *aren't* busy have better things to do than sit in meeting rooms while you convince them you're the second coming. Stick to what you're there to do.'

I have a writer colleague (who's written some of the best speeches I've ever read or, indeed, heard), who downs a glass of Chianti and says, 'Agencies need to be specific in pitches and add value: statistics, facts, expected results, measurement ideas, cascade programmes, legacy. Not too much detail, but enough to whet the appetite. Don't be afraid to be specific and then back those specifics with real data. Another glass?'

'I agree,' offers an agency leader, when I discuss the same issue of pitches with her. 'People do get hung up on details on both sides,' she says as she walks – so fast that I have to effect a small jog to keep up. 'Facilitating and managing a pitch is a great art', she says, speeding up her pace. 'The last thing we want is a carefully built pitch to sink beneath the waves because the client understands what you've said and really doesn't want to dwell but wants to move on. The stifled yawns, the clock watching, the perpetual doodling, or the BlackBerry action under the table should give you a clue. But, by then, it may be too late.' She's right, this speed walker. Make it deft, keep it light, and (so important), connect the benefits of your proposal to the project itself and the brief. Then leave it.

IF YOU'RE VISITING THEM, BRUSH YOUR HAIR …

An agency managing director and I are in his London office and an account director has joined us. We're demolishing pieces of rather delicious birthday cake. The hustle and bustle of the agency disappears when the office door is shut. It's calm. I ask if he, the MD whose birthday it is, thinks that pitching's hard all of the time. He nods and I smile, tapping my recorder with my pen. 'You have to say it out loud; it won't pick up nods,' I say (kindly). 'I think it is if you take pitching seriously,' he says, looking warily at the recorder. 'Let me tell you a pitch story.' My interviewee leans forward from his chair and then decides to stand in front of his desk. I jiggle the recorder about. He seems not to mind the tiny machine any more. He begins. 'You've arrived at a business park, let's say near Reading. The security guard at the gate can't find your pass, so there's that hassle, then he tells you that he can't get the person you're meant to be visiting on the phone. Then you're told that visitor parking *is* available and you sigh with relief, but when you drive towards the visitors' car park you discover that it's full, so you experience a panic moment, where you're late even though you're early. You have to park in the main car park where each of the spaces has a number and you pray to some deity that number 378 won't return that day. The executive you're there to meet, Hermann or

Lizibet (because let's imagine that this is a German car manufacturer with German folk in situ), is even later, so you wait in reception with a dry mouth and damp palms.' The storyteller sips some Berg mineral water.

He continues. 'You are asked by an assistant called, let's say Jeremy, if you would like some water or coffee. You say yes to the water and your colleagues um and ah about their hot drink requirements. You glance at your watch and wish you'd worn the other outfit you started to wear, the one that says 'I'm hip, I'm happening, I wear black and I'm not going to get overly dressed up just to suck up to you automotive people to talk about a management incentive programme.' Instead, you chose the look that you hope says, 'I'm so talented and successful, I don't even have to dress down,' but the new shoes really hurt and you cut yourself shaving. (You are a man by the way in this small episode.)' Birthday boy sips some more water and settles himself on his desk.

'You sneak your notes out of your slim briefcase. Your "leave behind" is still pristine in its expensive see-through folder. It's a 65-page A4 document that, like all pitch documents and leave-behinds, is decent enough copy, designed to present and sell your story enthusiastically. However, you know that it's a little vague and contains too much sales information and, worse, case studies that have no bearing on this task. It describes the main points of the creative idea and covers all of the main headings that the brief indicated should be covered. The visuals in it are good, well art-directed and executed with flair. It does go on a bit about the sixteen offices your company has round the world and every single skill that everyone on the team has. It does extol the virtues *ad nauseam* about the awards that your agency has won. You won't get this document/leave-behind out, nor tell them you have one, until the end. And, anyway, they've had a version before now because they asked for one and you sent over six, but you know in your heart of hearts that they won't have read it. They'll have misplaced the copies they had and, anyway, the main decision-maker will have skimmed it. The executive summary will tell them little because it's not really an executive summary but a message of gratitude that your agency has been invited to pitch. But they'll be eager to get the document today since then they won't have to remember anything.

So you try to scan your own notes while waiting for the meeting, but you know them off by heart. You videotaped yourself doing this pitch, timing it, practising it, until you have the pauses down to a fine dramatic art along with the ad-libs, the current observations and the jokes. You've got it down to twenty-two minutes, wishing it could all get said in sixteen.

Finally, the nice assistant, Jeremy, says that your potential client is ready to see you. You quickly slip your leave-behind document in your slim, tasteful briefcase, look round for your colleagues and go in to the lift where nobody speaks.

'Hello everyone!' Lizibet says, rushing in holding a folder, expensive pen and a styrene cup marked 'latte', in case there was any doubt, and greeting you warmly. She says, 'I'm so sorry to have kept you waiting, but there's some stuff going on, you know ...' (Translation: I have the power to make you wait, so I did and, just so that it's clear, I have more important things to do than this.)

'Hey, Lizibet, I understand,' you say, and of course you do understand. No security pass ready, no place to park, keeping you waiting. You understand: they are gods, the potential client is on Mount Olympus. You are a peasant and a mere mortal. More indignities will follow, including the 'Taking of the Calls' or 'The Reading of the Texts' during the pitch, probably once you've got to the budget part.

Lizibet now gestures that you and your colleagues should sit down round a table in a room that is still warm from the previous incumbents. The chairs are all over the place and, while there are new refreshments, you wonder how fresh they are. Lizibet takes the power chair that is at the top of the table. One person from marketing rushes in all sixes and sevens and with huge swathes of documentation, none of it to do with you or this meeting. It makes you feel slightly disenfranchised. Then the earth must stop turning while Lizibet summons an assistant and describes in great detail the type of tea for which they are in the mood, saying 'My coffee is horrible.' (Translation: I can say this even if it's not true because someone will bring me whatever I want.) Then Lizibet says, 'Could you ask Shannon to join us?' These are all just little displays of power and you and your team smile as if this is the most amusing situation and then you stop smiling when you see that Lizibet isn't. You then make idiotic small talk in which they and you have no real interest. Someone has turned the air conditioning off saying, 'Brrrrr', and you're sweating.

Tea is now on the table and Shannon's now in situ. Lizibet turns to give you her divided attention, plus 4.8 minutes of more small talk – but most of it is about her company's recent activities and you can't really join in because you have no idea what she's talking about. Shannon by the way is a younger person who has a pad and pen and will take notes. Finally, 'The Mystery Person Who Occupies an Undefined Niche in the Hierarchy' also joins the meeting. A quiet, well-dressed, perfectly groomed gentleman is introduced to you by name (let's call him Clive), but no mention is made of exactly who he is or why he is there, other than to lend an additional Kafka-esque element to the proceedings. The problem is, as someone who wants to get the pitch underway, you now don't know where the lines of power are in the room, so you don't quite know to whom you should play, or why.

'I really liked your proposal. *Wirklich gut*,' Lizibet says, and this is the only completely sincere thing to be said here today. You don't get inside this company's walls to pitch ideas to executives unless the proposal is good. So they have read it. You say thanks, and then someone from yet another department arrives, creating another choreography of who sits where. They get settled in, there are some more snatched German sentences and then they all stare.

'OK, over to you, but first perhaps we should update you on the objectives,' Lizibet says. 'We've had some further thoughts since we sent you the brief and also since we last met.' Then there follows half an hour of information that makes much of what you've proposed redundant. Then someone other than Lizibet (you think it's Clive) says, 'But enough of us. Over to you.'

Curtain rises, spotlight is on you and you now have twelve minutes to talk this audience through your sixteen-minute pitch that will take twenty two. And your father, who sold dental appliances in the north of Scotland for decades, thought he had a tough sales territory.

'I'm very excited about a contemporary adventure,' you say, launching into your pitch, including all the pauses, hesitations and moments of passion. But you can't sound over-rehearsed and it all sounds a bit hollow since much of the detail is now out of date. You have to play to their comfort zones and you suddenly realise that you don't really know what they are. But you have your two colleagues nodding vigorously at everything you say, perhaps too much. They look a little like the dogs you sometimes see with nodding heads on the rear shelves of cars. One is also fiddling with his coffee cup and it's getting on your nerves and maybe Lizibet's.

'That's bang on message, good,' the note-taking Shannon says after a while, to remind the others in the room that she is there, a power to be reckoned with, and they'd better watch their corporate step because she is on the up and up. You are shocked because you thought that Shannon was very low in the pecking order. Everyone looks at Shannon for more insights but she is looking hard at the notepad and writing something very important. Shannon looks about twelve years of age. You consider the point that maybe youth is everything in the Dorian Gray world of automotive communications and events.

Your eyes are now aglow and you smack some energy into your voice and continue. As you're talking, you try not to be distracted by the fact that the friendly, animated faces in front of you have turned into a Madame Tussaud set of waxworks. This is their fixed game face, when they hear pitch presentations. It's not personal. But, you feel that it *is* personal. A mobile phone rings. Lizibet answers her phone. The mysterious Clive suggests in a low, important voice that you should continue anyway. But you're just smart and brave enough to say, 'No, let's wait.' And you do wait. Lizibet eventually hangs up and apologises ('*sehr leid*'), but your sales momentum has all but disappeared. No one remembers where you were. You certainly don't. You must instantly regroup, recap the story and still sell this incentive programme to Beijing and you've only just got to the Beijing part. The PowerPoint onscreen behind you shows venues and Chinese tea girls, The Great Wall and The Forbidden City. You pause, letting this sink in. You talk faster, and then finish. Then your two colleagues get their short turns – logistics and budget. You're way over time and people are looking quite openly at their watches and the room's clock ticks.

They ask a few off-the-wall questions, but you've learned, even when stumped, to say, matter-of-factly, 'That's a solvable problem,' and not let the audience pause on negatives. When they offer a suggestion based on the new information about which until half an hour ago you knew nothing, you say, 'great idea,' whatever it is, displaying overt excitement about it, because you want these execs to attach their egos to your pitch so they'll want it and fight for it. But who knows what they're really thinking? You can't tell. They finally say, 'Thanks for coming in. We'll get back to you.'

You now offer up the pristine 65-page A4 leave-behind document, with a certain 'gosh-you-won't-want-this-but-hey' manner, so you won't seem too slick. They eagerly take it, but you're not certain that's because they want it or they want you out. Handshakes, smiles, you leave, having no idea if they love or hate what you've proposed, or what they think of you now. It's impossible to tell. And then you find yourself in the car park.'

The MD smiles and, sipping more of his expensive water, says, 'They're not all like that, of course, but pitches are hard. All of them – and they require a lot of work.' The group account director smiles and says, 'It's all down to *really* answering the brief, ensuring that the brief is in date, that you have *all* the right information and rehearsing. Rehearsing is key.' I think I smile back because she's right.

REHEARSING AND PRACTISING A PITCH IS SO IMPORTANT – DON'T EVER JUST WING IT

I know that not all pitches are like the MD's reminiscences that you've just read, but certainly there are some simple ways of getting them right:

Believe in your pitch

If you don't really, wholeheartedly believe in your pitch, your audience certainly won't. I know that there are those from the world of advertising and marketing who may say that a good account man or woman could sell anything, but I never believed that. Even the faintest whiff of doubt will be easy to smell – so before you begin make sure that you are confident in your own idea (or those of your company) and in your delivery. Actually, make sure that you are not just confident, but *passionate*. If you don't believe in your or your agency's ideas, who will? Who should?

Concentrate on your audience

Despite the fact that you are talking about your business, your expertise and your company's ideas, the pitching process isn't really about you – it's about your audience. Think about what your potential client wants and highlight the ways in which you can give that to them.

Steer clear of clichés

Maybe your business is going to set the world of events alight. Maybe you're pitching something that's never been seen before. All these things might be true – but it's imperative that you avoid tired clichés. Avoid the likes of: 'eat the elephant one bite at a time', 'let's not compare apples with oranges', 'we're going to leave our footprint on this project' and 'there's no "I" in team'. They make me squirm. Here's a simple test: is there anything in your pitch that sounds like it could come from the mouth of a candidate for the TV programme *The Apprentice*? If so, bin it.

Be honest

It's imperative that you are honest throughout your pitch. Don't exaggerate. Any inaccuracies will come out eventually anyway, and you simply have to know that exaggerations sound ludicrous. Clients aren't stupid, mostly not anyway.

Identify a need

Make sure that you explain the potential client's need for what your proposal offers and outline exactly how it satisfies that need. If the brief has invited consultative approaches as to how it's answered, say so, and say why you've approached it that way. If you're challenging part of the brief, say precisely why but don't do it in such a way as to make your listeners feel inadequate.

Be concise

The purpose of the pitch is to grab attention and make the potential client believe in your idea. This is often best achieved in just a couple of minutes. The best pitches are short, snappy, easy to follow and absolutely to the point. My cousin, who has produced a few events in his time, mostly in the United States, says, 'The purpose of the pitch isn't to give a detailed breakdown of your financial assets or the offices you have round the world (unless that's really, really relevant) and neither is it the time to go on about your best anecdotes of what happened to you when you were last in Stockholm. Few people give a damn and, while they may smile politely, you mustn't think that's encouragement to tell another witty story.' My dear cousin, with hair dyed the colour of a fresh satsuma, gets back to his buttered muffins.

Avoid jargon and speak plainly

You're likely to be pitching to people who may not know the world of events as well as do you, so don't presume that they are familiar with the technical ins and outs of your business. Explain your pitch using clear language. Don't use acronyms and don't be patronising. You're not bigger than the company you represent and you're not better than those people in front of you. Good language is like good vodka: clear.

Don't be (too) gimmicky

Gimmicks tend not to work. Those big foam pointy hands you were thinking of using? Get rid of them. That huge bag of Mars Bars that you plan to empty on the table at the end of your pitch …? Maybe, but you've got to know your audience pretty damn well, and understand how people in it might react. Clients want solutions – clever solutions certainly, but often simple and straightforward. Props and mock-ups can be useful in some circumstances, but they should only be used when really necessary, when you really know that they add some value to your case. Certainly, clients and potential clients like a laugh but don't take too many risks because the laugh may not be forthcoming. Oh yes – and if you need PowerPoint (and you probably don't), keep it very simple.

Get the important stuff in early

A great pitch grabs the attention from the very first second. Consider beginning with an 'elevator pitch' – a short overview that explains exactly what your idea is in less than a minute. Explain very briefly why your business or idea is exciting, before getting down to the nitty-gritty.

Practise

You should remember that pitching doesn't come naturally to everyone, so practise and rehearse. If you don't then you're out of your mind.

Using PowerPoint in the pitch

The late Steve Jobs was often cited by media and pundits alike as one of corporate land's greatest presenters and that's simply, they said, because he understood how to tell a story. He also used PowerPoint cleverly to help tell stories. Like any great sales pitch, an effective PowerPoint presentation offers a compelling narrative; it elicits an emotional response from the audience, even if the subject is, say, debt consolidation or finance derivatives. The trick is to understand how to engage your listeners, keep them focused and use the right visual imagery to support your message. And 'support' doesn't mean 'repeat'. So whether you're pitching an idea for a major marketing conference or an event introducing a new product to your potential client's customers, or simply trying to convince the potential client that you can deliver a brilliant AGM, a strong (but short) PowerPoint presentation may help to reinforce your proposition.

Now, it's worth saying that I loathe PowerPoint. Did Kennedy use it? Did Demosthenes? But, I grant (whilst gritting my teeth and thereby necessitating another expensive visit to my orthodontist) that it can have its place if used well as a support, but *only* ever as a support.

POWERPOINT IN PITCHES (IF YOU MUST)

An old salt of the event management world (who originally trained as a lawyer because he thought that Atticus Finch was the best character in fiction bar none) is currently discussing twins in mythology with a junior producer. 'You know of course,' he says 'that twins have appeared in mythology since the very dawn of civilisation. Romulus and Remus, Apollo and Artemis, Castor and Pollux – for ever immortalised as Gemini in the night sky.' He turns to me, 'Ah yes, PowerPoint, PowerPoint, that wretched device. Bob Gaskins and Microsoft have much to answer for. Creating a great PowerPoint is simpler than you might think. What is needed is an understanding of how to capture an audience's focus – and perhaps a bit of their imagination.' I ask whether he could give me an example. 'Sure,' says he. 'One thing I like to do is make sure there's a logical story. Just like any piece of good writing, there needs to be a beginning, middle and an end to your presentation. One tip is to use five words per line, and five lines per slide, *maximum*. A strong PowerPoint presentation should have ten slides, last no more than twenty minutes and contain no font smaller than thirty points.' A normal pitch presentation might have various headings:

▶ Showing that you understand the client problem or issue;

▶ Your solution to that specific problem only (and nothing else);

▶ Your track record (salient only);

▶ The plan showing how you'll deliver the event or campaign, to do what's needed – and how;

▶ The underlying magic and technology that will make the event work brilliantly; examples of where these (or similar) things have worked before;

▶ Other specific methodology for achieving this brilliant event, including logistics and high points;

▶ How will the event be measured? What legacy will there be?

▶ Your team;

▶ **Projections and milestones: key points of delivery or achievement; timeline;**

▶ **Costs.**

Your pitch needs to accomplish three goals: framing the issue, presenting the challenge and explaining how you will solve the problem. A Group Head of Communications with a famous and worldwide brand of soft drink agrees. 'At some point or another,' he says, 'we've all had to sit through a PowerPoint presentation during a pitch – flooded with an endless stream of bullet points, sentences or even full paragraphs – with images and bits flying in and out and colours galore. When that happens I can't remember any of it. I want to hear what the people in the room have to say. Any PowerPoint must only reinforce that.' He's right. Mr Jobs was famous for using virtually no text at all – an icon of a new product or a couple of big picture words were all that he ever used. The soft drinks chap says, 'People are afraid to use a slide with just one word on it, but it has merit because we have to process information before we go on to the next idea.' I totally agree with him. 'It's very important,' he goes on, 'for the mind to be able to rest on an idea or a thought, so if there's a constant flow of words or babel, people will grow tired, confused and then bored.'

I asked a client of mine her view on this. She and I have worked on strategies and events of all shapes and sizes over the years. 'Oh I hate PowerPoint,' she groans theatrically. Well she did go to drama school and, for a while, was an excellent actress. 'People simply stop paying attention to slides with too much text on them,' she says. 'It's like wallpaper.' In other words, it becomes easy to tune out. And, darling, save us from Clip Art, slide transitions and other tacky animations. That's the best way to pollute an agency brand's message and a PowerPoint presentation. Whatever's on screen must be straightforward. We did an event for an insurance company last week where the simple wouldn't do. Despite our best efforts, the client kept erring on the side of caution and the boring. Nothing as succinct as, "China: Up 15 per cent". No, they wanted: "Our sales in the Pan-Asian region are up 15 per cent over the same period as in 2010, according to our market research firm AsiaReportInc."'

A television writer friend, who used to write hundreds of executive speeches, says, 'When you listen to executives talking on stage, do you watch *them* or stare at their slides or presentation? Probably the latter, and it undoubtedly lulls you into a zombie-like state where you're hearing what they're saying, but it's not getting past the first layer of your brain and being processed. Those people in the audience would get parts in *World War Z*. The speaker has to compete with the slide for the attention of the audience and, often, the speaker loses. If you can't be more interesting than some dull slide, well, maybe you have a bigger problem, but it's a sure bet that you're not selling what you want to sell, be it an idea, proposition, campaign or product. Now, imagine the same presentation without any slides at all. There's not much you can do other than pay attention to the speaker, is there? If he or she is lively and excited enough (remember, passion is the most important factor in a good speech) and if the lighting and room architecture aren't terrible, your attention will be 100 per cent focused on what they are saying.'

He's right of course. Forget the transitions, the floating graphics, the text that slides on from the side, the too many bullet points at a time, the complicated circles and arrows. For goodness sake understand that a single picture or word can be a great introduction to, or reinforcement of, a point. I would passionately encourage those of you who make presentations to either try flying without a safety net, and skip the PowerPoint completely – or really work hard to minimise your slides. Tell your clients this. Tell them to make the slide reinforce one key point. If I wanted to read slides, after all, I'd ask a speaker to email them to me.

MAKE THE PITCH SIMPLE

A production company account director says, 'I talk to a lot of our clients about our pitches and also those of other agencies. While I'm obviously not told confidential details, I do get to understand what potential clients are looking for. There's no hard and fast rule, but there are some factors worth bearing in mind.' I ask, 'What, for instance?' The account director smiles and is about to sit carefully on the edge of his glass-topped desk. I espy a rather nice Waterman fountain pen with its cap off. After acknowledging thanks for my alert, he says, 'When someone on the client side asks a question mid-pitch or mid-presentation, invariably the person on the agency side who's speaking will say something like, "I'll get to that later in my presentation." This really irritates: just answer the question. A pitch is a dialogue, not a lecture. The more engaging a pitch is (and provided you get the core elements across), the better. And, besides, you're fighting human nature. The guy who's asked the question is going to spend the next couple of minutes thinking about why you won't or didn't or can't answer his question; he certainly won't be focussing on what you are presenting.'

I'll tell you something for nothing – it's also worth avoiding the lengthy introduction of the team with vast amounts of detail along with an elaborate repetition of the brief. And having too many people on the agency team always seems to suck the very air out of a room. Also, the bringing of a gaggle of creative, logistics and production people makes clients think, 'What on earth do all of these people actually *do* that they can afford to attend these meetings?' So, bring/take two other people maximum – unless there's a very good reason for more. Whoever is there needs to contribute.

Clients also hate it when agencies say something like, 'Well of course we have a virtual team.' Far-flung teams are sometimes successful, but they are the exception, not the rule. It's very difficult to get anything done if your producer or project manager is going to bed when the account director is just waking up. 'I also don't like it,' says a procurement executive from a health care company, 'when agencies go on and on about the fabulous satellite offices they have around the world when all my colleagues want is a sales conference in Manchester. Reach is only really good if a brief requires reach.'

A client project manager who works for a confectionary company which has factories around the world says, 'It's quite annoying when agencies say things like, "We don't have any competition." If there is no other company in that agency's space, it's probably not a very attractive niche. Also, it's a very big turnoff when people say, "We have a director who knows your CEO." I want the agency team to focus on solving *my* problem. It's very, very annoying when people get names wrong or confused. I resent being confused with someone else and I resent people calling me Steven when my name's Stuart.'

A young intern comes in and says, 'There's a guy out here from accounts who says Gaspachio was Pinnochio's father.' A beat, then, 'He wasn't was he?'

After getting the opportunity in the first place, pitching for business is the core element of any event company selling any aspect of the event cycle. Pitching needs to be taken seriously and it needs to show your listeners that you're passionate about what you do and what you're selling. Passion (not idiocy or arrogance) is contagious and affirming. But, remember, keep things to the point and be brief. Few audience members ever shout for more at the end of a speech or pitch. Or if they do, then it happens rarely and there needs to be an extraordinary emotional reason for it. Most audiences listening to most speeches or pitches can recall little beyond the first five to ten minutes. So, obviously, you have to make that five or ten minutes engaging and captivating. Rhetoric is the art of using speech and writing to persuade and influence – and that's exactly what your pitch should do. The good pitch calls for performance and, if you're performing because you love what you do and want to be successful at it, then preparing, becoming confident, overcoming nerves by knowing your stuff, rehearsing and understanding the brief are all part of the process. I wish that all agencies would get that. Pitching is performing and performing is bringing a bit of theatre and inspiration to your would be client. If you don't much care for pitching in an inspiring way, there's little chance that it will inspire the Lizibets of the world.

CHAPTER TWO
THE VENUE

THINKING ABOUT A PLACE TO DO THE SHOW

If pitching is all about persuasion, then talking to clients about event venues is all about needing the persuasive talents of Cicero. Venue choice can be a conundrum. Choose a venue to match your client's needs or, actually, the needs of the brief and proposed audience. If you want creativity, interactivity and an alert audience, then (amongst other things of course) choose somewhere that reflects energy. It's an obvious point once again, but you can't find a (right) venue without being crystal clear about the event's objectives. There are other factors to consider and we should get them fixed as a consideration list now. Take the following, for example, which relate to a more or less standard corporate conference:

▶ Location – from where are the attendees coming and how are they travelling? Does the location need to be near an airport, railway station or motorway junction? Is parking important and which is better for your purposes – a city centre or a country location?

▶ Attendee profile – very important – the venue needs to be appropriate for *delegates* and not for you or your client or your client's CEO.

▶ Flexibility – is there any flexibility in the chosen dates? Are they really fixed? Check public holidays, other holidays, other events, industry exhibitions and anything that's going on in the city or area that might be on at the same time as your event – particularly anything that might compete for hotel and venue space. Importantly, check what else is going on in the client company. Unfortunately, many clients fix dates before taking any consultation with anyone apart from the event owner's diary. They should be marooned on a desert island.

▶ Make sure that enough time is available (and booked) for setting up the staging, lighting, set and so on. Similarly, if an exhibition is planned as an attachment to an event, ensure that (sufficient) space has been booked for that too. I know, I know, but you'd be surprised.

▶ Measurement – consider how the success of the event is going to be measured and put the steps in place to achieve the objectives from the start. It really is extraordinary that a) some clients couldn't give a fig about measuring anything and b) that some agencies wouldn't know where to start. So, if measurement isn't your company's expertise, get some help, training or professional advice. Measurement will apply to a venue's suitability and everything else to do with the event's environment as much as anything else, including content.

▶ Registration process – think about how members of the audience are going to be invited and how will they reply – the registration process needs to be managed and managed well without any errors whatsoever. Errors at this stage are a killer because the CEO of the client company will find our very quickly – particularly if people's personal details are going all over the place. Also important – give consideration as to what needs to be told to delegates beforehand and, as appropriate, think about how to keep the impetus going *after* the event. Legacy of a piece of communications is critical these days. Less and less can clients just tick the box of 'event done and dusted'.

▶ Budget – is this realistic, fixed and does it match the detailed requirements? If there is no set budget, you'll need to create a core set of costs along with explanations and a list of options.

▶ Risks – what are the minimum numbers and cancellation terms? What are the other risks – such as flights, weather, inoculations, visas, other travel issues, political issues, general health and safety – and similar? Risk assessments all round are very important. Dull as cold toast, but important, although actually my cousin quite enjoys cold toast. If you don't know anything about risk, you must talk to someone who does. Clients expect their agencies to manage and/or advise on risk. Volcanic ash, social unrest and 'what if' scenarios are a great way to focus thinking.

▶ Complexity of turnarounds – if the same meeting area, auditorium, ballroom – wherever – is being used for your conference in the day and for your gala dinner in the evening, do leave sufficient time to turn the room around. Your venue will advise.

▶ Set-up and get-out time is essential of course, but you also need to allow time for rehearsals. There *should* be rehearsals – every time – no matter how small the event. Always. Without exception. Tell that to your client. They may take little notice, but it's so, so important. Would you watch a play in which the actors had never rehearsed and had only looked at their lines and moves ten minutes before show-time? Ok, you would. Most wouldn't. Ask the lady sitting next to you if she would.

▶ Consider carefully: the layout and style of the meeting, the greeting and registration/reception areas, the eating and drinking spaces plus any syndicate or breakout rooms. How many people will attend each part of the event? Do participants need to make notes, work in small groups or just listen to a presentation? Will the technology you're putting in front of them (say, voting system handsets) be easy to use? How much space is needed for anything and everything?

▶ Does the venue offer free, unlimited Wi-Fi access?

That's a rough list. There are more things to go on it as we'll see, but it'll do for now.

An always cheerful and happy logistics director is off on holiday. 'Where are you off to,' I ask? She smiles mischievously, 'White water rafting in New Zealand and then shopping in Paris.' She says of venue finding that there are some core dos and don'ts and these reinforce my own views. 'You need to establish if the venue fits the client company's image,' she says, 'as well as the event's needs. Image is important. Is the venue on brand? It's important that the venue gives the correct impression for a particular event. Will it appeal to the target audience? Will the venue's staff add to the attendees' experience in a positive way? Is the seating capacity suitable and are the venue's spaces large enough to provide a comfortable experience for those attending? Or are they too large? Too small? Are the spaces well laid out? Do they allow for good views of what's going on stage without any obstructions?' She stops and smiles. She knows what happened when I first started out in the industry. When I first started out, I had to book a venue. I wasn't trained and had no clue whatsoever, but I was mustard keen and knew Shakespeare inside out but quickly discovered that this had small use in event production apart from standing on stages when I thought nobody was looking and doing a bit of soliloquy. The venue (a conference hotel) was in a big city in the north of England and the event was a travel company's annual sales conference. The room had nine pillars and there was no way that four hundred people could have an unhindered view of the stage. I had booked the venue without seeing it or even asking the obvious questions. I had seen no floor plans and had discussed the booking with not one person. It was a big mistake. Another big mistake was that I had been charged with thinking up a theme for the event. Hours that will never come back were spent searching for the elusive theme that would magically connect travel vouchers, the balance sheet of a company in some difficulties, and the case against a narrowly realist conception of travels in Egypt – or was it Mozambique? I couldn't do it but then came up with something like "Going for Gold."

Of course, the travel company client wasn't happy, not least because the 'l' from 'Gold' fell off the set backdrop right in the middle of the CEO's main presentation and later I received one of those one-on-one lectures that headmasters or favourite teachers sometimes give, or when a parent sits you down for *that* chat about drugs, money or sex. I recall that I said sorry a great deal, looked at something really interesting on my shoes and listened (for hours and hours it seemed) to a talk on a) care, b) attention to detail, c) not letting the side down, d) not using clichés more than necessary and e) not shouting soliloquies when I thought nobody was looking and when I should have been somewhere else. Anyhow, my client not only forgave me (as did my boss, bless him), and both allowed me to be involved in the next event and the one after that and, indeed, we went on to produce (I like to think dazzling) events together for many years, even though I do say so myself.

My friend knows all this and her smile has become a fat grin. But she continues with her thoughts on venue finding. 'It's important to establish if attendees can move around without bottlenecks and delays. And venue parking in city centres can be a problem. Does the venue have enough parking spaces? Are they free of charge? If not, is the client aware? Many venue questions can be answered by a visit to the venue's website and by asking for a quote. If it's a venue you've never used before, you may want to ask the opinion of Destination Management Companies (DMCs) or other companies that have held conferences there to find out what their experiences were like. A visit to the venue is a must, if not by you, then by someone else who knows what to look for on your behalf. And the client should go too.'

SOME VENUES CAN CAUSE FRUSTRATION

A special events director from a large agency says, 'Some venues are the same the world over – the same carpet that shows no stains because the purple, lime green, ultramarine and amber swirls hide everything, the same burnt corner of a ceiling where a lighting designer once went slightly overboard, the same old single, sad and deflated, seasonal, pink balloon hanging from a chandelier, that slight but pervading smell of industrial cleaning fluid and old vegetables. Now, this isn't a prevalent state in many hotels but, once in a while, you do come across a conference hotel or venue that is not only tired, but downright exhausted. Such venues cause depression – not helped by rude management and staff who aren't interested in getting resolution to problems.'

I can't disagree. Venues can be annoying even when you've done everything that you possibly can to ensure service is smooth and the smiles are real. You assume that whatever you've booked for your event is ready and understood, but sometimes it isn't and nobody knows what you're talking about because it's a different management team on duty. You assume, after all your hard work and that of your colleagues, that the process of event management and onsite logistics will be fabulously easy. But it isn't. Whether it's one thing or an amalgam, that's no good for your client, and no matter how much you apologise, the result will be harmed and therefore the experience too. And, look, we're in the business of theatre and everyone wants the experience of theatre to be brilliant, nothing less. Whatever *may* be a problem ensure that you get the answers you need before the event and the reinforcement of information that your event will require. Whatever the problem onsite ensure that the venue knows that your expectations are very high. Attention to detail is an absolute must. If you're working in a largish agency or event management/production company there is a strong likelihood that you'll have logistics experts in-house. Alternatively, make sure you get the right advice and buy that in if necessary.

Additionally, you don't lose anything by hiring a venue finding agency in the first place; the finder will get the venue commission and you'll get paid event management and/or production fees from your client. But, even if you do use some help, ensure that you establish answers to the right questions:

▶ **A sales conference is very different from a shareholders meeting. Is the venue you're considering on (your client's) brand and fit for purpose?**

▶ **What's the décor like? Is it appropriate? Will you/can you compromise?**

▶ **Is the venue management flexible to your needs? And will they recommend ideas based on their experience?**

▶ Will external noise be a distraction?

▶ Is your client or potential client really looking for venue advice from you or have they got several lots of companies or people seeking out the same thing? That's really annoying because everyone will be chasing the same venues. Playing off people in this context is unhealthy and unhelpful.

▶ What rates are on offer and what conditions apply? Will the venue guarantee prices? What are the payment terms/options?

▶ Is the venue *really* available for the dates you want – including set-up? Sometimes internal departments at venues say different things.

▶ If you're planning on doing anything away from the venue, what's the distance and how long does it (genuinely) take?

▶ Can you see how this venue will add value to the delegates' experience?

▶ If the venue is a hotel, can you accommodate everyone there or will you need another hotel (or more)? Will that work or will people in the second hotel feel disenfranchised?

▶ Do you (really) know what's included in quoted prices and, just as important, what's not?

▶ Does the venue, and indeed all parts of it, have good accessibility?

▶ Is the venue easy to find? Are there other venues with similar names in the same area?

▶ Is the catering good? By whose standards? Can the catering offer exactly what your client wants or expects?

▶ Have you been offered a site visit? These days, even if the venue is in another country far away, a good recce (of probably several venues) is valid and should be built into the budget.

- ▶ Will you, or a logistics colleague, have one main point of contact at the venue or hotel?

- ▶ Has the venue any valid experience of the kind of event you're delivering? Can you talk to someone who has experienced the service?

- ▶ What can you (and can you not) do in terms of onsite banner displays and signage.

- ▶ Is there a business centre? Will you have sole use of it? Are you paying for it anyway when your client doesn't need it?

- ▶ What about storage (for production, materials, technical requirements)?

- ▶ Is there access for large trucks if the technical aspects of the event are big? Can you actually get the car on stage for the reveal? Well, it's not such a stupid question actually.

- ▶ Has the venue a policy on sustainability? Does it practice what it preaches? Do you? Does your client?

- ▶ Is the venue honest about what can be achieved – for example numbers of people in a particular space?

So, that's for starters. Think on.

HAVING FOUND A VENUE

As indicated, many clients decide on (and even book) a venue before briefing an agency like yours to deliver the event. They may have gone directly to a venue finding agency, but that agency will possibly be booking a venue without knowing the full event facts or needs. This is madness. But logistics companies or the venue itself (if it's part of a chain perhaps) or indeed a DMC (Destination Management Company) can offer specialist advice about a particular country, area, city and venue – and most of the time the advice is solid providing that the brief is robust. Most venue agencies under whatever guise will earn their income mostly in the form of a commission by receiving a percentage of the money your client will spend with a venue. Don't ever pretend to a client that no commission is payable and then try and keep it as extra income for your company. Be honest. Most clients will know how the commission system works and (rightly) will be less than pleased if they think or know that you're trying to pull a fast one.

If your potential client *has* booked a venue directly or indirectly, chances are that they won't have considered get-in times (usually because of cost or ignorance) or the amount of space required for what will inevitably be a growing number of participants. I've mentioned this already and will do so again way after this book has been published, because it really gets up my nose and just makes the preparation for an event really hard and, of course, it diminishes any real chances of rehearsal. Also, and invariably, a client will begin with thinking about an audience of, say, 300 souls and this number will creep up with the additions from the Marketing Director, Managing Director and worthy folk who have no idea of the consequences, and your contact at the client end won't challenge this but will just tell you to sort it out. So if the space that's been booked is fine for 300 people, but not for 400 people, there's a problem.

When you've found a venue you like, see how quickly the venue's sales team replies to your or your company's enquiry. Any aspect of service and speediness of response are important. It'll be the mark of the venue's way of doing business. If you're not offered a site visit, then ask for one. You must. Or someone on your behalf must. Site visits are very important because they give you a chance to see the venue (obviously) and an opportunity for you to decide whether you like it or not and whether it'll fit your and your client's requirements and the event's needs. It gives you a chance to see what added value exists in terms of food and beverage, service, ambiance, detail and extras.

A logistics manager friend says, rummaging round her bag for her phone, 'When you've booked a site visit or recce, it's important to always make a note of the most important things you want in or from the venue, a few days before you go to view it. Discuss this list with your client. That way, you won't get distracted on the day and you'll know exactly what you're looking for. When you get there, consider the welcome you receive from reception and your sales representative (as it's likely all your client's delegates will be greeted in the same way). Check out the car park, and see how full it is. Have a very close look at all common parts, various rooms, technical support and so on. Try to have lunch there to assess the quality of the food and menu choices. See how the staff behave in a variety of scenarios. See the venue through delegates' eyes.' Her phone rings – the theme from *Titanic* – and she waves the instrument triumphantly.

SOME VENUE JARGON

Shakespeare lived some 400 plus years ago and words he originated are still used today. He left 1700 or so strong words, words like abstemious, academe, accused, addiction, alligator, amazement, anchovy, arouse, assassination and auspicious – and those are just a few of the As. So, when I trip over words that are used as jargon and clever-clever speak in the event industry, I cower and cringe. My American cousin, who runs a very good American marketing and communications agency, however, just says, 'Get over it. C'mon, it's just the way it is.'

Well, I'm not sure about getting over it and I'm not very sure over what I should indeed be getting. But there you are, trying to do your best to avoid jargon and then, smack, you walk into a whole load of it. The events industry, like any other, is rife with it. I'm not going to give you chapter and verse on every single weird phrase in the events industry – we'd be here all day and you'd miss your plane/train/bus – but, because the sun is shining where I am on this fine afternoon and you're waiting for your plane, here's a useful list of venue-related phrases of which you may be aware and some not:

▶ **Room only: You'll know this of course. This is the rate for bedrooms at a hotel or conference centre and is for accommodation only. When quoted 'room only', you need to be aware that there is an additional charge for any meals or occasional food and beverage. Obviously. Yet ...**

▶ **Bed and breakfast (B&B): This rate is based on double or single occupancy. This can be two people in a twin room, two people** in a double room, one person in a single or one person in a double. Whoever's responsible for booking the venue/hotel, it's important to state, when making the enquiry, what the requirements are, because the rates for each option will be different. Also check whether the breakfast is continental or fully cooked, buffet or à la carte, and what time breakfast is served in the morning.

▶ Dinner, bed and breakfast: This rate is as above, but also includes dinner in the/a venue restaurant. Within the rate, the client will have a certain allowance for food in one of the venue's eateries. Any amount in excess of this allowance will be charged to the client separately. If it's a rate quoted for a party of guests, invariably there will be a separate charge for private dining. Equally, there may be discounts for a buffet service.

▶ 24 hour delegate rate: The basic rate normally includes two servings of tea and coffee (one in the morning and another in the afternoon), conference room hire, two-course hot and cold buffet lunch, three-course evening meal, accommodation and breakfast.

▶ Day delegate rate (DDR): This rate normally includes two servings of tea and coffee (one in the morning and again another in the afternoon), conference room hire and a two-course hot and cold buffet lunch. As with the 24 hour delegate rate, this package will differ with each venue.

▶ Rack rate: This is the venue or hotel's published rate and is negotiable, although the extent will vary according to the time of year, the day of the week, the number of delegates and confirmed bookings for the time of the booking.

▶ Activity site hire: This charge for using the venue's external property or special facilities can sometimes be included in a delegate package but, more often than not, the venue will make some form of charge. This can be per head or a fixed amount.

Some venues don't charge for using their grounds – depending upon the nature of the event, the grounds and the value of the booking. Never assume that you can do anything you want on venue grounds. If you've planned for an army regiment to set up zip wires and death slides in the beautiful grounds of a large country house for a sales conference activity, do ensure that the country house is agreeable and get the confirmation in writing!

▶ Syndicate or breakout room hire: Syndicate rooms differ in size and price. Some venues may include one or more syndicate rooms within a 24 hour or day delegate rate; others, of course, won't. Some venues will agree to the provision of breakout rooms (with or without some equipment) only for you to find that they are not rooms at all, but just open plan areas or converted bedrooms (awful), or have unsuitable furniture (dispiriting and uncomfortable). Every venue will have its own arrangements and its own deals. As with most headline rates, costs vary and a good venue agent, or intermediary agency, will (or should) know which venues are most cost-effective for your specific requirements.

Says an ex-logistics manager who has retired to France to write a book on etymology, 'When I was learning my craft, my then boss, having had time on his hands serving time in Malta because of an incident with a car launch, gave me a good list of venue jargon phrases and words and I found it useful. Have a look.' I'm handed over some typewritten notes and these are the edited highlights:

▶ Blocked space: sleeping rooms, exhibit, event, or other function space reserved for future use by an individual or organisation.

▶ Comp rooms: complimentary room(s) provided by a venue or hotel without charge, usually based on the number of booked rooms.

▶ Complimentary ratio: the number of rooms provided at no cost based on the number of occupied rooms.

▶ Room pick up: the number of sleeping rooms actually used by event attendees and/or exhibitors.

▶ By the person: a fixed price per attendee; covers all consumption of food and beverage at an event, within a given time frame – usually includes beverages, snacks or hors d'oeuvres – that sort of thing.

▶ Cash bar: private bar set-up where guests pay for their own drinks.

▶ Corkage: the charge placed on alcohol brought into the venue, but purchased elsewhere. The charge sometimes includes glassware, ice and mixers.

▶ Covers: actual number of meals served at a corporate or event meal.

▶ House brand: any brand of alcohol served when a customer requests a drink by its generic name – you know, like gin and tonic, scotch and soda.

▶ Limited consumption bar: the client establishes the maximum to be spent at an open bar which is then closed or converted to cash when the set limit is reached. ('By the way,' says a venue manager who works for a big hotel chain, 'always remember to tell delegates that this is going to happen, otherwise chaos follows.')

▶ Open bar: a bar in a private room where drinks are paid for by the client or a sponsor.

▶ Service bar: a counter from which alcoholic beverages are served or collected by waiting staff – located outside a function room, usually in an area not visible to guests.

▶ Wet bar: in a hotel room, a bar or counter area with running water, used for preparing drinks.

▶ Acceleration clause: a provision sometimes used in contracts to accelerate the deposit payment schedule or to demand full prepayment of the master account in the event of a default or lack of credit by the client or whoever's paying the bill.

▶ Attrition: this is the difference between the actual number of bedrooms taken up (or food-and-beverage covers) and the number agreed to in the terms of the venue's contract. Usually there's an allowable shortfall before any shortfall is assessed.

▶ Cancellation clause: a) the provision for both parties in a contract that outlines penalties if cancellation occurs for failure to comply with the terms of the agreement and/or b) the provision within an entertainment artist's contract that allows that artist to cancel within a specified period of time prior to the performance date.

▶ Force majeure (or act of God): an unforeseeable, unexpected or uncontrollable event (the obvious examples of which are wars, strikes, extreme weather and other disruptive circumstances outside anyone's anticipation or control).

▶ Option date: date by which confirmation must be received, contract signed or payment made to secure a reservation.

▶ Lanyard: a cord worn around the neck, with an identity badge attached. I put this in because they make you look terribly important and I once wore one that said 'Access All Areas'! These days you can find wonderful electronic badges. Ask yourself if you could ignore a message that was scrolling along on a badge clipped to someone near you? Also you can get badges now where messages can be sent to the wearer.

▶ Authorised signatory: a person who is authorised to legally bind an individual or organisation to a contract, to sign for meals and services on behalf of the client or agency, or charge items to a client's master account. Sort this out before you go onsite.

▶ Going onsite: going to the venue to begin setting up and preparing for the event. Sorry – bit obvious this one.

▶ Master account/bill: a record of transactions during an event where the resulting balance is paid directly by you or your client. This may include room rate, tax, incidentals, food and beverage, technical equipment, décor and so on.

▶ Cancellation or interruption insurance: insurance that protects an agency or production company or you as an individual against financial loss or expenses incurred when contractually specified perils necessitate cancelling or relocating an event, or cause a reduction in attendance.

▶ Deductible or excess: in insurance this is the amount the customer must pay before the insurance kicks in.

▶ Liability insurance: an insurance policy that protects you in the event that there is bodily injury or property damage to other people. The liability can be because of negligence or a failure to live up to promises made under a contract. You need specialist advice on this.

▶ Set-up/breakdown: you know this now – it's the use of a meeting/conference room/venue to set up or break down – and may be charged for at a different rate. Clients often forget that this set-up time is necessary and, if they do know that it's required, they'll often insist on too little. You'll need the strength and persuasive skills of Pericles to get this right.

▶ Dual set-up: arrangement of duplicate set-ups in two or more different locations.

▶ Pre-function space: area adjacent to the main event location – often used for receptions prior to a meal or sometimes for coffee breaks during an event.

- ▶ Room turnover: the amount of time needed to break down the room (another bit of jargon that means to take down or dismantle the equipment, set and staging) and reset a function room or auditorium.

- ▶ ROI: Return on Investment – the financial (or other) return made from running an event set against the cost of producing and managing it. This is very important and you will need to understand how to sell the ROI of events to potential and existing clients.

- ▶ Banquet event order or function sheet: a document providing complete and precise instructions to a hotel/venue for the running of an event – the venue's event Bible really.

- ▶ Function book: in a hotel or venue, the official record that controls room assignments for meetings and other events. It won't be a book these days.

- ▶ Dress code: required style of dress for an event – set by the client. Business casual is the most confusing and 'slacks' have caused the most questions.

- ▶ 1st or 2nd/3rd option: where a hotel or venue already has a provisional enquiry being held for another client when you want to book space – this is a total pain in the proverbial if that's the only venue you really want.

- ▶ 24 hour hold: a term used to describe the type of reservation made on function space within a hotel, convention centre and so on. An event organiser who has 24 hour hold on a space has exclusive use and access to that space for a period of 24 hours, usually from 12:01 to 24.00.

- ▶ All space hold: all function space at a venue is reserved for one client.

- ▶ Convention & Visitors Bureau (CVB): an organisation responsible for the promotion of a town, city, area, region or country to potential visitors, event managers and convention organisers.

▶ Destination Management Company (DMC): a local company that handles ground arrangements for tours, meetings, transportation and activities for groups usually originating from overseas. If you have a good DMC it's smooth as smooth. If you have a bad one, then hang on to your change and your hat. And your client.

▶ Ground operator: a company that provides land services such as sightseeing tours, transfers from the airport to a hotel, limos, taxis and some concierge services.

▶ HBA: Hotel Booking Agency.

▶ Release date: date beyond which a venue is free to sell function space to others.

Suffice to say there is undeniably an argot of vocabulary that goes with event management and, indeed, with production and communications as a whole too. I weep, gentle reader and clutch my wine glass all the harder. In his book, *Ogilvy on Advertising*, the late great advertising guru David Ogilvy wrote, 'Our business is infested with idiots who try to impress by using pretentious jargon.' He wrote much in 1983 that is as true today as it was then and a great deal of it can apply to the world of events.

GETTING DEALS FROM HOTELS

The demand for hotel services around the world has steadily increased over the past few years – despite the economic downturn – tilting the negotiating leverage in favour of 'preferred properties' (what those not in the industry call a hotel or venue) rather than the agencies or production companies. This has put extra pressure on agencies and production companies (and actually end clients) to find ways to negotiate with hotel sales to lower some of those expenses. Depending on your circumstances, there are some tips that may help you achieve some measure of venue savings:

▶ If you can, leverage multiple events at the same location: one of the more effective strategies for saving money is to hold more than one event for the same client at the same venue, preferably back to back. That's not always possible of course, but it is worth suggesting to your client. Venue sales managers are looking to achieve certain revenue targets, so they are likely to show more flexibility to a client willing to buy more space.

▶ Leverage the total number of guest rooms for the event: the venue will show flexibility on meeting room space costs – and even some catering expenses – if they know that an event will utilise a block of bedrooms. Obvious really.

▶ Leverage (good word, leverage) additional discounts on bedrooms: hotels/venues (particularly large chains) may discount guest rooms or offer you a lower rate. Ask.

▶ Negotiate food and beverage requirements: many agency people (and clients too) will cut costs by adjusting this category. But 'adjusting' often means 'cutting' and the results aren't always beneficial to the event. Most given menus are designed to be 'adjusted' to more or less meet anyone's budget. 'However,' says a high street retail communications manager charged with buying many events utilising hotels around the UK, 'in my experience, it's better to identify your preferred food and beverage needs and then request discounts rather than just cutting out bits and pieces. Hotels understand this; you're in the business of keeping your client's audiences happy and therefore so is the hotel.'

▶ Negotiate the in-house technical costs. This is a tricky area because the agency or production company for which you work might be providing all the technical support in which case the venue will supply nothing. But sometimes, for small events, it can make sense to use the venue's equipment (providing it's good and also providing the technicians are experienced and on the ball.) But lighting, sound, projection and staging are areas where hidden expenses can quickly add up with a venue – and sometimes can be negotiated, but not always. Renting LCD (Liquid Crystal Display) projectors, for instance, varies from venue to venue and they can be priced quite outrageously. But be bold and ask for a discount, preferably with the advice of someone who knows what things should cost. Also ask for some items to be waived, if they're not needed. Usually day rates for any personnel or technicians are non-negotiable. Says the high street retail communications manager, 'Venues are aware of client frustrations with A/V and technical provision costs and often outsource operations to third party companies instead, thereby eliminating any negotiating responsibility. But, if you know what you want and are precise, then you can get decent deals with the third parties.'

▶ Be extremely flexible on time, space and dates if you can. You probably can't, because the client or the client's Chief Executive's diary is fixed, but if you *are* flexible then costs will undoubtedly reduce.

▶ Compare quoted hotel bedroom discounts to online consumer travel search engines. It's amazing how often search engines such as Expedia or Travelocity may offer more cost effective rates than those offered by a hotel central sales operation to a corporate client.

▶ A good and obvious tip: don't get involved in negotiating with venues unless you really do have some experience. If in doubt, rely on a logistics expert, preferably within your agency or company,.or you might need to hire a freelance expert.

CHOOSING A VENUE-FINDING AGENCY

If I had a pound or indeed a dollar for everyone who's told me they can no longer afford to shop solely at smarter supermarket chains, I could afford to shop solely at one of those supermarket chains. Rake, say, 5 per cent off soap powder profits for a month and one of said chains could fund the entire UK national debt. The same goes for venue finding. If I had a pound (or maybe some yen) for every time a client said, 'Oh, we've booked the venue already. The show's on Tuesday and Wednesday and the get-in is 02:00 on Tuesday morning. Now let's discuss entertainment ...' I would be a happy man.

Similarly, following those sorts of conversations, if I had some loose change every time I visited the venue chosen by a client only to find that the banqueting suite of the Such and Such Inn, Cardiff has walls in clashing primary colours with hundreds of hostile-looking sofas, complete with gilt velour curtains, I'd be rich as Croesus. Seldom can venues have been so badly ripped off by their decorators. Seldom can clients have been so foolish.

Someone has to actually find the venue. Some clients clearly do their own thing and will have signed a contract before you arrive on the scene. That's so irritating because you will be presented with headaches straight away – usually because there is sufficient space booked for 500 people standing having a cocktail, but there isn't room for 500 people sitting at table rounds with a set/staging along with rear projection and all the corporate event trimmings. Of course, sometimes clients do know what they're doing (not least because they might have in-house specialists) and that's fine, but it is true that many choose the wrong venue to suit their or their audience's needs. Finding and buying space is a skill. Buying the right space is a special skill and I have huge respect for those who do it well day in day out.

Some clients buy the services of a specialist DMC, venue-finding company or logistics agency, and others rely on the skills and experience of their production company or their event delivery agency. Whatever and whoever, there are certain criteria that you or someone should take into account when sourcing a venue finder.

The most important factor when looking for a venue-finding agency is the quality of their employees. You need to identify quickly whether the venue-finding agency is a systems-based, impersonal call centre employing dozens of staff who have never been to any of the venues they are so heartily recommending, or maybe it's a team of experienced, passionate professionals with wide experience of finding venues for a wide range of events. If the answer is the former, then keep looking. It's critical to deal with someone or a business that has proper first-hand experience of the country, city, town, venues, hotels and environs for wherever and whatever it is that you have in mind.

Event management agencies often take the time to send their employees out on what the industry calls familiarisation trips or 'fam' trips for short. Such trips are paid-for visits with a small group of others from the industry to view a country, city, area, venue or hotel. Some fam trips are superb, some are ghastly. Much depends on the people who are in the group with you and obviously the organisation behind the trip. However, the idea of such trips is an excellent one and ensures that the employees of the venue-finding agency have visited a wide range of venues and have been shown around. Fam trips also apply to checking out airlines and other forms of transport and activities in and around particular venues, including restaurants, bars and entertainment. 'This process ensures that the staff from a venue-finding agency,' says the director of such a company, 'have personal contacts at a variety of venues and centres of interest, ensuring (in principle anyway) immediate, accurate information and often better financial or availability deals. That's the theory. In practice some fam trips are poorly organised, cheaply funded and are just overt selling opportunities, but those who attend are gradually demanding better content and delivery, and that's good. It's in everybody's interest that these visits are top quality.'

Clearly, it is not always possible (for you) to have seen a venue before short-listing it for a client. However, by gaining experience of seeing a number of different venues, the employees of a good venue-finding agency can sift through the endless venue choices on your behalf and make an informed decision when putting together a shortlist. The final venue choice is rarely the venue-finding agency employees' responsibility – it's yours or your client's, and the quality of the shortlist is vital for the success of your event. As a reminder, most venue-finding agencies will earn their money from commission from the venue, hotel or facility.

Apart from assessing the level of employee knowledge at a venue-finding agency, another key factor to assess is its service efficiency. A good agency should provide you with a number of references so that you can speak to others about their experience of the agency and also a venue or hotel in which you or your client has an interest. Broadly speaking and unremarkably, the benefit of an effective venue-finding agency is that they should find the venue that's perfect for your event. That means that you have to know what that is. The client too has a responsibility here. They need to be clear about what venue they are seeking and where. You must help. The client shouldn't use the finding exercise as a long-term (and free of charge) 'We'll know what we want when we find it' approach. Neither should it be allowed to say, 'Well, let's have the choice of six four-star hotels in six cities round the world and, if they're not right, we'll have another six.' That stinks and you need to be firm in helping the potential client or client to define the *precise* requirements. After all, that kind of advice is in your own interests to give.

Your venue-finding should be a pleasurable experience. There are many, many companies that pride themselves on high levels of service and passion for finding the right venue. Be wary of some venue-finding agencies just looking up (probably slightly out of date) information on their systems or using venue websites – you can do that yourself. You want to use a professional company to make your life easier and you also want to take advantage of expertise and experience.

CHAPTER THREE

TRAVELS

GREAT CITIES FOR GREAT EVENTS

My cousin (New York, reddish hair, runs a communication marketing agency, knows about events, talks non-stop – sometimes sense, sometimes not) and I are discussing (actually arguing about) the best cities in which to hold a conference, an average corporate conference. He says, 'A grand ballroom in a Las Vegas hotel maybe? Anything Disney? Berlin? London? Saratoga Springs? Johannesburg? Budapest is good. Melbourne, Sydney: you think that they're too far from Europe?' What I think is that it's very strange that he's talking to a family member in staccato half sentences. Choosing an overseas city for an event is hard and the options these days are wide – obviously depending on where your start-point is. Sometimes the decision's made for you because the client chooses a city for reasons of ease of travel, or because the client has heard that a particular venue in a particular city is good or because a city/country is dictated by a wider communications strategy.

You'll need to make sure that the city you're considering can offer conference attendees an experience that is hassle-free, offers some level of entertainment and is affordable within your client's budget. The last point is obvious but it is often the case that producers, logistics people and project managers find a great property at a 'great' price and try to sell it back to the client and that, in turn, can cause abrasions.

A logistics expert who works for a large DMC in the United States says, 'Cities like Las Vegas and Orlando end up being ideal settings for meetings not because of all the excitement each city has to offer (although that can play a part in a decision). They work out because they are built to host and service delegates. And that can be really, really important.' A good host city will be one in which you will want to attend a conference. But you have to know your client and your client's delegates. The city should be relatively easy and inexpensive to reach, particularly by air. Delegates should also be able to travel within the city once they get there, and safely. Also, and do forgive me if I am making an obvious point (as my cousin keeps telling me I am) but it's important to make sure that the city has enough rooms, restaurants and other facilities to meet the needs of your attendees. Also, and this is key too, keep in mind that, just because an event for a client was a hit in a city once, this doesn't guarantee that it will be a hit the next time for the same client. You should take note of variables that may have made the first event a hit – like a place that many attendees had never been before, the time of year the conference was held, content, approach and so on.

'An important thing to remember,' offers a well-travelled industry colleague who's been producing all sorts of conferences for an age, 'is that you should see the city and the venue in action before committing to anything. Visit them during their peak seasons to make sure they can appropriately accommodate your group for your event. This has the opportunity to offer you either piece of mind or a chance to get out before you're in too deep.'

I am now sitting at a formal dinner that is celebrating industry awards. The food's horrid, but the company is fun and we're drinking some strange Icelandic wine called *Kvöldsól*. It says on the bottle that it's an organic wine from Iceland made from antioxidant-rich berries. After many glasses, it doesn't matter. The people around me are discussing their preferred locations and cities for corporate events in the United States. Some are saying that hip is good, places like San Francisco, Seattle, Portland, Santa Fe, Austin and Boulder. Some say Vegas or Atlantic City. Others speak fondly of Disney properties.

Someone waxes lyrical about New York City. 'New York,' she says, 'is home to many hotels and leisure activities ideal for businesses that want to hold corporate meetings. Being both a tourist destination and international business centre, New York provides the best in terms of conference facilities and leisure activities.' 'Las Vegas,' contributes another member of the party who reminds me of Al Pacino, 'provides one of the best mixes of corporate event and entertainment facilities in the world. Bar none.'

'Vancouver is another favourite corporate destination of mine,' shouts cousin Maier down the phone. 'The city has spectacular scenery ranging from oceans to mountain views. The air is good and the people helpful.' He talks to someone with him in his office. There's a shout then he's back with me and he says, 'Barcelona is one of the leading destinations to hold corporate meetings. Being a major fashion and tourism destination, it offers some of the best world-class hotels and accommodation facilities. Ah, and another Spanish city that ranks among the best corporate destinations is Madrid. Like Barcelona, it's a major tourist destination. London is also rated to be among the best cities for corporate events with some excellent facilities, venues and hotels. Then there's Berlin, Singapore, Johannesburg, Pretoria, Milan, Rome …' He stops and tells me that he has to go.

Whatever city you choose or whichever one you select with your client, the rationale should be a business and strategic case. It will protect your event, mitigate risk, may help you reduce costs and ultimately manage all stakeholder expectations. To help you, you can set up a destination feasibility study – a great way of identifying requirements within your event profile and of having a structured approach for destination analysis. The study should revolve around the event profile and that in turn should include the event's goals and objectives, the attendees' demographics, programme content, available budget, available historical data, preferred dates, space requirements, bedroom requirements, range of acceptable rates, catering needs and quality, size of exhibition (if there is to be one) and an outline of the preferred social programme, in terms of gala dinners, partner programmes, teambuilding and the like. Congress and convention centres or associations in each country, and sometimes in each city, can be very helpful in advising which venue is most suitable for your needs. They can very often provide unbiased and free information about hotels, traditional (and indeed non-traditional) venues. They can also often help make introductions to local dignitaries and business leaders.

After short-listing your destination choices, a site inspection of those locations and venues is always recommended. You've heard this before and it's important, hence the repetition. The destination should have a proven track record in hosting conferences and it's possible (highly recommended) that you talk to someone who's held a conference there.

Oscillation of currencies, particularly these days, is always something of a risk, so it's important to keep a close eye on the currency of a destination and keep your client in the loop. Some clients will want to fix currency exchange rates at an early stage, but do take advice if cash and currencies aren't your skill areas. Also remember to check out visa and inoculation requirements. Check out if there are any clashing festivals, trade exhibitions or sporting events and don't forget that these might influence hotel and venue prices. In addition, and this is ever important now, check the venue's policy on CSR (Corporate Social Responsibility) and the environment. Someone at the client end will want to know so it's best that you do. 'Also,' says the Financial Director of a large event management agency, 'the whole issue of VAT and TOMS (Tour Operators' Margin Scheme) will need to be checked, and you should do that with an expert – probably someone in your company's finance department or an external advisor. I'm not even going to begin to explain. Up to date information on VAT prevailing rates, any impending changes and the process for VAT reclaim is vital information to have. This can save a lot of money in the conference budget.'

A TRIP TO DUBAI

On a recent working visit to the United Arab Emirates, mostly Dubai, I met a number of event industry experts and I took the opportunity to ask a few for their view of using venues and hotels throughout the world for corporate events. We sat in the coffee lounge of a hotel belonging to a major Dubai hotel chain – enjoying fruit juices and, in one case, a large vodka and tonic despite the fact that it was eight thirty in the morning. 'You have to be careful when choosing an overseas venue,' said one member of our experienced group. She went on, 'Most overseas destinations have a host of DMCs offering transfers and off-site programmes. Beware! The quality of services and performance varies immensely. If you can't decide between holding your event in, say, the United Kingdom or overseas, there are additional considerations. Apart from transportation costs, visas may be required, adding time and more expense. In dangerous times or during periods of social unrest, the nationality of your speakers may create additional difficulties getting them in and out of the country. Don't forget the weather – it may be too hot, humid or cold for your delegates' comfort – as anyone who has tried holding an event in the Middle East during Ramadan will attest!' She continued with her valuable advice, 'The main challenges are knowing the culture, the correct legal procedures and the political situation of the country in which the event will take place. You have to know how the people operate and how to deal with vendors and other people … how to do things effectively without offending people. You also have to use common sense. Not that long ago a major computer manufacturer insisted on not cancelling its regional management conference being held in Athens, only to find that two days before the event, there was rioting in the streets nearby and the building next door was ransacked. Foresight and good sense are essential and cancellation is not the end of the world if safety is involved.'

This colleague is fluent in Spanish and can greet people in French, Mandarin Chinese and some Arabic, but she mostly does business with people who can speak English. 'That's one of the benefits of the twelve countries with which my company works,' she says. 'We have local business and social contacts and they give us real-time information about what's going on, things we need to know and what we should avoid.' She pauses and stands to greet in Arabic two local gentlemen who are passing, deep in conversation. After they have smiled at her in recognition, she says to a quizzical me, 'It means "Hello and how are you this morning?" It helps to be friendly and speak some of the language. Not essential, but very helpful.' One of our circle accidentally tips his pomegranate juice all over my neighbour's soft leather Gucci bag and the air is tinged light blue with language from all over the globe.

Another in our group, a German logistics specialist of many years standing and for whom I have huge respect, picks up the discussion: 'Before sending clients overseas, the agency for which I used to work held orientations so that the client project manager or producer could understand cultural differences and avoid potential pitfalls, thereby increasing chances for the event's success. Of course, some clients (such as international banks) are very well travelled and often know places better than their agencies. Also, security is an important consideration nowadays. With conferences, private security is sometimes hired, especially when there are dignitaries involved. More and more, clients are looking for agencies with people who understand global culture and international mores. Understanding culture and the different ways of doing business makes you more versatile – more flexible.'

Later, outside, in the sodden heat, I pass hundreds and hundreds of regimented palm trees and idly I wonder who waters them and with what. The skyline, in the dusty, beige haze, looks like a poster for a remake of *Roller Blade*. It's very quiet and very hot. Once, everyone thought that Dubai was going to become much like Singapore – a commercial and financial services hub with fabulous hotels, apartments, cars, servants and food and drink of any kind at any time – and a city in which many conferences would be held year round. But it hasn't quite worked out, although I think it's on the rise again and many businesses are holding important events here. I see the current tallest building in the world – it was going to be called Burj Dubai, but it's now called the Burj Khalifa, named after Abu Dhabi's ruler who put up the cash. I really like Dubai. I actually like the casual opulence and I like the people very much. I like the service ethic that's prevalent in venues and the 'can-do' attitude that goes with that. This may not be everyone's view, but I'm holding on to mine.

Delivering an event here can be refreshing. There is a positive attitude amongst venue managements and, while most of the hotel auditoriums or banqueting rooms aren't quite my cup of tea when it comes to design and décor, the end results can be very good. The same goes for exhibitions and the desert activities – 4x4 racing, dune buggies, sand surfing, camel riding and the like. There are also a number of very good dry hire companies out there. Dry hire means that you can hire equipment with or without technicians, but with no creativity or added services. There are a couple of excellent fully-fledged production companies too which have excellent reputations and can deliver very big projects as well as small. Of course there are also some poor companies as indeed there are everywhere – out to make a quick buck (and they do) but to hell in a handcart with quality or truth.

MILAN IN SPRINGTIME

The Galleria Vittorio Emanuele is a shopping arcade. At one end is La Scala and at the other the Milan Duomo, apparently the second largest church on the planet. The Galleria Vittorio Emanuele is no ordinary shopping mall. This is no large aircraft hangar that the United Arab Emirates, Saudi Arabia, or Qatar might offer. This is the biggest walkway in Italy. People, young and old, particularly the old, parade up and down. They show off clothing styles that you may want immediately, but can only drool over, or else discover that the fantastic soft tweed jacket with leather patches on the elbow that you espied sold out months ago and, anyway, would have taken a year's salary to purchase.

But what's brilliant in Milan, particularly in the sunshine, is that there's a free fashion show everywhere you walk or visit. The world seems to be here to try and see what the latest fashions are. Some try to wear all those fashions at once. All parade up and down Milan's shopping malls to capture the essence of what's 'in' and what is, for most of us, 'out' because it's just totally unaffordable.

It's to here (well, Milan) that a large group of executives from an international computer software retail business head-officed in the United Kingdom are attending their annual marketing conference. This time it's also seen as part of a new incentive programme, and a visit to Milan's fashion centre is part of that process for one part of the overall group.

Milan is known as Italy's fashion and design capital. It is also a major influence in the world of music, industry, art and literature – oh yes, and sport, particularly football. The city has a plethora of wonderful museums, university buildings, churches and libraries. The shops, bars and restaurants cater for every taste, and there's always a buzz in the air – a sense of excitement, verve and vigour. It's by far the largest metropolitan city in Italy and has served as the hub for many of Italy's famous fashion houses such as Dolce & Gabbana, Armani, Gucci, Prada, Versace and so on. The art galleries are brilliant – I'm sitting in The Church of Santa Maria delle Grazie where Da Vinci's *Last Supper of Jesus and the Apostles* is displayed. I honestly do stare in wonder and think of the mystery.

Milan is a major railway hub with the busiest station, Milan Central, giving access to much of Europe. There are three international airports. The Milan Convention Centre, 'Fiera Milano Congressi', is one of Italy's leading conference centres and can manage large-scale international events. Just outside the city is Lake Como and a panorama that's superb. Bergamo, an ancient city, isn't far away and Vigevano is worth a visit. There are few cities that I know as being superb for any type of corporate event, and Milan is one I'd use in a heartbeat. This is of course subjective and you'll have your own favourites. The most important aspect of a city for a venue for a conference is transport, safety, style, interest and event facilities. Milan has all those. The Hotel Principe di Savoia, for example, offers the largest meeting and conference space available of five star hotels in Milan. Its Sala Cristalli is equipped with the most advanced audio-visual solutions – and I do mean advanced. All the fourteen different sized meeting rooms can be equipped with the latest technology. Then there's The Crowne Plaza Milan Hotel – a four star hotel, situated near to Milan Linate Airport and a few kilometres from Piazza Duomo. The Crowne Plaza Milan has thirteen conference rooms and the famous *Il Teatro*, one of the biggest structures in Italy, able to host up to 2000 people. The Leonardo Da Vinci Congress Centre is great for conventions, seminars, meetings, fashion shows and big association banquets. The Congress Centre is equipped with the most advanced technology for projection, sound, recording and simultaneous translation in ten different languages. The main room has no pillars and seats 1200 people. It can be divided into six different rooms by means of sound-proof mobile divides. There are a myriad of smaller venues dotted around and just outside the city. Service at each is excellent and the city really does understand corporate events. You don't get that everywhere in the world.

NEW YORK

The expression on my colleague's face suggested that give-and-take was an unpleasant concept to which she would never ever subscribe. Her jaw tightened, jutted and went pink as she turned, muttering, 'Look, I've told the client New York and nobody's going to stop me.' Another colleague professed a preference for Paris given, she said, that there were venues and activities that suited our client's needs perfectly.

So New York it was. This was some years ago and New York was still off the beaten track for most corporate events. 600 senior executives duly rocked up to the Big Apple. It was when everything about the United States was brilliant, and I personally think that mostly everything about the United States is, by and large, still brilliant, although I'm aware that this view can be contentious at dinner parties. I've seen extraordinary technological developments in America, amazing art and theatre. I've heard the intensity of Arthur Miller, David Mamet, Edward Albee, Lillian Hellman … the list is long. I've witnessed poetry and experiential theatre – brilliantly, cleverly, passionately done. I've explored every nook and cranny of New York and I think that I've still got a lifetime of exploring yet to do. My large cousin, who will tell anyone who cares to listen, that he hails from the 'siddie', says that there are more nooks and crannies left to feed several lifetimes of discovery, and I believe him.

But it's not just the city that attracts. New York State is rich in history and its lush countryside provides the perfect backdrop for events large and small. It's a state where nations were planned, treaties were signed and islands were famously acquired. It's a state where, in 1825, the monumental Erie Canal opened a viable avenue for transportation of goods from the Atlantic Ocean to the Great Lakes, and it's a state where huge conurbations coexist with rugged mountains and wide tracts of land. Because of this fortuitous confluence of commerce, culture and nature, New York State sets the stage for events of every type, from intimate corporate retreats to massive association conferences. Whether a venue requires a more urban landscape or one that nestles comfortably into the countryside, New York State has everything you could need for a corporate conference.

When considering New York State, many think of Buffalo, Rochester and Syracuse to the west, the Adirondacks to the north or Albany to the southeast. When seeking out an east coast venue alternative to the high stress and expense associated with New York City, New York State gives us the perfect mix of rural and urban, technology and education, food and culture. Sales pitch over. Well, kind of.

I've been to NY many times and it is, without question, my favourite city, closely followed by Venice (Italy). I like New Yorkers. I like the airports – crazy I know. New York City is serviced by three: JFK and LaGuardia in New York and Liberty International in Newark. Don't let the fact that Liberty is in a different state scare you off. You can take a cab ride, train or even helicopter and make it to Manhattan in no time. 'Public transport is the way to travel in New York,' says my cousin. He tells me over a pastrami and mustard on light rye brunch at a famous deli on East Houston Street: 'The subway and rail lines connect the city nicely and can save you hours (almost days) in traffic. If you want to stay above ground, take a cab. Parking causes difficulties and there's just no need to have your own car when you can get around twenty four hours a day with someone else driving.'

Anyway, back in the day when I produced that event for 600 or so bank executives, the show was filled with dry ice pumping down shiny stairways and there were dancers doing some big numbers during the awards ceremony. There were lasers and those were the days when you had to be quite careful; there was a lighting rig to do justice to the East Street Band that was playing up the road led by 'The Boss'. I remember the hotel where we stayed and the bar lined with ranks of people. It was the best of times apart from the moment when a man at the concierge desk asked which part of Australia I was from.

New York City is indeed one of my favourite cities for events of all kinds. It has the venues (nearly a million square feet of exhibition and event space) and bedrooms (some 80,000), the infrastructure, the added buzz and entertainment. It's safe. Catering is great and this is a city of huge imagination when it comes to ideas for a buffet or fine dining. Here there is the Statue of Liberty, the Empire State Building, Times Square, and the Metropolitan

Museum of Art. Here are places to find your inner Zen should you so wish, places to dance away the night (and day), places that offer brilliant burlesque or the burlesque can come to you. You can shop, see the New York City Ballet, see The American Ballet Theatre, go to Carnegie Hall (where the ghosts of Isaac Stern, Benny Goodman, Duke Ellington, and the Beatles survive), the brilliant High Line Park, the Brooklyn Bridge, Prospect Park, New York Transit Museum, MoMa and much more. But, you might well be saying, there are many of the world's great cities that offer great theatre, architecture, venues, food and atmosphere. You're right and this is a subjective view. My cousin puts it as well as anyone, 'New York has a special charisma, a buzz that delights, and whenever I've been involved in an event here, they've always worked well – the technicians, the creatives, the delivery and the can-do attitude are brilliant.

Most of my clients over the years and many in the events industry love New York. In my mind's eye I see a bustling metropolis with a plethora of yellow cabs, underground subway station entrances and buildings that stretch high. I see Brooklyn, Staten Island, Queens, Manhattan, The Bronx. New York can really look beautiful and on a clear, sunny day, the light's almost golden.

CHAPTER FOUR

PROCUREMENT, THE REQUEST FOR INFORMATION (RFI) AND THE REQUEST FOR (A) PROPOSAL (RFP)

WHAT DO YOU MEAN, PROCUREMENT, THE RFI AND THE RFP?

Sounds like a series of other world police forces doesn't it – or something out of *Star Wars*: 'The procurement general will see you now captain – in the RFI if you please but, be careful, because the RFP is malfunctioning.' Procurement makes many an event industry newbie blanche. It makes many an oldie go somewhat pale round the gills too. There's an event management agency based in the north of England, led by someone who achieved a first in Mathematics from Oxford. He entertains me to coffee and cheesecake. I crumble the cake on my plate much as Louis Pasteur might have done in his early stages of discovery. He says, 'There's a group of mathematicians campaigning for the mathematical constant pi to be replaced by tau, the latter being the ratio of the circumference to the radius as opposed to that of the circumference to the diameter. As tau is simply twice the value of pi ... did you know that a value for pi is mentioned in the Old Testament – relating to the construction of the Temple of Solomon, around 450 BC?' I must be staring and the cheesecake is as dust. 'Anyway...' the mathematician says, and he stares back for a moment. 'But you don't want to hear about pi or tau do you?' I shrug my shoulders, indicating that I'm easy. He then says, 'Thought not. OK, well, many young entrants to the event production, management and delivery businesses have been bloodied by being charged with helping to complete many an RFI or RFP, which is daft really because these things require seasoned hands, not new people who will know little.' What he says (now) is important and I want to spend time on this area because it's obviously a focal aspect of the process of winning business as well as a necessary discipline. It must be done well – not only to have a chance of winning, but of competing to get onto tender lists in the first place.

My mathematician friend explains his view on procurement difficulties: 'People get confused by the jargon. When, for example, is an RFI (Request for Information) an EOI (Expression of Interest) and when is an RFP (Request for Proposal) an RFT (Request for Tender) and when should an RFQ (Request for Quotation) be used, and what is an ROI (Registration of Interest)? Even more questions arise on how to respond to each of these tools that are used in a procurement process. I should also point out that most event projects purchased by a corporate or public organisation will go through an RFI and RFP process and you'll only get the first of these, the RFI, if your company is on the Purchasing or Procurement Department's list. As for the others – EOIs, RFTs and ROIs – they rarely turn up in the events industry.'

A procurement director who works for a major airline says (I sense a little wearily), 'A Registration of Interest (ROI) *can* be used by an organisation wanting to "buy" the services of an event supplier (or a company offering services to the event industry) to determine which organisations would like to register to be part of a procurement process. Clear? Information in a standard template (normally provided), and limited to a few pages, is all that should be required from respondents. An EOI is very similar, although more detail might be requested in an EOI as it's more than just registering – respondents are able to express their views and capabilities. Again a template should be provided and respondents shouldn't be expected to provide volumes of information. But to do these things properly takes thought and some time. Now, an RFI should be taken very seriously, and anyway, it's a chance to explain how your company approaches design, provision of solutions, capability, specific and relevant experience (note the "relevant"), company information, references, pricing policy and indicative implementation times.'

Most important, in connection with any of these requests for information, is that the buying organisation is crystal clear about what they are setting out to achieve at this stage of the procurement process and they should make it clear to respondents. That's you or your company, in case there's any doubt. The workload at this stage should not be a burden if you and your colleagues are organised and if you read the requirements carefully. One thing that is most peculiar is that many event businesses don't have a well-greased system for responding to an RFI, and they don't actually answer the questions properly but just cut and paste from older responses. That's really foolish these days because potential clients have people on board who really *do* read the RFI answers and grade accordingly. They also know what they want and are experienced in the events field.

OH PROCUREMENT – *CARPE DIEM*

There was a time when, and not that many years ago, but certainly in the last century, I was having dinner with the CEO of a high street bank along with one of my producers. We'd delivered two or three mid-sized events for his bank and he liked our style and the way that we ensured that communication really worked, and the way in which we wrote speeches, came up with cost-effective creativity and attended to detail. The London dinner focused on some mundane matters – such as which celebs were dining at this particular brasserie that evening. At one point our client went over to say hello to a mainstream TV presenter whom he knew. When he returned, the CEO began to talk about getting his vision and mission across to many thousands of staff and his need to effect substantial change in attitudes towards what the bank needed to become. My producer and I listened and within a couple of hours we had sketched out a way of delivering what the CEO wanted to achieve. It was literally a plan drawn out on the back of several napkins. I'd like to be able to say that the serviettes were kept and framed but, no. Within two or so months we had a programme rolling and some of that involved event production, film making and much else. The point is that we didn't go anywhere near procurement. Now, I'm not suggesting that was the right or wrong way. It was just *the* way that it happened. These days this would really occur like that. Certainly, sometimes projects *do* get the nod from on high without the usual processes, but not as a rule, and it's the rule that drives the industry these days.

I talked recently and at length with the head of procurement at, as it happens, a major bank. She said, 'Procurement is the acquisition of goods and/or services. It's favourable to the buying organisation that the events or event-related services are appropriate and that they are procured at the best possible cost to meet the needs of the purchaser in terms of fitness for purpose, quality, quantity, delivery and track record.'

A request for information (RFI) is a standard business process, the purpose of which is to collect written information about the capabilities of various suppliers. I'm reiterating this because I know from speaking to client companies that they often despair at the nonsense that gets sent back, mostly because suppliers don't answer the questions accurately or at all. Normally RFIs follow a format that can be used for comparative purposes – and that makes sense. The problem is that, inevitably, the process is rarely fair and not really comparative – not least because each company charges slightly differently and also, creatively, will be different. 'It *can* be like comparing apples with oranges. An RFI is primarily used to gather information to help make a decision on what steps to take next,' says a procurement manager at a European automotive company. 'RFIs are therefore seldom the final stage and are instead often a precursor to an RFP.'

THE REQUEST FOR AN RFP

An RFP is issued as an invitation for suppliers who have usually got through the RFI stage (often through an email or online process), to submit a proposal for an aspect (or all) of the delivery of an event. The RFP process is meant to bring structure and, one would hope, fairness, to the procurement decision and is also meant to allow the risks and benefits to be identified clearly upfront. But, overall, the RFP is looking for an answer to a specific brief, along with a creative response and detailed costs. That would normally be great but not all briefs are indeed great and many leave huge gaps – and that causes confusion, anxiety and mistakes. If the duty of an event supplier is to give an RFP time and effort, then there is a duty (sometimes disgracefully ignored) from those on the client-side to prepare an excellent brief. Anything less is inexcusable.

Says the CEO of a major UK event and design agency with fully operational offices around the world, 'An RFP should dictate to varying degrees the exact structure and format of the supplier's response. Effective RFPs typically reflect the potential client's strategy and short/long-term business objectives. Those will, or should, provide detailed insights on which you will be able (and will be expected) to offer a view – in the context of a specific event or conference. But most RFPs throw up more questions than they answer and there are usually strict rules about the number of times you can ask questions of the potential client. Essentially, you simply have to know what that potential client is thinking about and that means a proper meeting before you even put pen to paper.'

Most RFPs will ask for a statement of work – a document that captures and defines the time-line for delivery of various parts of the programme or event. The RFP might also point out the need for specific deadlines and penalties for exceeding deadlines. The event and design company CEO again: 'It's important that the potential client, the purchaser, doesn't always lay down the golden rules. You, as a supplier, need to define your company's terms and rules of engagement as well. That's tough if you're a small concern and pitching for a piece of major blue chip business; it's hard for you to dictate any rules. But there's no point in agreeing to something that you can't deliver or something to which you can't adhere at a later stage. That way madness lies.'

Procurement can be a dusty old process and fraught with potholes including e-procurement and e-bidding. E-procurement is managed with a software application that includes features for supplier management and complex auctions. E-bidding is a financial war via a client website whereby you put in your best bids over, say, three rounds. Very often the e-procurement and e-bidding processes are managed by a third party consultancy company. 'That's not always a benefit to you,' says an executive producer, 'because you'll never know what the consultancy regards as important and the consultancy will rarely engage with you directly or properly.'

Event companies tend to hate RFIs and RFPs for two reasons. First, the time they require can be significant. Second, current selling prices and margins are likely to be pruned to the bone. However, the successful supplier who wins the award may capture significant increased amounts of additional work that was previously unavailable. Smart senior management at the client end, including procurement managers, increasingly recognise that certain suppliers can represent a strategic resource. So, aim to be one of those then. Most buyer organisations don't receive the full value available from their supplier – and suppliers tend to fail to provide their target customers with maximum perceived customer value – including useful information and proactive thinking. The executive producer, wearing, I might point out, a petrol blue suit of exquisite cut, adds, 'I fail to understand why supplier organisations don't see RFP requests as a brilliant opportunity to not only win business, but to differentiate themselves – to separate themselves from their competition. If the issue is the time required to respond to an RFP, then maybe a supplier needs to rethink and reorganise how its resources are positioned in order to properly and successfully respond.'

My cousin rings from New York and tells me (loudly) that RFIs and RFPs are important and that I should tell people to take them seriously. That's all he has to say on the subject.

GETTING NOTICED

If an RFI is your agency's shop window for the client or potential client, there is little opportunity to demonstrate your company's personality and to engender that all-important chemistry. That only happens if you succeed in getting through to the next stage. Given that several competitors may be responding (more than five is too many) and given that most competitors will be saying much the same thing as you, what do you need to do to optimise your chances of being noticed?

I discuss this with a retired UK government agency procurement specialist who tells me that, in her view, the answer (and her list) are relatively simple.

▶ Examine the brief, read it again and get someone else to sense check it. If you can't answer all the questions thoroughly and precisely (not just saying what you *want* to say, but saying what the question demands), then you probably shouldn't be responding to it.

▶ Question the brief. That's not the same as challenging it which you can only really do if you know the potential client very well or if you're *absolutely* sure of your ground. RFIs and RFPs are often based on templates designed to find suppliers in completely different sectors, so the information asked for can sometimes be irrelevant. By asking questions, you may even help the client reconstruct the RFP in a more meaningful way but that happens rarely. Often though the potential client will ask for questions by a particular date, following which no more are allowed. They may also share your questions and their answers with all competitors. They may also decide to get all suppliers in one room in order to openly discuss the brief and to air issues and questions. That's a galling experience and nobody ever asks what they really want to ask in front of competitors not least because everyone's trying to shine in front of the client.

▶ Be honest with the client if the RFP is outside your scale or scope, but say what your scope is. You will be respected for it and the potential client may come back to you when a more relevant need arises.

▶ Use case studies to demonstrate your capabilities, especially when using partners to help you fulfil the brief. The case studies *must* be relevant. Too many agencies put forward an award-winning show as a case study that has no bearing at all on what this potential client might want.

▶ It's not just about prices – demonstrate clearly how you add value but keep adjectives to a minimum.

▶ Be clear about your points of difference from the competition – difficult but important. Put yourself in the client's position: why should they pick you?

▶ Often there's a section asking for additional information. Seize this with both hands as an opportunity to make your business come alive by, for instance, including other relevant areas of expertise, major accomplishments and, if you must, awards. But don't go on and on, and don't forget, awards are really for your clients, not you. Be graceful enough to acknowledge that.

▶ Potential clients are often looking for a long-term partner beyond the duration of the RFP contract, so show how you can deliver value year-on-year by expanding the proposition, but *don't* go off on a long tangent.

▶ Invest time and money in making the RFP look good, but not flash or superfluous. Include presentation-style documentation that makes it easy to follow and understand. Too many responses look good, but require instructions as to order, sense or how to get the box open! What you think is highly amusing may get put in the bin.

▶ When looking at KPIs (Key Performance Indicators), ensure that you are being asked to respond with things you can actually measure. For example, you can't say what savings you will make if you don't know what was spent before!

▶ If the RFP follows an RFI, ensure your responses are consistent. Yes, really.

▶ You can be assured that failure to respond professionally to either an RFI or an RFP moves your organisation to the back burner of potential suppliers to the buyer organisation – possibly for years to come. Procurement executives aren't fools and they don't like having their chains pulled. Deal with the process with the utmost respect.

ISSUES TO REVIEW AND MATTERS WITH WHICH YOU MUST ENGAGE

It is quite extraordinary that big agencies often have little idea whether they've done any work for a potential client or not. That's because there's no guardian of information and, if there ever was, when he or she leaves, and times are tough, the role is made redundant or lies dormant and with it the information. Even smaller event production companies struggle sometimes to remember what went on ten years ago apart from the owner who recalls most things in a rosy hue anyway. But I'm being cynical and slap my wrist for doing that. But, it *is* worth considering if there's a history with the potential project or account. Why did you receive the RFI or RFP in the first place? Was there a previous connection? If your organisation *has* a history, and particularly a recent and successful history with the account, then you probably have some healthy and valuable information to use in the RFP.

Clients tend to dislike changing suppliers, particularly suppliers which have a strong, successful track record – so to win the business from the incumbent, you really need to score (very) highly in all departments. I speak to the editor of a British event magazine and website. He says, 'A good bit of advice is this: if you want to improve your probability of winning a future RFP, conduct periodic business reviews with the target account's senior management. There are always issues that defy quantitative analysis and the key value in that process is trust and relationship. Also, it's undeniably the case that potential clients (and indeed clients of course) do, from time to time, want to know what views you have on an aspect of the events or communications world. If you can end up being an adviser to a potential client or client, then you are more than a provider of events – and that puts you in pole position.'

Of course, you may have a successful history with other accounts like the one you're trying to get. Successful agencies tend to specialise in customer markets. Not always, granted, but often, so if, say, you have several financial institutions on your books, you're likely to know a fair amount about financial services and that can be used as a great asset. Success tends to build future success and you can't 'unknow' what you know. What you learn and accomplish by working on one account tends to be recognised and valued by a potential client that's similarly positioned. Recognition of these issues can provide you with a competitive edge that can separate you from a slightly lower priced competitor if you explain these issues in terms of buyer benefits in your response.

You do of course need to ask yourself whether the potential client fits the profile of clients you or your company are working to supply. Does that sound silly? It shouldn't, because not every client will suit every agency or production company – and vice versa. By the way, every agency should have communicated to all of its staff the kind of client the business seeks and why or why not. It doesn't hurt to create a written profile of this so that understanding is absolute. If a current RFP has lots of possibilities, but doesn't fit the profile of the kind of organisation you want to supply, you may want to think hard about whether it's in your interest to respond.

Potential revenue volume should *not* be the critical factor for investing your precious resources into a demanding RFI/RFP process. There's no value in winning business that you can't satisfy. I know of event agencies where accounts were won with great fanfare. In one case the agency was out of pocket by several million dollars after 18 months because the account team had no real clue how to manage and satisfy the account, much to the client's unsurprising anger and frustration. Certainly the agency had had no cognisance of the resources required and absolutely no real idea of how to charge properly for the services that it was providing. An agency financial director says, 'You have to consider whether there will be negative (even indirect) fallout if you *don't* respond to an RFI or RFP. Another point – can you offer products, services and programmes that can elevate this potential client's performance even if the potential client didn't ask for them in the RFI or RFP? Some RFIs and RFPs imply the question, 'What can you provide us – that is economically valuable or value added – that we didn't ask for?' It's a terrible question and nobody knows how to answer it properly. Be very careful, because wittering on and on about non-relevant services won't endear you to anyone. On the other hand, if you do have connected and relevant services or expertise, make sure that the potential client knows. It's a sensible balancing act. Your potential client is interested in developing suppliers able to elevate economic or strategic performance. I suppose, from experience, your responsibility is to determine how you can be meaningful and useful to this potential client over time and, if that's the position, then go ahead and explain those issues in compelling, business performance language.'

My cousin, ever loud, tells me that I must tell you that procurement presents issues with which any agency should have already engaged. He says that this is one of the biggest problems – that agencies and event companies don't, as a rule, think about the questions that an RFI or RFP pose. This is a good point and actually, now I come to think about it, it's a common scenario which can be easily addressed and will make any agency's objectives and modus operandi clearer.

WHAT *REALLY* SEPARATES YOUR AGENCY, OR EVENT COMPANY, FROM THE COMPETITION?

I'm in New York again, staying with my cousin, who has decided eventually to give proper vent to his views on matters to do with RFPs. 'One of the most difficult things is to describe your company's differentiation in terms that are meaningful to any RFP. It's a fundamental question that very few agencies can answer properly. But *every* event business has some clear differentiation. It may be size or scope (but don't just say that you have sixteen offices around the world if there are only two people in each or if they're just loose associations with another business). Be honest about size, scope and resource, but make your answer specific to what the erstwhile client may want or need. Your advantage may indeed be overseas presence or it may be specialisation in, say, the retail industry. Don't overlook the detail of your resources, security say, creative track record or processes, provided they are relevant. With a particular background that is marketable, buyers may work hard to bring you in as a supplier.' We decide to visit his favourite deli in Greenwich Village where the brunches are amazing and where the plates are the size of trays.

How well a supplier's documentation looks is important and you could get an excellent reputation for clarity and well-organised, good-looking information. Also, if there are five members on the evaluation team of an RFP, send six copies, not just one, unless you are asked specifically for only one.

As indicated, don't keep on reinventing the wheel. When you develop information for one RFI or RFP, keep it and maybe use it again as a source for subsequent RFIs and RFPs, but remember please that you absolutely *cannot* just regurgitate the same information for any response. Many of the complaints about RFIs and RFPs focus on the time they require an agency to complete. Take a step back and begin preparing general information in advance. If you prepare in advance, not only should the quality of information improve, but you'll build up a library of material and your ability to successfully engage with the whole process of pitching for new business will grow.

Ensure that you keep a record of your company's management team, their experience, credentials, very brief CV information and photographs. Buyer organisations prize suppliers with good, relevant credentials. Make a note regularly of any intellectual content that you or your colleagues have prepared or published. Create thought-pieces from time to time with titles such as, 'Our most recent fifty performance improvement initiatives and what they mean for our clients.' If these are really good pieces, put them on your company's website under the heading of, say, 'Insights' or send them to potential clients from time to time. Clients and potential clients want value in all its senses – that's not only a cost thing, although of course cost is a driver. Competitive pricing certainly counts, but overall strategic contributions to a client's business performance count too. My cousin says over pastrami on rye, 'We've moved into a world in which suppliers and buyers are developing informal partnerships. Long-term relationships are prized; they tend to allow for reliability, trust and continuous improvement.

Smart organisations are looking for suppliers who can best contribute to the buying company's long-term performance. That understanding goes far beyond pricing and requires us to understand the potential client's overall strategy, business priorities and sources of pain.'

Each and every procurement person I know separately and collectively says (and of course I paraphrase), 'He (or she) who takes little care and attention over RFIs and RFPs will find the gates of hell electrified.'

CHAPTER FIVE
BEFORE THE SHOW BEGINS

PROJECT MANAGEMENT

In Shakespeare's *Henry V*, Act IV.iii, Henry tells his troops before the great battle of Agincourt that, 'All things are ready, if our minds be so'. The event industry, outside of very big productions, hasn't put a whole lot of stock into strategic management. Managing a project, or indeed strategy, is as important as creativity. It's the process of getting everything ready, and to do that properly requires a clear and powerful mind-set. I'm assuming that you understand that an event may not be the answer to *all* communication issues, but I'm also assuming that, by now, you've got the green light to produce or manage an event.

Conferences and events are often unpopular in the minds of communication executives in client companies because they take up time – often that of many people, certainly one – usually your day-to-day client. These same executives see the event preparation and project management as additional to what they call the 'day job'. 'These folk wouldn't last very long if they worked for me, I can tell you,' says a friend who's deputy CEO at a very large health-care business. He becomes so apoplectic at the thought of the 'day job' brigade that he has to calm himself by discussing with me the problematic orchestration towards the end of *The Magic Flute*. The deputy CEO and I discuss the nature of project management over a calming cup of tea and a couple of slices of Dundee cake. As I consider the art of project management, I realise, not for the first time, that most of it is logic and common sense.

Project management is all about the planning, organisation and management of the resources required to deliver an event or programme. Cousin Maier says that, 'A key skill required toward the final stages of a project is the ability to analyse the impact of changes brought about by the project. You must never, ever, underestimate the knock-on changes and effects that a major project can bring about. Being able to analyse and then manage a project is a skill that must be mastered by anyone delivering any aspect of an event. When a project runs smoothly and in the right order, then that's fine, but throw in a change, then another, and another – and the result can be messy. Changes to the specification of a project after it has begun are all too easily overlooked or ignored and you will need to constantly revisit your plan to incorporate them. Amongst other things, any change to the original specification or brief could have a knock-on effect on a multitude of other factors relating to the project, not least cost and perhaps aspects of delivery. Project management is a complex task and the bigger the project, obviously the more complex it becomes.' Of course, he's right. You must be able to keep track of progress on the project from all the various sections of it that are ongoing. This can be done on paper, but in all reality you'll need to learn and understand how to make the most out of one of the many pieces of project management software that are available. I can't confess to be an expert here and neither might you be, but there'll be someone in your office who undoubtedly is.

Having said that, two warnings stem from a single danger. One – don't enjoy the planning so much that there's no 'doing'. Two – don't enjoy the computer-based project management process more than dealing with project managing the project. A client of long-standing, someone who really understands the holistic nature of corporate communications in which events sit, says, 'If you can't communicate supremely well, I'm sorry but then you'll never become an effective and successful project manager. Any manager, but especially the project manager, producer or account manager, has to understand that, although he or she is charged with ensuring the successful completion of a project, there'll be a multiplicity of people and suppliers who have to be brought together in order to achieve the project's aims and objectives. If communication doesn't happen effectively, either in speech, emails, texts, briefs or presentations, then you won't provide the information that your colleagues and suppliers need to fulfil their jobs, and things won't get done.

Understanding how to use a budget is another essential project management skill to possess. The three key stages to a budget are preparing it, selling it and monitoring it. Whilst your finance department and others may well be ostensibly charged with doing these things for and with you, as project manager, producer or whatever, you might have the ultimate responsibility for the budget and therefore you need to be able to understand what you are being told. You will need budget skills because you'll need to know how to, for example, rationally and logically challenge budget over-runs and negotiate with suppliers, as well as being able to sensibly monitor the budget as the project progresses – not least so that you or your company makes a profit.

The essence of any good project manager is to be a good team leader and certainly a good team player. Whilst decisions will probably remain your responsibility in many areas (and some may not, depending on your level), that's not to say that you shouldn't encourage input from others or be prepared to work with them to help them achieve their goals too. Someone very senior and well known in the world of advertising holds this view: 'In the context of project management, intelligence is your ability to have a clear vision of all aspects of the project, whilst at any one time being able to keenly focus on a specific aspect of it. Put another way, just having the big picture will not help when you have a decision to make on a specific matter. You won't always have the time to spend hours researching and re-reading material in order to make a decision at the time it's needed.' He continues as we watch London rain from the comfort of his office: 'It's almost inevitable that, at times, a project – an event or an advertising campaign – will be stressful, if not highly stressful. Being able to work calmly under such conditions is an absolute pre-requisite for a good project manager. A key point to reducing your stress levels is your ability to move on from a setback. If something goes wrong, or not according to plan, don't waste time worrying about whose fault it might have been – or get involved in a cycle of what could have been different. That can come later in your project evaluation – unless of course there's someone in your team who's doing harm. Instead, move swiftly on to keep the project absolutely on track.'

Time management is important too and I've witnessed many a producer or project manager running around like a headless chicken towards the end of the preparation stage of an event, realising that not everything that should be ready is. Time management is much more than simply allocating portions of time to certain jobs. You need to analyse exactly what it is you're spending your time on and how important those tasks and portions of time are to the successful completion of the project. For example, you could easily spend up to an hour a day just reading emails. This is a task you can delegate to an assistant if you have one or perhaps you could get into the office early, as do I. This is a great time to get through administrative tasks without interruption and email reading and writing in the peace and quiet of the day is beneficial. You must apply a healthy time management philosophy to most things you do. Do you need to attend that meeting or can you delegate attendance to someone else? In what order should things be done or achieved? If people want slices of your time and you need to get on, tell them so – politely but firmly and that includes senior management unless there's a matter of urgency that requires your presence or attention. Remember, you're the project manager and you are primarily there to manage the strategic planning, the overall monitoring and delivery of innovative solutions to problems. Much is expected of you – and your senior managers should understand that.

CONSIDERING EVENT FOOD AND BEVERAGE (F&B)

I do remember (all too clearly) working with a logistics colleague whose speciality was F&B and whose breath always reeked of garlic. Not just a gentle whiff, but a potent pong – as if she was sucking on a perpetual clove. In meetings and moments when she would want to talk closely about something or other, I found myself leaning away or backwards to the point of toppling. She, of course, leaned in so that she could continue her conversations. I am minded of another of Shakespeare's lines, this from *A Midsummer Night's Dream*, Act IV.ii when Bottom says to his co-actors: 'And, most dear actors, eat no onions or garlic, for we are to utter sweet breath; and I do not doubt but to hear them say, it is a sweet comedy. No more words: Away! Go, away!'

Rarely have I become heavily involved in the F&B aspect of event management and delivery, but I have always disliked the spoken nonsense that goes with the important decision-making process that accompanies many a discussion about food and drink. The pretence is baffling and there have been several times that I have been told of a client eating his/her way through a taster meal with no clue as to what they should be doing or offering by way of commentary. Also, they tend to eat everything rather than tasting the dishes and judging the wines – which is the whole point. Of course, that sort of scenario might be the fault of the logistics or project manager, but clients should also be given some idea by our industry as to what they are supposed to do. It's also another case of sheer common sense. Invariably these days, most venues have a choice of set menus to suit most budgets, although there's no point going to a five star hotel and expecting three star prices for F&B. The key is to keep the whole thing moderately simple and don't be persuaded to do what is outside your or, more particularly, your client's delegates' comfort zone.

Food (and the beverages that accompany it) can be nearly as important to an event as the purpose of the event itself. As the event planner, producer, logistics manager, project manager – whatever role you play – you will have a view or some involvement in the choice of what to have eating-wise for your event. If you work for a big agency, there may be people in the team who'll do all this for or with you, but it's worth knowing what's what. One of the first things to remember is that the choice of food is absolutely not what *you* or your direct client may want to eat. It's all about the delegates and just because the managing director of the client firm is enormously fond of foie gras consommé and mackerel with salsa verde doesn't mean that this is what the gala dinner fare should contain. But, as we shall shortly see, that's not the biggest headache.

Whether you're working with a private caterer, the catering manager or banqueting director at the venue, it's helpful to consider several factors before building the menu. My cousin, no mean trencherman himself, says, 'The first thing to remember is that the menu options presented to you and your client are almost always 100 per cent flexible, at a price. Even though most caterers will allow you to confirm the menu and head count about three weeks prior to the event, I suggest confirming the menu early in the planning phase. It probably won't happen like that because your client won't let it happen like that – but you can dream.

Menus for most average events should include several set meal options and perhaps a few à la carte selections developed by the venue's executive chef or your catering specialist. Set menus for breakfast are usually more cost-effective and easier to select, including continental options, hot buffets and breakfast stations. My cousin, now hitching up his trousers over a burgeoning tummy, adds, 'The content of 'continental' of course depends upon where in the world you are. Most breakfast options these days revolve around a help-yourself buffet arrangement with specific order chefs able to create, for example, varieties of egg dishes. If your breakfast is privatised then it's definitely going to be a buffet. You hungry?'

Lunches at events these days tend to be brief and rarely longer than an hour. This is a good thing because it means that people can get on with the business of engaging with the event. On the other hand, some feel that networking is key – although networking never works in the way that most clients think that it will and I'm not convinced that people untutored in how to network do so with any useful conviction. Those from Birmingham, Alabama will talk to others from Birmingham, Alabama. I exaggerate, but actually not by much. So for lunches, they too might be buffet or sandwich-based, or something simple like a selection of salads accompanied perhaps by one or two hot dishes and easy-to-eat desserts. Recently there has grown a habit of delegates taking food and drink back into a breakout or plenary session. I disapprove; unless the event is deliberately casual and everyone's eating and drinking whilst working, it's discourteous to presenters or colleagues and enormously irritating to everyone who has to listen to the mastication and clinking of cutlery. Some event discipline is a very good thing.

'For dinners (depending on what the dinner is for),' says a highly experienced logistics director who works for one of the biggest communications agencies in the world, and who used to be director of events at a large group of international hotels, 'you will always have a choice of pre-packaged buffets or plated dinners and both will offer a choice of three to five courses. This is where you'll find items that reflect the executive chef's personal preferences and the choice might be confusingly wide. For a gala dinner the courses can't be too many otherwise the content of the evening – awards, speeches, entertainment acts, dancing, more speeches, announcements – just wouldn't fit in, although clients do try and overfill dinners with activity where many among the audience would like a chance to chat.'

My personal view is that coffee, tea and comfort breaks are always too long – even allowing for the fact that people need to get out of the auditorium and go somewhere and then come back. People always try and drift off to do the necessary with iPhones and BlackBerries. Heaven forbid that they should close down and be incommunicado for a day. But a pastry or two or some interesting biscuits do always go down well during breaks. Fruit – preferably easy to eat fruit pieces – are a good option, as are a small variety of finger buffet savouries. During drinks receptions (perhaps on the evening of delegate arrival), most caterers or hotels will offer à la carte options for chilled and hot hors d'oeuvres and hosted bar reception packages (often charged hourly per person or on consumption). They will also offer cold and hot platter service points, as well as dessert stations. Again, the reception fare will depend on how long people are expected to stand talking and drinking – or how long they will have to wait until dinner is served. Also people need to know if there is going to be dinner, otherwise they'll fill up on bits: an obvious point but one frequently missed in the communications to delegates. By the way, offering cheap and curled up food at receptions (particularly if the reception is shortly after arrival, or after a long journey) is a short cut to justified bad moods and no small irritation all round.

Regardless of the meal in consideration, I've encountered numerous situations when the client management team has requested (or insisted upon) the wrong (and lengthy) times to allow for meals. A breakfast window can be forty minutes – and tough if anyone misses it. A lunch doesn't need to be more than an hour, as mentioned, although this depends on purpose (that is, other than stopping for fuel). Dinners are different in that there are usually all kinds of add-ons like an awards ceremony, for example.

I honestly have to say that when I started out in the events industry I really can't recall there being so many different opportunities for delegates to say 'no' to meals – and I'm not *that* old thank you. The choices of dinners were either regular or vegetarian and that was it. Now, trying to cater for all those folk with nut and various other myriad allergies can be illness inducing (to you) although, these days, most good venues, caterers and hotels are able to cope admirably. When you add to the list of 'difficult' eaters those who can't eat various comestibles for religious reasons, this aspect of event delivery is a minefield. Plus there will always be many at a table who will say 'Mmmm, that veggie option looks better than the chicken I ordered. I'll ask for that instead' and will declare unflinchingly (with a glare that could maim) that she or he had always asked for the veggie or non-gluten option way back and how dare the minion, who looks exasperated and holds two plates of cooling chicken, argue differently. It is critical to incorporate and notify your catering manager about any special requests and needs that your guests may have as early as you can. Good luck with that and may your God go with you.

A high street retail communications executive with some decent experience of sorting out event and banqueting F&B says, 'When considering budgets and costs, remember that most meals will require a minimum headcount and the venue or caterer will charge on a per person basis. There will also be a charge applied to set up your event even if it's in the same room or auditorium in which the plenary part of the event itself has been held. However, these fees are often negotiable and even waived if the event spend is good. It doesn't hurt to ask. Sometimes a fee is charged if a sous chef or chef is present at a carving station. Similarly bar fees may not include bartender services and these may be high if not negotiated in advance. The room or auditorium rental fee will have been negotiated in advance obviously, but always ask about extras, and if you're not sure what they mean or what they are, ask again and/or take advice from someone on your side. Often room rental is negotiable depending on your event's numbers. Then on top of the final total there'll be obligatory or suggested service charges and local or national taxes to pay.' She has a disarming smile, uses it, shakes my hand and goes off to a meeting.

ON THE GROUND

I've always been in awe of colleagues who have the task of organising large-scale event logistics, getting people from A to B (where B is usually far, far away) and back. Let's face it, most of you aren't in the business of coordinating the actual logistics of shuttling event guests from port or airport to venue, or from station to venue, or from venue to venue, but it's a task that may fall to someone in your team. Ground transportation companies are often hired to handle these sorts of logistics for the duration of an event. And if your event lasts several days, the details are many and onerous.

About thirty years ago local transport companies (coaches, buses, taxis) began working closely with event management agencies and production companies – and indeed with end clients directly. Most of these companies have evolved into DMCs and you'll recall that DMCs, different ones based in cities around the world, will partner with an event planner or producer to develop and execute nearly every aspect of the local logistics of an event, obviously at a cost which is sometimes high. A Spanish logistics director explains, 'Even though event planners, producers or even logistics managers can do an effective job in managing transportation and other logistics matters directly, it's a good thing to know that you have a local company which will understand more about the intricacies of working in a particular city than you. Given their roots in the transportation business, most DMCs are excellent at arranging airport arrivals/departures, coordinating manifests, porterage, event transfers and handling most transportation needs. They will also recommend the most cost-effective transportation options including limousines, mini-coaches, large buses and long distance coaches, vans and taxis. Most DMCs also offer good advice on venues, entertainment options and various activities – all interesting and useful to the event planner.'

Relying on a DMC is a wise use of time (and money) to ensure that everyone is being transported appropriately and on time. Hiring a DMC makes sense whether your event is big or small. If the need is small and you can handle things, then fine, but using experts is going to be important for your reputation and it will also make life easier for you and your client. Of course, the investment is part of delivering an overall excellent experience and that's what you're in business to do.

GIVE-AWAYS AND CORPORATE GIFTS – SUCH A WASTE OF MONEY

It's worth mentioning this topic now because it's something that can get left to the last minute – often because it's only at the last minute that your client will decide to offer delegates a something by which to remember the event. So many things have been given away which gather dust or hit the bin, or get given to kids. Some don't make it out of the venue. So, it's important, not least of course because gifts are a great cost. Cousin Maier has a view (of course): 'I would venture that the annual corporate spend on such gift items must be in the region of billions, and tens of those at that. For every idea you have, there will undoubtedly and undeniably be several suppliers happy to take your client's money. There'll be a supplier of everything from cheap pens to refrigerators. I have seen men, executives, leaving events looking like they dressed in a cupboard without a light, in all the finery that the organisers have given them as freebies: berets, cowboy hats, shirts, golfing shoes, tie-pins, garish ties, cufflinks, wind-proof jackets, rain jackets, branded socks, even underwear, although I hasten to add that the latter tend not to be on (full) view. For stylish women, while the only designers they would normally consider are French or Italian, they now wander towards their limo to the airport sporting garish flat shoes and hats with some strange motto writ large, while tucked away in their branded, tasteless handbags will be a fountain pen with her name along its barrel that will never be used. It used to be calculators and pads. Now it's iPods and health club vouchers.'

An executive producer of corporate events is pushed into commenting, 'I never really know why people need a giveaway at all. Is it a thank you for attending? Is it a keepsake? Is it a reminder of some aspect of the event? Anyway, let's assume that you have to find something: which supplier do you choose? Often, producers and project managers rely on personal referrals or their own online shopping efforts. That's fine, but it's more effective to understand who's who in this gift industry and who will help make you look good in the process. Promotional product distributors serve as brokers between suppliers of promotional products and event agencies or the end client. They are independent firms and work directly with many different industry suppliers, or they might be independent representatives of national distributors managing industry-wide relationships and leveraging big buying power. But there are some dubious players out there, some offering inferior products, so it's wise to get to know a distributor before buying. How long have they been in business? What kind of discounts can they offer? Are they reliable? Do they deliver what they promise? That sort of thing. Ask around.'

There are also incentive and promotions/gift companies that offer a good level of event support, such as graphic design, branding and other planning services. What they do may conflict with what your firm does, so be careful. These companies tend to be boutique businesses that specialise and help event project managers and producers with corporate gift needs. Some of these businesses create online catalogues and allow direct buying.

'The essential thing,' reinforces the marketing director of a pharmaceutical company based in the UK, 'is to consider what you're giving a gift for. If it's because you want the delegate to love you then it's a waste of time. If it's because the item has some relevance to the conference or event, then perhaps OK, but just giving things for giving's sake is a waste of money and can actually do harm. If the gift is wrong or is seen as 'cheap' or pointless, then that can reflect on the event and the people holding it.' She adds, as she departs, 'The reason for offering give-aways is to cement a relationship between the event and the delegate. If what you're considering doesn't do that, forget it. Key rings, pens, conference folders, even smart electronic gadgets have very limited appeal.

INVITATIONS AND REGISTRATION – GET THEM ABSOLUTELY RIGHT

I attended an event industry conference recently in Brussels and it wasn't particularly bad or good, but what made me nearly not go was the invitation. The invitation, unusually these days, was by hand, which was fine, but it was accompanied by a treatise pamphlet all about Europe. The tenet of the pamphlet, beautifully and expensively produced, was meant to entice attendees to 'think European'. I know that Euroscepticism has been marching rapidly through national parliaments across the EU. This document maintained that it is European parliaments that are setting the pace in the UK, not the country's own. Support for the EU is collapsing, it went on, among the European public – and populist Eurosceptic parties are being elected en masse in countries from Denmark to Austria, from the Netherlands to Finland. The euro crisis, the pamphlet cried out, has transformed European politics to the extent that even mainstream MPs, who normally yell for closer union, are discovering the joys of saying 'non', 'nein', 'nee', 'ne', 'ikke', 'den' and 'nie'. Whereas being Eurosceptic would, until recently, have stopped an MP's career in its tracks in most European parliaments, it's now the making of them. The pamphlet went on (and interminably on) in this way. Well, this was all well and good (or not), but had very little to do with the conference's content and, as an invitation accomplice, verging on advertising or propaganda, was something of a damp cloth. This is not good practice I thought and should be avoided in the process of sending out invitations. It's the equivalent of junk mail so into the bin it went and I cringed at the cost involved to deliver little result.

Good attendee registration practice and payment handling (if applicable) is crucial. There are many internet or computer-based schemes and systems that can be utilised for event registration. Some are simple, some more complex. Some are available off the shelf and others are purpose-built. I don't propose to go into the options here, but be warned – do your homework and make sure that whatever you do consider, get specialist advice and support.

You can use a registration process to collect attendee data for all kinds of reasons: dietary requirements, workshop or breakout choice, event content, questionnaire information on objectives, marketing activities post-conference and so on. However, some people ask rather pointless questions and the information is useless or never used. Delegates, unsurprisingly, don't like that.

Creating a clear, concise, well-defined registration process is imperative to the success of most events, unless they are very tiny. The registration process is an extension of the event itself and is another component that can add or subtract from the overall experience. Remember that the registration website is likely to be the first or second contact with a delegate and vice versa. Therefore, as with other relationships, first impressions do count. Apart from a 'save the date' email, the next bit of communication will be a website hopefully telling the delegate all about the event, the venue and proposed content. The website needs to be warm and non time-consuming. It needs to be easy to navigate and the detail must be straightforward. The structure of language must be excellent so that everything is crystal clear. Also, if financial (credit card) information is required, then the delegate needs to know that everything will be safe and sound.

The managing director of an American delegate management company that specialises in computer-based registration systems has this to say: 'Event organisers, project managers and producers often worry that high-tech registration options will alienate a portion of their target audience. Yet you'd be surprised how quickly even your most traditional users will adapt to online registration. In fact, many event organisers have found that removing paper registration altogether has led to higher attendance, happier attendees and much fewer complications at events.' Well, she would say that of course and I respect her knowledge and ardent sales talk, but what she says is, in my experience, very true. After a few glasses of very good Armagnac and Cognac (for research purposes only), we discuss registration processes once more but in slower motion.

'Ever lengthy and arduous paper registration processes are usually frustrating for attendees and costly for the client organisation,' she asserts. 'Also, responses are variable and people seem to reply less to paper-based requests for information than they do to online registration processes. Paper-based systems are also a pain in the neck for the event company because mistakes can be made and the whole thing is very time-consuming.'

To reiterate, there are two important items that your memory must not fail. First, make registration as easy as possible. Second, make sure that no mistakes are made. There is nothing more likely to really (and I mean really) anger the client, and at a high level too, if your system makes public what it shouldn't make public, gets someone's name wrong, or sends material out to the wrong person. Mistakes will get reported upwards quicker than you can say 'Shall I look for a new job then?' Seriously, don't make mistakes; ensure that whoever or whatever is providing your system is very good, and managed by superb practitioners.

Make sure your system is set up to send confirmations and reminders to the delegates and, obviously, part of your plan in agreement with your client must be the frequency of contact with those delegates. Ensure that the client signs off what you're going to send and also ensure that the language and information are precise and correct. As mentioned (and it is worth repeating *ad nauseam*), a single miscommunication can destroy an attendee's experience at an event, and your career. 'So, why,' asks a producer colleague, 'do some event organisers still rely on manual processes to manage things like meal preferences, room blocks and nearly every attendee preference? Take the time to set up a way for your attendees to choose their own preferences and make self-service changes to those preferences before the event. The best registration systems will make this process easy for attendees and some systems will even provide reports that can be shared with hotels, caterers and event organisers in real time. These shared reports ensure that all preferences are updated and accurate at all times, leading to happier attendees and smoother events.'

Many event delegates become frustrated by the length of time it takes to fill out a registration form. Yet many of these same registrants are previous 'customers' of the organisation/company holding the event. That means there's no reason why you should require them to re-submit every piece of personal information. Instead, all event registration systems should be using an auto-recall system to pre-populate personal and business information whenever possible. Not only does this practice dramatically reduce time spent in the registration process, but it also decreases the number of people who abandon the process and reduces errors in your reporting. 'Anyway,' says my visiting American cousin who, if I haven't told you, runs a very large communications agency in New York. 'This simple feature – the auto-recall system – can improve the attendee experience while making sure you, as the event producer, always have accurate contact information for follow-ups and content promotion.' We sample some good Righetti Amarone 2000 from the Veneto region of Italy. The bottle's label declares, 'This is a fantastic Amarone with rich, dark flavours of dried cherries and a warm, spicy finish.' Neither of us can taste cherries.

YOU'VE SORTED REGISTRATION, BUT ON THE DAY PEOPLE MAY NOT TURN UP

No-shows (people who don't turn up with or without valid reasons) are a dull topic and there isn't a lot you can do to legislate against it – provided that you've managed everything else well and that you're safe in the knowledge that the joining instructions are good and clear. If you're like most event organisers, seeing a stack of unused name badges at the point where the first plenary is well under way is a pain and somewhat depressing, and actually very frustrating. There is a way to reduce no-shows before the event – yet it's one of the least-used features in event registration. The feature is called a 'click-to-confirm' reminder and it allows event organisers or logistics managers (whoever is in charge of the registration process at your end) to send a series of triggered email reminders leading up to an event, asking attendees to confirm that they will be attending. This practice allows organisers to weed out people who have changed their minds and open up spaces either to allow others in or not, but at least you can better manage accommodation and meals. 'In addition,' pipes up cousin Maier, 'the extra action taken by your attendees reminds them about the event and reaffirms their commitment to attend. Obviously last minute problems – family, ill health, travel delays, business crises – can always be a difficulty, and there isn't much you can do about those scenarios, but invitees are let off the hook too easily in their attitude towards attendance.'

I ask an international corporate communication executive normally based in France, his view. He's about to lead a special events team with a major French technological development business. 'As social networking becomes more important to attendees both before and after events, event organisers and project managers increasingly depend on good networking opportunities to make their corporate events get talked about. Some are confidential and so that wouldn't apply. Obviously clients have to approve the use of Twitter or Facebook or whatever for any social networking, but social media is being used widely now to generate awareness and discussion. Those opportunities start during the registration process and can continue way after the event itself.'

If you do get involved in social networking for event purposes, ensure that you enlist the help of experts. You really don't want the wrong thing to go out to a myriad of people who shouldn't be receiving that 'wrong thing'. Like all communication tools, treat this one with ardent respect. It can work for you and it sure as hell can work against you. No? Then riddle me this dear reader. In 2011, in early February, 200 Hell's Angels arrived at a glass manufacturer's management conference in Manchester, UK because of a prank Facebook player. Yes, they did leave. Eventually. Rumour has it that six months later one Hell's Angel married a glass manufacturer sales executive from Seattle.

Make sure you provide a quick link to a directory of event attendees both during your registration process and in your confirmation email. The kind of information you provide on that directory will vary, but many organisers include names of attendees, email addresses and even a list of the sessions that people are attending. This technique immediately engages your attendee with your event, allowing them to reach out to friends or set up meetings with colleagues. That's where social media can work a treat.

BADGERS

I'm sitting in a departure lounge at Barcelona airport. One of the advantages of Barcelona airport is that it's really close to the city centre, just 14 km away. The airport is specifically located at El Prat del Llobregat, the town that gives the name Aeroport del Prat to the airport, the second largest in the country after Madrid's Aeropuerto de Barajas. In the departure lounge I'm chatting to one of Spain's top corporate communications specialists. We talk about badging, and my Spanish friend says, 'This has become part of the registration process and a badger is a badger'. She smiles when she realises her mistake.

'Well it isn't actually,' eventually admonishes a senior producer with whom we're travelling. 'A badge isn't just a badge' she says. 'Top event producers and managers are realising that badges can play a crucial role in tying registration information to the event. Most sophisticated registration platforms will allow you to enhance your badges with group information, colour coding and even an agenda. You can get name badges with a scrolling LED message. These are programmable to say what you want. The message can be changed immediately using onboard control buttons or can be altered remotely. Other electronic badges have barcodes holding relevant information such as whether you're attending a particular session or going on a trip or whether you have reserved a place at a function or what menu you've chosen. You can also get badges that allow you to connect with stations throughout a venue and you'll receive your next day's agenda on a screen, on your phone or even on the badge.'

My Spanish colleague adds, 'Yes, but you have to consider cost and you also have to decide if any badging is really necessary in the first place. Often badges become redundant not least because they hold too much information in a font that requires a magnifying glass. Invariably, the only bit of information needed is the first name unless there's a *very* good reason why there should be more detail. The rest can come out of conversation. It may be a good idea to brand your badges, agendas and signage to match your registration form. Many client companies decide to throw any old theming or branding on all kinds of event collateral – branding that has nothing to do with the event. That's a mistake and does nothing for reinforcing brand values or the event's message or theme. The use of brand or a theme needs to be designed and managed, like anything else – with care.'

CONDITIONAL LOGIC IS CLEVER

A senior producer is angry at how badly some agencies manage registration. 'Attendees struggle with long registration forms, even online' she snaps, 'particularly when those forms contain information that isn't relevant to them. More and more event companies are using something called "conditional logic" to avoid that pitfall.' She sips her iced tea. 'Conditional logic' she says, 'is based on statements which use triggers within the registration form to dynamically display appropriate information. Conditional logic (also called "if/then logic") means that you can display a certain field or fields on your registration form based on how a registrant responds to a previous field. For example, suppose you have an awards dinner and a delegate, the registrant, has the option to bring a guest. Conditional logic allows you to display fields prompting the delegate for the guest's information (such as name, menu preference and so on) but only if the registrant ticked the box to indicate that they actually planned to bring a dinner guest.'

'Conditional logic is great – obvious and simple,' continues the producer, 'and allows you to show or hide a field based on what users select for another field on a web page form. For example, you might have a field asking, "How would you rate the service we offered?" If a user chooses "Poor", you might want the system to display a field for comments so that the user can say *why* they thought the service was poor.'

An IT specialist from the event division of a Dutch marketing agency says, 'You can use conditional logic on event registration forms for all kinds of purposes. Very complicated events use conditional logic to dramatically streamline registration – and actually people like the process where logical questions or pieces of information follow certain inputs.'

When I get to New York and talk to my cousin over some chicken noodle soup, he says, 'By the way, if you're using old-fashioned conference name tags, use a big font. Use a bold, sans-serif typeface with the largest possible letter size. Badges and event buttons should be easy to read from at least 12 feet away. The whole purpose of a badge is to make it easy for people to meet, mingle and say "Hello!" No sense giving out badges that require conference participants to squint and stare at your chest.' Later, we see an extraordinarily good performance of *Death of a Salesman* and, not for the first time, I marvel at brilliant stagecraft, script and acting. I wish business executives who profess to be great speakers would see this sort of delivery.

CLARITY RULES IN REGISTRATION AS IN EVERYTHING ELSE, BUT YOU'D NEVER KNOW IT

Years and years ago I attended a conference in Birmingham, and at the registration desk I was (eventually) attended by a smiling and effete young person in a smart red blazer who said that, to gain entry, I had to pay for three books and all accommodation and meals, up front. 'But I don't want the books and I may not want all the meals, and I've already registered,' I said brushing snow from my hair and coat. Half an hour later I was getting no further and, because there was a large lady behind me complaining vociferously about being kept waiting, I paid up. 'Sign here, here and here. Oh and here,' said one of the effete crew. I handed over my credit card and did sign here, here, here and here. The books were awful, my hotel room was next to the lift shaft on one side and a paper-thin wall on the other, through which I could hear the occasional squeak of skin sliding on the plastic bath. The majority of the guest speakers failed to turn up due to the weather. Needless to say a refund was not forthcoming. As I left the event, the same desk people, now sporting blue blazers instead of the red, asked every departing guest if he or she would like to register for another, similar conference at which there'd be more good books and thin walled rooms. The registration form would only take, ooh no time at all. I fled.

Registration is better than that these days, mostly. I talk to the MD of a delegate management business. She says, sighing a little, that, 'As others will have undoubtedly said to you, any and every question on a registration form must count. There is absolutely no value in asking a question where the answer might be confusing (to you, your client or the delegate) or where the answer may be superfluous and of no use to you whatsoever.

'Another thing,' says a Brazilian colleague who now stops to talk en route to Passport Control. 'Consider,' he says, 'if the event registration process should be closed to people not invited. Requiring a password to proceed to registration is a good idea. The password could actually be a constant to be used by the delegate throughout the event – and beyond.'

The MD of the delegate management business rings me to add some more thoughts. 'It's really important not to forget that payments via the registration process can be a pain, but do consider accepting different currencies if that's appropriate. For attendees in different countries, it can make their experience better when reconciling expenses and it will make them feel more welcome. Ah, yes, and add flight and accommodation booking options to the process, again as appropriate, obviously. This can save registrants time and give you even more information about their experience. But as with anything to do with data collection, the bywords are confidentiality and accuracy. Tell people who read your book not to muck this up. Oh, and it hopefully should go without saying that the website should include more than just the online registration form. It should at least display the agenda, speaker, directions and similar information.'

I get an email from my American relative. It says, amongst other more familial things, 'As providers differ in service, producers and event project managers should choose a registration management system which can offer automated payment handling, billing, a discount system and a cancellation handling process. In order to find the right provider, it's helpful to create a checklist with features that are relevant for you and your conference. The timing of sending out the invitation is important and this should be built into the event plan, and further reminders of the event should also be planned and added to the project timeline. Certain (particularly more senior) audiences may require at least three months notice (or more) of the event, with reminders sent out to the undecided as you near the event date.'

Confirmation of attendance should be urged immediately as you will need to build up a communication channel to the delegate leading up to the event, both to promote the event (obviously) and also to reduce the inevitable drop-out rate. Communication should be regular and involve email messages from, say, the event's 'owner' or sponsor, along with, say, newsletters and further details about the programme, speakers, other participants, joining instructions, travel and accommodation details, hospitality arrangements and any relevant information that you'd like the delegate to receive before the event.

I receive another call from the MD of the delegate management services company. 'Usually, the delegate attendee list will also be created from the registration list and can be analysed and produced as necessary. The contact list is most important if there is a crisis during the event and should be up-to-date and available to all those concerned in dealing with a situation if the need arises.'

I'm now in France and driving to Avignon to attend a forum on event management, registration and content development – an odd mix. One of the interesting areas of discussion will be Facebook invitations to events. As I approach my destination, the view in every direction becomes increasingly stunning: wooded hills, orchards, meadows of yellow and bright green. I've had a lunch of steak and aligot (potato mashed with cheese, garlic and butter) and am at one with the world. I think about some corporate events in which I've been involved and decide, not for the first time, that clarity of content is probably the most problematic and, at the same time, the most exciting part of an event on which to work. Developing content to create great experiences is not an easy task. You have to put yourself in one of the attendee's shoes. What will make the event fun, exciting, informative, engaging, interactive and memorable for you, the attendee? What content would you want? I let the question float and wonder what answers there might be in Avignon.

CHAPTER SIX
CONTENT

THE IMPORTANCE OF QUALITY CONTENT

Why do people attend conferences? 'Oooh, lots of reasons,' says my cousin. 'Let's see,' he says a tad smugly, 'to network, to learn about best practice, to share best practice, to feel part of a group, to feel wanted, to feel necessary, to understand the future, to understand the present, to put the past in perspective, to get new ideas, to test new ideas, to change your mind, to change the minds of others, to inspire, to be inspired, to know that you had no choice because the event was mandatory…'

'Providing opportunities for attendees to connect is important,' says the marketing director of an aircraft parts company. 'At the heart of every conference,' he continues, 'is the exchange of information and ideas achieved through its content. Content is at the very heart of the event's brand and its eventual reputation in the minds of attendees.' He's quite right of course about the need to focus on content. An event producer or project manager and their team must stretch widely and deeply to imagine, source, shape and then deliver relevant and timely information – and information that exceeds the expectations of the audience. For 'information' read message, proposition, anything that the event is there to do. However, that's all well and good given two important conditions: one, that the client actually wants help in content and messaging (many don't or assume that the event production company or agency wouldn't have a clue, and that of course may be true) and two, that the client listens to the agency and then waits for the client CEO to tell everyone what he/she wants no matter what and that's (boringly and self-seekingly) that.

Besides the provision of great speakers along with value-added, relevant communication and exciting ideas, the other reason people attend events, apart from fun of course, is to network.   As an event producer/project manager, you can help your client's attendees get the most out of the occasion by making networking easier before, during and after your event.   Quality content discussions can be had using existing social networks, like Facebook pages, Twitter hashtags and LinkedIn groups. The digital materials you or your client might use to promote the event are important to substantiate content and to drive interest. Where this undeniably fails is not because of the tool or medium, but because the content is not delegate-relevant or is simply not on message.

CONTENT HAS TO PROVIDE FOCUS AND WE HAVE TO FOCUS ON CONTENT

When I was a small boy I loved reading adventure stories – anything from *Treasure Island* by Robert Louis Stevenson to John Buchan's *The Thirty-nine Steps*. Adventure often meant imagining the dark and mysterious lands of Europe's east – harbouring trilby-wearing spies and villains with stubby guns on fast steam trains crossing borders fraught with danger, and always at night. Knowing looks would cross dining cars, mysterious packages would appear and duplicate briefcases would disappear. These days much of Europe is the same as anywhere else in Europe. Yes the world has become a very small place. The EU has ensured that congruity is a byword and it is often decreed that even countries that aren't particularly 'old' European should be new European.

So, what has this to do with event content? Well, event content is one of those strange elements that has hordes attacking it and rarely is it allowed to take its proper and leading place at the seat of other component parts of an event. Clients will hijack a morning or an afternoon at the drop of a hat or at the drop of the MD's hat; committees will stuff all sorts of garbage into an event – a comedian here, a management guru there, a chap who climbed the foothills of the Ulugh Muztagh mountain range in the Qinghai-Tibetan Plateau, four plenary sessions in one evening, nine breakout sessions which serve no true or recalled purpose, a gala dinner, some drunken awards that receive less and less applause after the thirty-second … and so on. Oh yes, an exaggeration certainly, but many an event is cobbled together as an amalgam of all things dreadful – just because someone at the client end late in the day wants it like that or because the client has been persuaded that it should be like that or because hey, this is what they've always done or because some consultancy which hasn't a clue has recommended such a course of action. Actually one of the most common reasons why content gets changed is because the client is so concerned to include the detail, data or output of *another* communication initiative that the other initiative takes over, totally subsuming the original reason for the event's existence.

Event agencies shouldn't be smug about this because it is they who often keep wringing out themes like *Simply the Best* and *Going for Gold* along with the tired comedian, the boring, overweight management guru who leans on the lectern so that he and it wobble, the chap who climbed that blessed mountain, the drumming troupe who claim that they're from South Africa, the breakout facilitator ladies who talk of Prada and the men of football scores, the big bottoms in tight designer nylon leisurewear posing in front of the client CEO, the client team in Police sunglasses, the lowly interns ensconced in breakout rooms and looking at flip charts.

Content is the driver behind all events. Without it, the event is nothing. Museum and gallery curators arrange art to create meaning and generate excitement. They produce thoughtful, intentional exhibitions with purpose and context. I have a curator friend who looks after classic Italian drawings at one of London's big museums. To listen to him talk of Raphael and Michelangelo is a treat. 'Curators who consistently create exhibits with relevance, meaning and context,' he says, 'establish a relationship with their audiences. Their audiences return the favour with more visits because of the experience and added value. I'd say that was similar to a corporate event experience.'

It's vital that we create conference experiences that have purpose, are contextual and make a proposition clear. Imagine then if we followed in a curator's footsteps, if we juxtaposed conference content and presentations against one another to create meaning and engender excitement. Cousin Maier says, 'Our job as communication and event producers is to help create narrative. We are there to evoke responses from the conference participants; we are there to help communicate messages. Successful conferences are intentional about the content. What that means is that nothing in the content should be accidental. It should be directed and rehearsed like a play or indeed any great experience, whilst allowing the actors and players to show their craft and be ever fresh. I always saw my job as an "audience-engager", a "helper of message conveyance" and a storyteller.'

CONTENT – BACK TO THE FUTURE

Walberswick in Suffolk. Winter. The metal-grey sea rolls under a huge, similarly grey sky. Lighter pigeon feather grey clouds scud on their way to Holland. The waves are brown-tinged with a deeper granite colour and the big rolling fists smash into the sand with a bomb-raid roar and explode in a shower of bubbles, whipped by the wind into a white, swirling cloud of what looks like soap suds. The two reactors in the distance that is Sizewell sit a) grubby grey squared and b) round, pearl white. I am told that there is no likely connection between the power station and the suds, but one thinks that there is and gloomy thoughts emerge.

What you see isn't what always is. The first step in planning compelling content is actually to take a step back. It's important to read, synthesise and really understand all the data available from the client concerning context, objectives, motivation and event history, if there is one. Reviewing as much as possible will help you to construct an *informed* (not, as is often the case, a guessed) perspective on what messages, themes, interactions, topics, formats and speakers succeeded before with a particular audience. You may have discovered some of this from the brief to which you responded to win the business. But, at that stage you won't probably have had access to drilled-down detail, unless of course you've known the client for a long time. If that's the case, then you'll have been proactive and will have kept in constant touch about your client's business and its changes.

You can develop shape with the client or you and your agency team can develop what might be called a straw man – a draft that can be knocked down and rebuilt. Invariably, clients don't know what they don't want until they see it – or rather until they see what they don't want. Not the best and most encouraging approach, I confess.

A well-known corporate event content development specialist and speechwriter says, 'If necessary, question the brief, but be careful here though. If you challenge a brief, you have to know *why* you're challenging it and you'll need very, very good reasons and back-up argument for what's wrong with it, or what should replace what's there. This isn't as scary as it may sound because clients invariably want good, reasoned advice. Then, there's this thing about getting back to the future. A pre-conference survey is a good way to establish a) a connection and engagement with the intended audience and b) a mechanism to solicit feedback from the target audience that will help shape the event's content. The (carefully prepared) survey should invite targeted event stakeholders to share what's on their minds and the challenges they face in their business. Preparation is key. In any questioning of stakeholders or a sample of delegates, there's absolutely no value in asking questions where the answers will be ambiguous. Simple is best and I often use Skype or get groups of stakeholders together. The results are often illuminating, bringing issues to the forefront that an event manager or producer (that's you) and client executives, may not have anticipated, but in any case are real, relevant and compelling.'

I agree. Occasionally, event questionnaires elicit responses from those who don't think through their responses and put down daft or nasty things that are impossible or undesirable to deliver. But on the whole (and provided that the questions are very good and carefully considered in their preparation), the results will provide an opportunity to identify challenges shared across the community that the event programme and content can be tailored to address. An HR executive for a shipping company declares that, 'Online forums are another rich resource for identifying topics to create a programme. Obviously it depends what the event is for and the intended audience, but social networking sites like LinkedIn are powerful tools for finding out what themes are recurring in corporate life – and what seem to be the hot topics (with the liveliest debates) taking place. Attention should be paid to which individuals are leading these discussions – they may be ideal conference presenters one day. I have to say though that content mustn't be ruled by flavours "out there". Content must be driven by real, relevant communication needs and the strategy in which the event fits.'

A long-standing colleague of mine who's delivered huge events round the world adds, 'A conference committee can be a terrific asset, delivering insights from the stakeholders each committee member may represent, such as attendees, corporate executives, franchisees, suppliers, exhibitors or sponsors. The committee should be vested with real responsibilities, such as holding regular meetings to discuss content planning, contributing to the topics list and identifying potential speakers.   But, if the committee is too large and unwieldy or meets too rarely, decisions will be hard to make or the decisions won't come to fruition. If the committee is not chaired with a rod of iron, it won't work either.'

EVENT SHAPE IS OFTEN IGNORED

'I often wonder,' mutters a publisher friend who's visiting London – part business, part not, and who doesn't know a vast amount about event delivery but has attended many. 'I often wonder,' he repeats, 'why people responsible for public entertainment don't ever take a tip from the sort of work you do.' 'What do you mean?' I ask. 'Well,' says he, 'take the cinema. You join a queue even if you've booked online. You attempt to get hold of the seats you've already reserved, but an attendant whom you would not want to meet in a dark alleyway tells you that your seats have gone, and is already looking past you at the person behind you. So you then have to buy two brand new tickets for the price of four. You go to another (prettier) attendant and buy a bucket of popcorn (and it really is a bucket and there is only one size) along with a carton of slushy sky blue ice chips that smell of chemicals. You'd actually asked for orange juice but the communications became muddled since this attendant hails from Peru. The chemicals and their price make your eyes water. You eat half the popcorn but the rest gets spilled on the floor. The blue stuff gets thrown away. You watch a film that has no real sense or content and it isn't funny or sad. The story is confusing and none of the comedy is comedic. Well, you wouldn't get that in a corporate event, would you?'

Well, the point is, of course, that he's quite wrong. You would and you do. Some corporate conferences are badly managed, the whole 'customer' experience is poor and the content is wrong or just dire. Many events have a depressing air of apocalyptic gloom. Some are stale, others culturally tuneless and many are just a repeat of what's gone before, year after year. Some are devoid of light or laughter. Many are dark, sombre and isolated – in all senses – with gothic menace lurking behind every stage stair's creak, shadow and flicker of low lighting. The coffee breaks offer coffee that is just warm. Men and women attendees become wild-eyed and gush or become listless and dull. The production crew, wearing ill-fitting company t-shirts, don't look at anyone and are constantly busy but never helpful. And so on. But I'm very pleased to say that any of this is rare these days.

It's a twist on the often-quoted line in *Field of Dreams*, 'If you build it, they will come.' Giving a voice to the audience and inviting them to help shape the event establishes an early level of engagement and investment in the event that, in my experience, is more likely to result in a content-appropriate event. When attendees feel they've helped to design an event or have had some input, their level of buy-in increases and they're more receptive throughout the conference lifecycle to the event messages. This is a *gross* generalisation – of course it is – but involvement helps with ownership. Audience involvement and excitement help to generate word of mouth and can increase the visibility of the event among the desired event community. However, you should strive to achieve the delicate balance between what the audience wants and what it *needs*. Relying solely on the target audience for conceiving the educational content, say, may lead to a short-sighted programme that only addresses current, immediate and controversial challenges. You can't build a whole event around what individual delegates want. You, from experience, and your client, from detailed knowledge, will have a clear idea abut what the event needs in terms of content. It's your job to give that content shape. My cousin says that, 'Producers and project managers should consider the optimal mix of content to address what the audience is facing *now* and what it needs to be taught to navigate future conditions. Once you know that, you can shape the whole so that the experience hits most of the audience in the best way.'

In the process of establishing the early shape of the event, you also need to see the event from the point of view of the delegate. Hopefully, you'll have done this already and that's partly perhaps why you won the pitch in the first place. Now, detail is critical and you can't just say people arrive, register and go somewhere. The whole delegate experience is what it's all about. If you understand the audience members properly you'll be able to consider what will press their buttons and what will work in the name of communicating a particular message.

DO CLIENTS KNOW BEST?

Establishing event content is hard. As JFK said, 'We chose to go to the moon. We chose to go to the moon in this decade and do the other things, not because they are easy, but because they are hard ...' (And, by the by, if you want to read a brilliantly crafted speech, go and find Kennedy's Rice Stadium moon speech (September 12, 1962). Like much of Ted Sorensen's speechwriting, this one is a peach.

Event content is our master (or mistress). Like all slaves we loathe our master (or mistress) unless he or she decides to like us, in which case we lie back to have our tummies tickled (etc). And we worry. We worry whether the audience will give a flying ferret for all of that which we've prepared. However, some clients just want to tick the boxes and don't give a fig whether anyone in the audience likes any of what goes on during the event. The thing is that content, in order to work, usually has to be sold hard to a client, a client who will invariably want a programme of things he or she likes rather than what will be right for the audience.

The producer of a number of high profile public and sporting events points out a common complaint: 'We've certainly witnessed instances where content has been pushed further and further out in the event planning timeline, as if it only needs to be finalised in time to issue the conference programme guide. To procrastinate on content development is a mistake and a lost opportunity for the client, the event and the event's legacy. You really have to try very hard to get a client to focus (and stick to focussing) on content.' Discussing, shaping, curating content – deeply, widely, intelligently and together – are key to the development and delivery of a good event.

CONFERENCE THEMES

A theme is the writing through the stick of event rock. It's the basis for all content, and all content should relate to it. It can be a strapline and an anthem. It should be something that lasts way after the event is finished, and probably beforehand too. I muse about the best themes and my eyes narrow Clint Eastwood style into my caffè tiramisu as I remember some of the stinkers. Well, I think it's Clint Eastwood style. The lady at the next table must think that I have a strange twitch. She edges away.

Leadership as a broad theme is one that has always worked and for fairly obvious reasons, although of course if the theme *is* leadership and no leadership is manifest at the event, then everyone looks a bit silly. An old salt from the rock and roll days of the events industry says that 'Leadership, or an aspect of it, is an excellent theme for any conference. Another major strength of any organisation is people working together in harmony without ego clashes and differences. Hah. Good luck with that. But the idea of making teamwork work is a good theme under which each component part of the event's content can work. And, of course, guest speakers and audience engagement can operate well within a theme like teamwork.'

Another interesting conference theme is 'change'. Then there's 'technology', 'service', 'globalisation', 'fast and furious' and 'sustainability'. There is no dearth of ideas for organising an event based on ecology themes. Depending specifically on the context and content (although theme often *drives* content), there are esoteric themes like Cabaret, Carnival, Masked Ball, Mexican, French, Spanish (and so on round the globe), Street Fair, Pink, Gold, Silver, Black, White (and so on round the spectrum), Silver Screen and Movie Stars, *Treasure Island, Pirates of the Caribbean, Gold Rush California,* or *Willy Wonka.* The last can be an amazing exhibition or gala dinner environment but you have to have the budget to do it very well. Most of the theme styles I've just mentioned are primarily for dinners or celebrations, but not always. Of course there may be a main theme for the bulk of the event with a slightly different or totally different twist or slant for the gala dinner or awards ceremony. Be very careful though. Don't mess with the main theme too much. Once you've got it and you know it works and that the client likes it, stick with it. My cousin has a word or two on the subject: 'Many a time I've seen a main theme, a sub-theme for the morning, a sub-sub theme for the evening and something totally unrelated the next day. Make the theme suit the event and, for goodness sake, the proposition. The proposition might well *be* the theme of course.'

My cousin continues, 'I get asked all the time for event theme ideas, but I say that you need content and messaging first or it doesn't work. But some themes that have proved to be good would include: The Winning Team, Beat the Clock, The Time's Right, Achievers, Better All Together – Altogether Better, The Sky's the Limit, Breaking Down Barriers, The Wall, and Teamwork Works. But the theme needs to fit the culture of the client and the nature of the event although sometimes themes can be used to shock or surprise which is fine provided there's a good reason.'

Corporate events may warrant imaginative themes that convey strong messages. Gala dinners or awards ceremonies can also benefit from imaginative themes. 'Once chosen, a theme should pervade every aspect of your event. That's important,' yells a producer who's invited me for a chat, a cup of institutional coffee, and a look at his latest creation for a high street bank sales conference (or training programme as it has to be called in case shareholders riot at the expense). He goes on, 'It's easy to get carried away coming up with imaginative themes for an event, but they should always be relevant to the client's business culture and brand. Many agencies suggest wild and wonderful themes that just don't relate at all, in any way, to the client's culture or brand, and they just can't be sustained beyond the event, and sometimes not even that far. Also, if there's a specific message to the event, the theme should strongly support it.'

Themes can be tied to almost anything: historical events, films, plays, TV programmes, music genres, racing, flight, speed, the sky, height, the stars, depth, breadth – be creative, but stay relevant. Once you've decided on a theme that suits your event, supports your message and upholds your client's brand, you'll need to apply it across the board. The theme should be incorporated into the registration process, any pre-event communication, all design, signage, décor, catering, music, maybe photography, videos, entertainment, promotional aspects and, if there any, give-aways. The important thing is not to force the theme down the throats of every aspect of the show, but good and natural connections are enjoyed by audiences – and that's where your creativity and that of your colleagues will come in. Don't forget that audiences can make quantum leaps in understanding. They do that all the time when they watch plays, TV and movies. Given certain sets of information, we get things; we understand connections. A corporate event is the same. Things don't have to be over-spelt out for an audience to connect. If they are audiences turn off and boredom or cynicism can set in.

I was once accompanying a potential client on a visit to Chicago. We were going to see a corporate event, the detail of which was top secret and the theme even more so. I understood this given that I was the 'competition' and I'd been invited so that I could get a better understanding of the potential client's culture. My companion's CEO was going to ring my companion with whom I was travelling to confirm the theme and the running order. Nothing to do with me – I was merely a passenger. Promptly, as arranged, my companion took the call on his mobile phone. Immediately, he held the handset with one hand, looked at me slyly and used the other hand to shield his mouth seemingly in the belief that I could lip read what he was saying. As if. And anyway, he wasn't saying anything but just nodding. I think that he thought that he was in a Robert Ludlum novel. The look didn't work terribly well because his sunglasses, perched on top of his hair-gelled head, kept slipping down over his face. Well, the theme that the CEO had imparted was *Back to the Future*, and they all thought that this was something worth keeping secret. It was around the time that the last of the trilogy movies had come out and, I suppose, from that point of view, there was a certain 'now-ness' about the theme but it related to nothing whatsoever to do with the event's rationale or reason for being – no overarching strategy, message, proposition or news.

You're going to think that this is sour grapes but the *Back to the Future* event, when it happened some three months later, was forgettable. No real content had been shaped and that which had just wasn't wedded to the theme. In other words the theme didn't work because it couldn't. Nobody in the audience really connected with the content because nobody had wanted to engage in designing an event that was relevant for this audience. Nobody had considered it important to consider what the audience needed or wanted. The whole thing was just a drop date in the corporate diary – because it always had been. The client took no advice, cut back on the wrong things and overspent wildly on give-aways and stuff that mostly ended up on the carpet. There was no congruity, no 'glue' and not much of it any good – just lots of set pieces and 'chalk and talk' presentations broken up by a number of well-produced but pointless vox pops, always preceded by two minutes of crashing thunder and swirling spray – which was brilliant as an effect (once), but nobody knew what it was for and, anyway, most in the audience thought that something had gone awry with the sprinkler system. And …. relax.

RELEVANCE

I'm spending time with the family and am really enjoying catching up on some reading and seaside walks. I talk to a well-known theatre director who has, in his time, delivered some excellent corporate and televisual events. He says, 'Relevant event content should be the crack cocaine of conference attendees. It should create an extraordinary euphoria – the sort of thing when you see an uplifting film or play or hear a piece of music that is brilliant for all sorts of reasons. It should create an alertness and an extreme craving for more. Delivering the right content to the right audience can deliver a feel-good rush that should be remembered for years to come. When relevant content is presented within context in a creative way, audience brains get going. You create a wave of pleasure.' This is so true. Any cognitive work (thinking) that leads to success creates a pleasant feeling in the brain that causes a flood of positive emotions. We feel good. There's a sense of satisfaction and accomplishment when we successfully think through an issue. The theatre director adds, 'What happens onstage, what we control as producers, should be all about helping make that sense of understanding and satisfaction happen. The brain even rewards us with a dose of dopamine.

Even if the news isn't good, the collective view about the messages can be positive if what happens onstage is done right.'

'I think that we have to consider what happens onstage as answers to relevant questions that people in the audience have about issues concerning content or message,' says a senior executive producer from a London events agency. 'If the content has been properly prepared and if we really know that we've got the messaging right, then what happens in an event should provide some solutions, or should help, but not over help, attendees to come to solutions on their own. What I do in my job I think is help organisations help their delegates to understand the relevant corporate questions, the problems.' The producer continues, 'Dopamine you say? Well, I do think that event delegates or participants get a rush of dopamine from solving a problem. Then they'll think of your conference with the pleasure that comes from learning. Conversely, when there are issues and the conference is meant to shed light or help with those issues and there is no light or help, then frustration and disappointment set in. That leads to disillusionment and a fed up bunch of people. Actually in that scenario people can get a dose of cortisol, the hormone related to stress. And, if the problem is too difficult to solve, or the content doesn't maintain interest, attention is lost.'

I think about the need to make event content interesting by explaining how it's relevant to attendees. People are naturally curious. We all like uncovering new ideas, solving problems and pursuing thoughts. Curiosity is actually fragile. Content may prompt interest but it does not necessarily maintain it. Content that is too difficult to understand can cause us to lose interest. It kills our curiosity, while content that is too simple causes boredom. The key is to engage by creating content that is totally appropriate to a particular audience (rarely achieved), is exciting in how it's delivered and makes people think long after the aircraft has left for home.

CHAPTER SEVEN
BEHAVIOUR

FAILING TO RESPOND TO AN RSVP OR GENERAL INVITATION

Just in case, RSVP means 'répondez s'il vous plait'. It's a bit like asking someone what the abbreviations 'e.g.' or 'i.e.' mean ('exempli gratia' 'for the sake of an example' and 'id est' meaning 'that is.') and if you knew, then I apologise. Now then, let's get on. Assume that you're a manager in a company and you receive a 'save the date' email invitation from the director of another division in that company, inviting you to attend an important event at which a new product is to be launched. The RSVP requests that you call a specific individual to confirm your attendance. You (genuinely) forget to respond to the email and to the one that follows it. Two weeks later someone from the inviting host's team calls you up and wonders why you've not replied. 'Is there a problem?' 'Not at all,' you reply, 'I just forgot.' They extend an invitation for you to get your finger out and decide whether you'd like to attend or not since places are disappearing fast. This time, after a quick check with your diary, you give an enthusiastic 'yes'.

Nothing very unusual in this of course but here's an etiquette tip: respond within five days of receiving any invitation for any event, personal or business. It's simply good manners. You may think that you saying yea or nay doesn't matter but if we all worked like that, not much would happen in life. Also, changing a 'yes' to a 'no' is only acceptable on account of illness or injury, a family crisis or an absolutely (really) unavoidable professional or business conflict. Call your hosts immediately. Cancelling because you have a better offer is not acceptable, no matter *who* you think you are. Actually, being a 'no show' is unacceptable. I'm mentioning this because, as a project manager or producer, you need to instill this into your client's thinking and, if you can influence the process, help shape the way that invitations to your event are worded and delivered. Undoubtedly you will have some delegate management expertise yourself or will have someone close to hand who has the right expertise, but ensuring that, from the very start, your erstwhile delegates get the message that the event's sponsor wants them to attend, is key. Of course, it may be that attendance at a particular event is compulsory but, even then, people need to commit mentally to the fact that they are attending (and feel OK about it) and not think that they can opt out at the last minute.

Invitations to delegates to attend a conference need to be personal and, above all, relevant (right spellings, right names, right details) so whatever registration system is being used, ensure that experts are in charge and make sure that the right information is sourced. This is so important since, as indicated earlier, nothing can cause more aggravation at high levels in company hierarchies than incorrect data about an individual being invited to attend an event.

FAILING TO FOLLOW THE DRESS CODE

People forget things and, for some reason, when it comes to events, delegates and potential delegates sometimes go very droopy in the head. They are suddenly three years old and can't understand things. They can't find bits of information that are staring them in the face. They want to be led, hand-held and comforted and, even then, they invariably get it all wrong. Some delegates will ignore instructions and advice on a beautifully created registration website. No, I don't know why either but moaning, 'But I'm too busy,' really doesn't cut it.

If the delegate had read the advice, he or she would know that the product launch is a two-day event at a good venue within reasonable distance from where he or she lives or works. Because he or she works at a software company where the dress code is always business casual, when he or she arrives at the event, he's (let's assume the male gender) wearing khakis and a beaten up but clean long sleeve soft cotton shirt. He's greeted at the onsite registration kiosk and then invited to step into a reception to find everyone else is wearing business attire. A colleague of mine laughs. She's a specialist in event registration and invitation etiquette. 'It does still happen. People are either arrogant or think it's clever. My advice is simple. Read the website advice on what to do, where to go and what to wear. It's hardly complicated. When in doubt, always overdress for most circumstances.'

Advise your clients accordingly. Dress code may be assumed but it's best to make it clear, particularly if there are various different social occasions to attend or indeed if there are any outside activities. And, by the by, what constitutes business casual or smart casual is something of a minefield – so establish with your client what you mean and what they mean; don't assume. Similarly, formal dress might mean black tie and sometimes not, so check. I well remember going to Harrow School to see a play that featured a now prominent actor and director. I turned up in a jacket and open neck shirt (yes and trousers). Unfortunately, everyone else was wearing black tie because it was a special school day or evening and I hadn't read the invitation properly.

I've just come back from a week in a Welsh holiday cottage with an octogenarian, two friends (and their toddler), my wife, three sons, and a dog. While in Wales, I was expected to attend an industry function and, because I didn't have time to check, a 'friend' said that attire was black tie. I happily obliged and donned the penguin suit indeed looking rather dapper even if I say so myself. Needless to say, nobody else was wearing anything remotely close to a black bow tie. However, I was able to lie through my teeth and say to anyone who asked that I had just come from an awards ceremony and had been recognised for my contribution to the industry. I then bowed a little to each questioner and wandered off as though exhausted by being famous and very, very talented.

FAILING TO ARRIVE ON TIME

It annoys me not a little when events don't start on time. I'm a fairly punctual sort of chap myself and while I have no problem waiting five minutes for a meeting to start, it pains me to see three hundred people waiting fifteen minutes for one or two other people who're late and, what's worse, who don't seem to care one iota. Also, when some people are habitually late, other participants start thinking 'Hey, tomorrow *I'll* arrive ten minutes late.' It's a downward slide from there and it's just plain rude.

Get your client to agree that, 'The conference starts at 15.00 hours' means that the conference starts at 15.00 hours sharp, and not fifteen or thirty minutes later. Emphasise this in the joining instructions. Start the event at the appointed time, regardless of how many participants are still missing. Waiting for them only teaches them that it's OK to be late. Make the latecomers sit at the back. If I had my way I wouldn't let them in at all unless there's an absolutely undeniable and valid reason. Make lateness visible. I don't know why CEOs from the stage don't embarrass latecomers in the same way stand-up comedians do: 'Ah a late arrival I see. Good morning to you sir. Now, shall I interrupt you and bang the door when you're interviewing for your next promotion?' Or 'Good morning to you. Geoff Prattley isn't it? My office please on Tuesday morning.'

A scriptwriter of many a corporate script says, 'Turning up for each aspect of the event is a courtesy and, again, your client needs to consider – with your help – how people should take their attendee responsibilities seriously. Showing up promptly is the right thing to do. Be present in the keynotes to which you've committed or at which you're expected. Be prompt for the pre-dinner drinks and the dinners you've said you'll attend and at each and every networking break. If you're in the room – be *in the room*. Don't chat incessantly and annoyingly to your neighbour, don't eat a bag of biscuits, don't drink juice noisily, don't bring your china cup and saucer in and then interrupt the speaker's flow as you deposit both on the floor.'

HELPING CLIENTS UNDERSTAND ETIQUETTE

You have to be careful here because you can't be condescending. However, some clients really just don't know the best way to advise their attendees how to behave. Some conference behaviour I've witnessed (as have many in the industry) has been disgusting and disgraceful. There's no excuse and I am always amazed that the client company concerned tolerates it, not least when the damage to the company's brand can be irreparable.

OH, BEHAVE

Excessive drinking at company events, inappropriate table manners, and lack of chivalry are unacceptable, whoever you are – client or agency side. You and your team/crew cannot drink too much – and definitely not in open sight of the client. Rudeness or bad language are not to be countenanced at any time. Good manners *do* count and I'm not being holier than thou here. Many clients will pick up on the fact that crew and teams are well-mannered, courteous and helpful during a time of no small stress. They will also note the opposite. There's not a huge amount you can do if someone from the client side is rude or demonstrates inappropriate behaviour but if it puts the event at risk or demeans a member of your team, you should address the matter with your client straight away and insist on action.

There are always times when we feel irritated with venue staff, suppliers, colleagues, crew, team members, the client – but on site you damn well keep that to yourself or have words very privately. Appropriate business etiquette is expected of everyone, especially at corporate events. However, it never ceases to surprise me how few people are trained in the art of good manners. Most people learn event etiquette on the job, but much of it is down to common sense and sensitivity.

There is a widely held view in the events industry that conference delegates tend to behave out of time and out of place. They feel that they can behave very differently than they would, say, at home and that leads to all sorts of ghastly misdemeanours. On the other hand, some people don't know *how* to behave full stop. On the other hand (OK there *are* three in this instance), some people feel that they can just let go and do what they please because repercussions are few. Well, having witnessed a few events go to bits because of bad behaviour, I would urge you to try and instil in your client that it's a total waste of money to provide an event or, more likely, the gala dinner part of an event, with no parameters or sanctions.

I would certainly understand your reticence to preach. Keep in mind, though (and, if you can, remind your client) that the purpose of etiquette is to create an environment that allows *everyone* to feel comfortable. Poor behaviour in the management and delivery of any event is bad news. Poor behaviour on the client side can be a disaster – and not just amongst the guests or delegates. A highly respected producer of large automotive events says, 'I was once producing an event for a major car company and it was a very large and elaborate marketing conference over a three day period. Cars on stage were involved and the attention to German detail was phenomenal – on our side as well as theirs. The evening before the show was to begin, and after exhaustive technical and presenter rehearsals, the Group MD turned up amid a great display of red carpet and accompanied by whatever the collective noun for a bunch of rather obsequious junior executives is. The MD was nice enough to begin with, shook my hand and many of my hardworking team's hands too. Then he went onstage to look at the huge set, a set of which I was and still am enormously proud. He was smoking a very large Nicaraguan cigar, which had a peppery smell and he coolly tipped the prodigious ash onto the pale blue stage carpet, carpet that had been lovingly and recently swept and cleaned of any mark by my crew. I politely asked this man to put the cigar out or preferably take it off the stage immediately. He refused and there ensued something of a verbal battle in English and German. As his cigar was still lit and still being puffed, I steered the gentleman's arm towards the stage steps (treads as they're called in the trade). I pointed out in perfect German that if he didn't take the cigar away there would be no event and I spun dramatically on my heel and walked off. There was a shout of something which, roughly translated, means 'What in heaven's name do you think you're doing and who do you think you are talking to? How dare you?' I turned, walked back and politely said something along the lines of, 'My team and I have worked very hard to make this event perfect for you and your colleagues in every single and small way. Yes, the overall cost has been high, but everything has come within budget. My (and our) attention to detail is exemplary, as is yours when you build your fine cars. Would you let me smoke a cigar in a brand new (I can't remember what series or vehicle I used as an example) that you wanted others to drive? I don't think so.' There was a bit of a hush and then in a beautifully filmic way, he smiled and of course came away from the stage, and I wish I could say that we hugged. But I did get that smile and the show was a success. We send each other Christmas cards still.'

Attending a conference, people may be tense and apprehensive because they're out of their regular environment or comfort zone and have been pushed into a social situation that requires them to engage with people with whom they may not normally interact. But there is no excuse for a drop in basic manners and some people have a very selfish attitude or a sense of self-importance that is pathetic. 'Oh yeah,' says cousin Maier. 'Many people leave their phones on during plenary sessions, creating a disturbance when they receive e-mails or phone calls. It's bad manners and unacceptable. Some people even leave meetings to take "important" calls. That's bad manners too. Nobody is that important and, anyway, unless you're awaiting a call that's about something very serious indeed, there are coffee breaks when you can ring someone back.'

A director from an international travel company says, 'Delegates often forget their business cards. I'm not sure what a producer or project manager can do about that really. But business cards are obviously ideal for conferences. However, having said that, with more and more events adding QR codes (abbreviated from Quick Response Code) to name badges, it's wise to consider suggesting to clients that delegates get digital with their 'calling cards'. Using a smart phone's camera on a fellow delegate's card can lead to a biography or links to all the networks and websites to which the fellow delegate belongs. Another thing that conference delegates often forget (or maybe just don't know) is the art of talking, of conversation. In conferences there are networking opportunities and it's extraordinary how many people, men and women, don't listen to, or aren't interested in, what another party has to say. Some people just stick to others with whom they work day in day out. Events provide an opportunity to really find out things, to establish new information, to learn and to meet useful and interesting people. That requires some planning and effort.'

EVENT OBSERVERS

Some event specialists and producers employ a meeting anthropologist for an event – obviously with the client's buy-in. It's often useful to have independent outsiders (trained and senior researchers, perhaps behavioural psychologists), to observe your conference participants' actions, behaviours, likes, dislikes, motivation, boredom levels, decisions and group culture. This isn't a daft idea. You and your client need to know how your attendees interacted with each other, how they responded to your schedule, how they reacted to your speakers, how they understood the content proposition and messages, how they aligned with or against your objectives and generally how they conducted themselves. It's good research.

Most event producers and their staff are too busy overseeing the management and delivery of the event to observe attendees' actions. Yet that data is valuable if only to help in the planning of future events and legacy communications. Usually producers and their clients rely on post-conference surveys to collect data from their attendees about the experience and there's nothing wrong with that, provided that the surveys are of real value. But very often these aren't enough. They only give a snapshot into that attendee's mind about the questions asked and only at the time that the questionnaire is completed. Some events ask that a questionnaire is completed at the end of each day or at different moments throughout the event – and indeed anything to make the overall picture accurate must be a good thing.

Corporate events take people out of their daily routines and force them into a new or different environment. Attendees suddenly face unfamiliar surroundings, a strange home base, untried schedules, perhaps unusual meal routines, different ideas, new connections, different sleeping patterns and unknown experiences. Cousin Maier pipes up during a transatlantic Skype, 'I think that it's sometimes an abnormal situation. The conference attendees form a temporary society with new rules and expectations and that can be something to which it's hard for some to adjust.' He excuses himself for a moment while he picks up a giggling child who then has to perform a new song about buses and wheels much to the admiration of her uncle. After my genuine congratulations, the stoic goes on, 'That "new society" can be culturally different as well as startling in terms of interaction, location, role, social status, work, different levels of peers, presence of senior colleagues or some other relationship positioning. There's likely to be a plurality of groups and small communities – and some delegates might feel alienated. These are factors of which a good producer or project manager needs to be cognisant. Efforts need to be made, usually by senior executives on the client side, to ensure that everyone feels engaged.'

MEASURING DELEGATE BEHAVIOUR PATTERNS

Rich data and analysis flow naturally these days in and around conferences. Now, producers and project managers can view immediate session evaluations on iPads and similar. Attendees Tweet about (and post on) the event via social networking platforms. We in the event industry have an unprecedented opportunity to learn from the rich veins of event intelligence that is available through technology. Now, as my cousin has often said, event producers and project managers can understand how the event is perceived, which element of the programme was most effective, and data can be developed for future planning. These elements can be managed by an event app. Deploying a mobile app before, during or after a conference has one obvious benefit – the cost (and environmental) savings derived from replacing some or all of the normal event-related printed materials. 'However,' said one of the best American event producers (who speaks six languages with equal fluency and has a degree from MIT), 'that isn't the only reason for event producers to consider a mobile app. If building an intelligent event – one that yields relevant, immediate and accurate information about audience reaction – is one of the client's goals, mobile apps are an important part of that strategy.'

I would agree, as does the corporate communications director of a very well-known carbonated drink brand. 'Using a mobile app to deliver electronic session and speaker evaluations,' she says with utter conviction while looking out of an office window at the busy London street below, 'has some significant advantages. Results are obtained in real time, which improves the producer's ability – and ours – to evaluate content just after it has been experienced. A mobile evaluation app can instantly collect feedback and tabulate whatever results you want. Another important factor here is that speakers can learn how attendees received the content shortly after presenting it, as opposed to weeks after the event ends. Is that a good thing? Yes, sometimes it is.' My fizzy drink friend has with her an event manager colleague who adds to the conversation, 'Evaluation results from all of the sessions can be combined at the end of the conference and presented in a digital format so that event analysis is straightforward. Other than a show of hands or via a voting system (both of which by the way can have their merits, not least that the former would be free), conference speakers have few ways to immediately gauge the audience's views. Also, I think that it's fair to say that we can encourage engagement and inclusion via the use of apps or smartphone devices to survey attendees from time to time during the event on, say, event content and delegates' experiences. A client may not wish to make everything public, particularly if immediate reactions to something are poor, so the warts and all approach – of telling an audience everything – needs caution.'

At a recent conference, a speaker was presenting a complex idea which he was making marvellously simple – about corporate communications. It was lively, entertaining and exciting, not least because he was pointing and touching parts of a huge screen, moving things around. He climbed ladders and crossed beams that made the process even more 'fun'. We all had iPads from an earlier session. His presentation finished and many in the audience were desperately trying to write his material down. Suddenly he waved both hands at the screen and everything whooshed off never to be seen again, or so we thought. There were shocked groans and sparks of anger. The presenter had walked off and there was something of a hush. Suddenly, each of the iPads came alive with all the content that he'd just rubbed out. Brilliant.

On the way home this evening I notice that a newspaper has it that social media is a minefield for brands, and that one pundit says that Facebook and Twitter are about 'building brands through editorial' as opposed to just being vehicles for advertising. The article also comments on the fact that mobile apps are being used widely at conferences around the world – for example at congress meetings, at pharmaceutical advisory boards and corporate events in general. I find this extremely interesting and note that a growing number of clients are using Twitter to gain insights into event success and to generate simple benefits during and beyond the event.

A group of similar people with similar interests or objectives is clearly going to be more interesting than any single member of that group. With an event, there's always someone out there amongst the audience who will have some added value information or refreshing point of view relating to the event's proposition. Sure, this level of insight will be captured through Q&A sessions, debates, discussions, breakouts and similar, but utilising Twitter is very helpful too and can be kept totally confidential to those who know the specific hashtag.

My cousin once more expresses a view. 'Being able to tap into the Twitter community is incredibly illuminating. Twitter is starting to replace Google for many people I know. In its broadest sense, Twitter becomes a news service. Some of these interactions lead to new ideas, others lead to temporary collaborations while still others have led to ongoing partnerships over time. When Twitter is used for a closed corporate event, those in the know find that this smaller community can act as an excellent pool for new thinking. Not only does Twitter open up new relationships – it's a great place to cement and deepen existing ones. Another factor that people seem to like is the fact that messages are out of necessity short. And Twitter is being used more regularly for event polls and evaluation – simple to do of course and immediate.'

I discuss Twitter with a technology consultant who spends much of his time with large event delivery companies. He says, 'Twitter polls should use a common hash tag (like, for example, #mypoll) that will tie the questions and answers together. In doing so, the followers of poll participants (event delegates) will be exposed to the Q&A and potentially participate. Keeping the hastag going way after the event's finished can bring relevant discussions and useful points of view – of use to the client company's planning and, of course, should be of benefit in many ways to the delegates. If a client has the resource or if they'll pay someone to do it, you should suggest helping event delegates meet their needs beyond the event via effective social networking. In a few years' time this will be commonplace.' He pauses and thinks for a moment. 'Yep. Commonplace,' he says.

CHAPTER EIGHT
SPEAKERS AND CONTRIBUTORS

INTERNAL SPEAKERS

For the purposes of this section, there are two sorts of speakers – those who are from the client company and guest speakers or contributors who are invited as external specialists. In both cases there are holes down which you (and they) can fall. 'Oh yes?' I hear you mutter. Well, young doubting Thomas or Thomasina, there have been many an occasion that I've witnessed professorial types who've not listened at all to the health and safety briefings, and have with full cheer trotted towards the rear of the stage area to touch a screen which is, as you know, normally not firm. In the process of their enthusiasms, they have then toppled, with just enough time for a brief shriek, down what can amount to a three or four metre drop, on top of lights and other various technical apparatus. No deaths yet but some red or very pale faces and, as memory has it, but one legal problem. Anyway, there *are* holes down which you can tumble.

There are other ways any speaker can fail in his or her presentation: a misconception about what the audience will retain from the presentation (due to a lack of knowledge about the audience), or the presenter might just be dreadful – in which case that's a pretty important reason for major failure. Just because someone is a senior somebody from the client side, or an author of some renown, or a famous person from the world of light entertainment or a major subject matter expert from across the Atlantic, does not by *any* means whatsoever prove that he or she is a great presenter.

Even if the person in question *is* a pretty good presenter, if what is delivered is the same presentation that has been boringly and routinely put out time after time, it's likely that the speaker will be a bit tired and perhaps unenthusiastic. If the speaker is bored, then the audience will hardly be electrified. Once, a very long time ago, a client insisted on using an internal senior executive as a conference speaker who spoke in rhyming couplets about current management techniques – this kind of thing if memory serves: 'Blessed are you whose worthiness gives scope/Being had, to triumph; being lacked, to hope', and 'So, till the judgement that yourself arise/You live in this, and dwell in business eyes.' So it went on – for quite a long time – to an unbelieving and open-mouthed audience.

Unfortunately, you may have little choice over internal speakers because the CEO, the marketing director and, say, the head of HR may absolutely have to speak (on the client's insistence) and you may not know how each is going to be until it's too late – and even if you knew how bad they were, there's not a lot you can do. However, you *can* (and must) ask questions at an early stage and suggest, if the runes portend unhappy times, that the speaker is perhaps interviewed on stage or maybe makes a short lectern-style presentation and is then interviewed, or maybe just works damn hard at rehearsing and practising his or her presentation. And, here's the thing. Most executives in most organisations anywhere in the world (and, for some reason, particularly in the UK and mainland Europe) just *won't* rehearse, and think that practising or going through a speech or presentation is for wimps. They're surrounded by acolytes, each of whom tells the executive how great he or she is at presentations – and the vain individual believes the hype. Or, more insultingly, he or she doesn't care two hoots because the audiences usually comprise their own staff and they, poor souls, have no choice but to sit still and receive any old dirge. Selfish executives like this need to mature, show some respect for their audiences, and grasp an opportunity to communicate well – with both hands. Such opportunities to communicate are golden. Why waste them?

So, internal speakers (by which I mean from the client end) are a given – although, as indicated, you can suggest alternative methods of getting the best from them. In any case, you will need to try (very hard) to recommend that there aren't too many lectern-driven presentations because quite frankly that's just boring and a speaker has to be so, so good to manage a fabulous lectern presentation. For any audience to have to sit through ten of these in one day (or, for crying out loud, maybe more) is enough to make grown men weep and drench their neighbours in tears. But, by the Roman Archaic Triad of Jupiter, Mars and dear Quirinus, it happens again and again.

Client presenters/speakers, whoever they are, need to prepare a presentation well and fill the allotted time (twenty minutes maximum but good luck with selling *that*). Actually what I should have said there is that the content of the speech or presentation should dictate the time, which should be no longer than twenty minutes. Some of the very best speeches I've ever witnessed have been around ten or fifteen minutes long. Occasionally, but rarely, you get a superb example where someone extraordinary can speak for an hour and hold the audience spellbound.

EXTERNAL PRESENTERS AND CONTRIBUTORS

Said the creative director of a London agency over a cup of excellent Nilgiri, 'We had a client who insisted on a demonstration from the Guangdong Acrobatic Troupe of China, followed by a management lecture that maintained that what we had just seen was exactly like a business in crisis. Then there was another client who was so taken with the film *Cowboys and Aliens* that she insisted on paying a lot of money to show extracts, and then had a management professor talk about analogies between what had been seen and management skills. We saw Daniel Craig – an escapee from the aliens' prison laboratory – use a glowing bracelet that doubles as a supergun. The audience was treated to watching warring Wild West folk hiding their differences in order to fight the space monsters. Well, the biggest talking point at coffee time was the creatures whose faces were made entirely from nasal cartilage, oh, and the spacecraft that abducted their single-toothed victims using lassoes rather than teleportation devices.' He cackles at the memory. 'Dreadful,' he mutters.

Sometimes, it's a good idea to have an external expert who will add value to an event's theme or who can underline an event's proposition. Sometimes it's good to have someone with whom the audience will identify and/or will respect for some aspect of *relevant* high achievement. This kind of thing rings the changes, can be very interesting (or should be) and might add corporate value to the event and its objectives. But do remember that relevant content *has* to be the overall driver. Many, both client and agency side, throw in a guest speaker to fill an empty slot. Silly and wasteful.

If hiring an outside speaker, event producers or project managers may either contract directly with a professional speaker or their agent, or rely on the expertise of a speaker bureau, of which there are many, but only a few which are really good and really know their stuff.

Says my cousin, 'A solid, well-planned programme or agenda should identify the need for an appropriate topic or theme to be addressed by a guest. Note that the topic will present itself and the speaker will follow.' The CEO of a major New York speaker bureau offers me this: 'There are some key determinants in planning for a guest speaker.' His office overlooks Central Park and the season is spring. The Big Apple is lit with sparkle and dazzle. 'First,' he says in a tone that insists that I move away from the window and listen to him, 'event producers should always understand what the audience will need or want so that you can relay that to the external speakers on your shortlist. This may sound obvious but I've witnessed many producers who can't be precise about objectives of the whole event and of particular sessions. The speaker will need to understand the event's objectives and you and your client will need to be clear about the expectations of the speaker and the methods by which you and your client can benchmark success.' He's in full spate now and he's making much good sense. 'Say you're looking for a keynote speaker, it's often good to choose someone who's a specialist in whatever your client does for a living – particularly if the information and the message to convey are highly clinical and industry specific. That speaker needs academic knowledge, specific background or education, to understand the nuances of the client's industry, history, politics and corporate culture. As all producers worth their salt will know, there are some common themes that run through events or which occupy executive minds. Themes and messages are broad and universal. Every industry cares about leadership, teamwork, behaviours, change, communications, conflict resolution, stress management, sales, growth, marketing, mergers, acquisitions, poor sales, great sales and so on. A quality guest speaker will (should) research and customise his or her subject of expertise to specifically address the client's needs with close reference to the client's industry and its current issues.' One of his colleagues comes in to join us, someone with whom I've often worked and who really knows her guest speakers for most eventualities. Pleasantries and establishing who's done what over, she remarks, 'Sometimes you will know, or your client will know, that an event's audience might perceive the conference message to be more valuable and inspirational if delivered by an "outsider". When internal representatives address difficult messages, audiences may suspect hidden agendas or wonder if the internal speaker has been coached or "got at" ...' (here she figuratively mimcs parentheses in the air) '... by senior management. In such cases, a guest speaker is perceived as more objective.'

WHEN CHOOSING A GUEST SPEAKER, CONSIDER A NUMBER OF THINGS

A popular British speaker on change management says, 'It's important to gather what it is that the people in the audience want or need to walk away with from what a guest speaker might say. Be clear about the event's themes and objectives to help you narrow down your guest speaker search. Some clients plump for a person, particularly a famous headline speaker, about whom they know little and then complain when that name doesn't really work out, so it's important to advise positively and gently – but with strong argument. Be persuasive but know what you're talking about. If necessary, take good advice and do your homework. It's important not only to consider the speaker's name and the topic but the positioning of the session in the agenda. A guest speaker works especially well to open or close a conference, or to provide a change of pace. Audiences enjoy events that are framed with universal topics, which help bring the energy together, or point the way ahead with enthusiasm. A guest speaker keynote of 45 to 60 minutes is very common, but that can be too long and should include a Q&A session. Some event clients want to buy a guest speaker by the pound or, literally, by the length of a presentation, and that's foolish. If a speaker is really good and engages the audience, then an hour can work well, but this needs careful planning and discussion.' He pauses briefly, looks moodily at his flashing smart phone and then continues. 'There's a difference between a professional speaker and a celebrity speaker, or a Canadian speaker, say, and a Dutch speaker or an American. Each brings his or her own magic to a conference. The way to ensure the best fit for your event is to ask yourself about the pros and cons of each type of speaker – what's best for your specific audience, what's the primary focus? Do we want this guest speaker to provide content or entertainment, motivation and inspiration or a mixture of all of those things?' Personality traits are a driver too; many an event has been spoiled by someone who looks brilliant on paper, but is a pain to work with. You also need to consider whether you want someone who is forthright, humorous, content heavy, inspirational, and/or perhaps motivational? Consider the personality and chemistry of your audience to ensure the right fit between audience and speaker. This can be easier said than done, but it is very important – not least because mistakes are not only expensive but can ruin the whole event and its legacy.

Price or cost is obviously an important matter and clients (and actually producers) have sometimes a totally unrealistic idea of what guest contributors might cost. You must research the market to get a realistic sense of which speakers cost what. Do that by gathering information on two or three shortlisted presenters. Try and see videos of the speakers in action and also try and talk to others who've used those people for similar purposes. 'Fees may differ,' says an affable British speaker bureau executive who's sporting a jacket the type of which one normally sees walking about in Henley during the Royal Regatta, 'and, if they do, it's important to explore the deliverables for each. The problem is that clients invariably plump for someone who is at the cheaper end of the market but is totally inappropriate for the event and its audience. Mind you going for the more costly end of the market doesn't always mean that the speaker will be right for your event. The same actually applies to event entertainment too. Mind you, it's also fair to say that clients sometimes get caught in the headlights of fame and choose an expensive someone for his or her name but who doesn't really deliver in terms of appropriate content or message synergy.'

Later that evening I discuss the matter with cousin Maier who is going to bed or waking up – I forget which. 'It's also important to find out exactly what the quoted fee includes,' he says under a huge yawn, 'like travel and accommodation expenses. Will the speaker customise his or her presentation? Is there an additional fee for that customisation? Can you video the presentation and, if you're allowed to, is there an additional fee for that? Will the speaker insist that you buy hundreds of his books to give away at your event? Will he insist on bringing his partner, uncle, secretary, aged parent?'

I talk to a researcher who is used to finding the most apposite speaker for a wide variety of international corporate events. She says, 'Always review the speaker's website to get a greater sense of his or her subject matter expertise, credentials, clients and testimonials. Are references available? Look for evidence of a diverse group of satisfied, previous clients. Has this speaker spoken at an event similar to yours? Is he or she published? View the speaker's work on YouTube and via other sources. Always, but always, insist on having the chance to talk directly with the speaker. Most bureau staff or agents will agree to arrange this, but often only once the speaker is booked. Insist on speaking before you make the booking. It can be a conference or Skype call which can include the bureau or agent. You probably won't be given the phone number so the agent or the speaker will arrange the call. If the bureau or agent says that you can't speak directly to the prospective speaker then, if you don't know the speaker and can't find anyone who can vouch for quality and whether he or she is apposite, consider moving on. *Never* take risks without doing your homework and, even with homework, there are risks with an unknown candidate. Just because someone is famous for a book, research or any kind of expertise, does *not* make that person a good conference presenter. I could give you chapter and accompanying verse on this, but laws prohibit me. Just take my word for it. It's a bit like assuming that a newsreader has great legs.'

There are times when the client ends up insisting on their own in-house expert, but choosing a prophet from one's own house has its drawbacks.

However, you may end up with little say over a favoured son or daughter and there is a time when you need to stop any protestations and just get on with it. Some battles you won't win. After the event, when the evaluations come in, if there are any, then you can smile to yourself knowing that the audience thought that the client's favourite was rubbish. But, of course, that's a bit late and it's a hollow victory because the failure may reflect on you and your company. If you're concerned talk about it openly with your client and also your line manager.

BE CAUTIOUS

Be absolutely certain that the speaker you are considering is able deliver with the focus that you expect on the subject that you want addressed. Speakers can go off-piste if allowed, so ensure that your brief is succinct and crystal clear. In truth of course, the guest speaker should be a continuum of what has gone before in an event and what will follow, where everything is seamless and high quality communication.

There's a place in many corporate events for sporting greats, novelists, adventurers (but please no more mountain climbers or folk with frostbitten fingers), scientists, specialists in this and wondrous people in that; there's no shortage of speakers in all categories, but, there is a shortage of *really* good ones. The ideal for conference producers and project managers is to find the correct category to fit the mix for the particular event (in other words, last year's mix might not be at all appropriate for this year's event). Most importantly, you must ensure that the speaker chosen is not just someone who is recognised for achievement in a particular field, but is someone who actually knows how to engage an audience.

A publisher who used to be a celebrity agent says, 'Be wary of people who think that they should get on the public speaking circuit because they have retired from, say, the world of sport. Some ex-sportspeople and retired business people of note are very good presenters, but only in certain environments, such as a dinner, or to briefly reinforce a key message. Some are good at getting an audience to relax. People have a fascination for celebrity, but that's only good if the celebrity can deliver a sentence. A great story will not fire anyone's attention if poorly delivered.'

Flexibility in a guest speaker is important. There's no shortage of 'one speech' presenters out there and one of these might be exactly what you need. However, and it is a big 'but', it's important to ensure that external speakers *really* do have the breadth of experience in their professed area of expertise or competency to offer the flexibility of topic range and to tailor a topic. I've worked with several international gurus, although I heartily dislike the term and the title tends to ramp up costs. In my experience, these people generally strive hard to assist producers or clients to make the event everything it should be. I've also worked with speakers who have a list of demands as long as an ego-centric, tempestuous pop-star, even down to insisting on bowls of only blue M&Ms or drinks that only begin with the letter 'B'.

Also, any event manager or producer worth his or her salt wants all those participants responsible for delivery – *including* guest speakers – to play their part when the going gets tough. When things go haywire at a conference (and of course sometimes they do), the project manager/producer wants people in all roles, including speakers, to pitch in and be part of the solution – and not to be some over-indulged prima donna sitting on the side-lines increasing the extent of the day's problems.

SO WHAT ARE THE GURU INGREDIENTS?

I'm in Manchester, where I spent some of my youth. I'm in an Italian restaurant with an old school friend who's now a management mentor and making a fortune. We order some decent Chianti. He says, 'This used to be a restaurant, but now calls itself a ristorante. Spaghetti has become pasta and cheese formaggio.' He pauses and then addresses my question concerning guest speakers. 'In an events industry environment of increasing costs and decreasing budgets, most conference producers and project managers would agree the ideal speaker would be one who:

▶ is a recognised expert with significant experience in the area/s about which he or she presents;

▶ presents with an engaging style, utilising the appropriate mix of entertainment and content for the particular client, the particular event and the particular objectives;

▶ is prepared to have a Skype or phone chat with you and, after you, with the client – with you in attendance;

▶ is willing to specifically tailor each presentation to the needs of the specific audience (and has a track record of successfully and specifically doing just that);

▶ doesn't argue for the sake of it or ever in front of the client (well-known broadcasters take note!);

▶ has the capacity to add value by perhaps running a follow-up workshop to a keynote or participating in a lively and relevant panel session.

The bullet points are mine of course but that's how he speaks – everything tidy and nicely arranged. 'Every speaker's specific requirements are different,' he says after downing another glass of the red and toying with his formaggio. 'At a minimum,' he continues, 'you should expect to be responsible for paying for airfare (usually business class), overnight accommodation (usually at least a junior suite), transport (usually a smart car/limo at either end), meals (usually room service) and AV requirements (usually last minute). Sometimes a speaker may have a flat fee for travel or may require specific per-diems to cover meals and incidentals. There can also be additional fees for hand-outs or the right to video his or her presentation – something invariably the client will want, but for which there'll be no budget – and don't even think for a nanosecond of doing this secretly. If you or your client gets caught, the penalties for infringing copyright can be huge.'

Fees for external speakers range from a few thousand dollars or pounds to over a hundred thousand. The speakers or their agents and bureaux set their fees and there are no specific criteria or standards for how they do that. They will charge what they can get away with, but there's always room for some negotiation. Always ask and be prepared to walk away if your budget can't run to what's being charged. Never think that an agent will reduce a fee just because you say so but, as I say, ask. Sometimes speakers are keen to take a commission because they want to work with your client. Or you.

Professional speakers are those who have chosen to speak for a living. Generally the bureau or agent will invoice you and the speaker will receive a fee less commission – that's a percentage of the fee that will be kept by the bureau or agent. It works like this because the bureau or agent will have secured and engaged the speaker for you and will assume all the contractual obligations. There are exceptions, as in any business, and there may be times when a bureau might charge their own fees in addition to commission when providing services – such as extensive research or strategic planning. Make sure you know what the rules are *before* you begin. Many is the time that I've been faced with weeping project managers or producers because they haven't really got a handle on a deal with a speaker bureau or agency and now clutch an invoice far higher than budgets allow.

Some speakers present as a result of specific expertise in a given field. Speaking is not usually their primary vocation and celebrities are an example of just that. Often, you will pay a lot of money just to have a celebrity on the platform. The planner (you) or the client – or both of you – have to determine the real value of that. Sometimes the benefit of a major celebrity just *being* there can have huge benefit and the experience will be remembered long after the event has finished, sometimes years later. There was a famous Manchester United and England football player called Bobby Charlton, later to become Sir Bobby Charlton. He was a huge star and the idol of many a young boy back in the 1960s – not least playing a major role when England won the World Cup in 1966. Unlike many football stars Bobby remained steady, polite, calm and kind. He was a hero. I invited him to attend a black tie awards ceremony for a bank and the event was important in terms of motivation and moving moments. Emotion needed to be high. Sir Bobby was introduced and he walked onstage to a standing ovation lasting for, oh, around ten minutes. He had a quick bit of dialogue with the bank's CEO and then a football was rolled on from the wings (rehearsed I hasten to add); the great footballer collected the ball with his foot, tapped the ball in the air and kept it in the air for a good couple of minutes – and then kicked it out into the audience. Another standing ovation ensued and a not a dry eye in the house as this modest man stood bemused at the fuss being made. This was a moment I will never forget and, I guarantee, neither will any of the audience, men and women alike.

Expert speakers and indeed celebrities may be very good at motivating audiences and, of course, motivating any audience is what a client will mostly want at any event – at some point certainly. But at other times that celebrity can be a waste of time because the event or the audience doesn't *need* the presence of a famous person. Also, obviously, a celeb can be costly and, just because someone is indeed an A list star and can fire the audience's zeal and imagination for ten minutes, doesn't mean that the experience is worth a small pot of gold.

MOTIVATIONAL SPEAKERS

Motivational speakers are universally popular. What changes from time to time is the style of motivation that clients want to hire. Once there was a focus on pure motivation – the 'yeah-all-of-you-can-do-it-if-you-really-try-type' – but that's rather old hat now. Most clients quite naturally want motivation, but with a message. Best-selling business authors, for example, are very often in demand. It seems that many authors – though not all – hit the speaking circuit as soon as their book starts receiving notoriety. It is assumed that, because they have written a business book that has sold well at airports, they must have a message and, for some unknown rationale, they must be fabulous conference speakers. Well, not always. Recently, a client of mine insisted (against all advice) on hiring a celebrity author who had published some esoteric tome explaining the recent dip in world markets. The celebrity author cost a fortune, dismissed any notion of any rehearsal or run-through, insisted on not wearing a microphone, didn't listen at all to advice concerning where there was light on the stage, refused more or less everything apart from his meals and first class travel. During the show he kicked a delicate piece of staging causing it to topple and break. He dashed a glass of water to the ground for dramatic effect causing a stain on his trouser front that would have been embarrassing anywhere public. He did the usual and leaned heavily against the lectern to the point where it very nearly toppled over and him with it. Oh, how the crew and I prayed to the lectern God for some help in making this happen. Alas, the lectern was solid and the author went on his pedantic, dreary and mostly unheard or unseen way. My only consolation was that in post-event evaluation, he received very few ticks in any box, and his second book was a flop, which just goes to prove something or other.

EVENT HOSTS, FACILITATORS, MODERATORS OR MCS

I once hired a well-known television presenter as a conference facilitator. His hobby was the weather – meteorology. On the second day of the event, at the very beginning, before the first keynote presentation, he began to let the audience, some 1000 motor industry souls, know of his interest in the thunder clouds gathering outside the venue. This wasn't scheduled or 'in the script'. He regaled the somewhat surprised motor dealer principals with stories of hurricanes, tornados, squalls, cyclones, twisters, gales, blizzards, thunderstorms, snowstorms and Shakespearian tempests. Then whatever it was that was gathering outside, decided to burst and thunder clapped and lightning lit. Our facilitator then quoted (very well actually) that wonderful opening piece spoken by Shakespeare's Lear (III.ii): 'Blow, winds, and crack your cheeks! Rage! Blow!/ You cataracts and hurricanes, spout/ Till you have drench'd our steeples, drown'd the cocks!/ You sulphurous and thought-executing fires,/ Vaunt-couriers to oak-cleaving thunderbolts,/ Singe my white head!' Well, that last bit didn't work so well because the facilitator had a thick head of black hair, but you can picture the scene I'm sure.

Our man then advised us that a storm was coming. Well, we knew that, but he explained that it had begun as a mild breeze from someone blowing their nose in Africa, how it had picked up power over the Arctic, strengthened somewhere over the cold seas and then whooshed into the United States, circling lower Manhattan, turned east over the Atlantic, enjoyed a meeting with a wind coming in the other direction and created a huge wave in the Bermuda Triangle and then, bored with that, smacked straight into London. There was a stunned hush and then funnily enough – because audiences do the strangest things – people began to applaud. Well there was a little confrontation at coffee time and the chap did keep to the straight and narrow thereon. The point is, you must ensure that any external person taking the stage is thoroughly briefed about what to do and what not to do. In detail. Of course, allow a little slack for the person onstage to amuse and delight the audience provided that whatever the facilitator or MC is doing doesn't go on too long or interfere with the event's purpose. Humour (relevant humour) is good in the right place and with the right content for a particular audience.

Usually, the clients or production companies/agencies that use MCs and facilitators for an event are looking to present a unified conference with excellent flow and continuity – sometimes with an eye towards clever and seamless linking between each component part of the event. Often, heavy content-oriented events will use entertainers as MCs to lighten up the atmosphere and make an otherwise daunting event rather enjoyable. This depends more about the type of event you're trying to create. Incentive programmes, for people who have had to earn the right to attend, will use more celebrity types to reward attendees with an unforgettable experience. More corporate and management-focused events will lean towards professional facilitators or TV-famous presenters, but again they will only be as good as the brief they receive and the focus they apply.

Facilitators will usually work very hard (with you) to ensure congruity and effectiveness. But one thing that all facilitators do need is safety. I know because I've facilitated many conferences. What do I mean by safety? Well, in many assignments where you are the MC or facilitator at an event, there are many people who feel that they can give you instructions. There's the CEO, a client committee of some sort and other prominent people onsite or in pre-production. I always establish early on with my clients that I will only take instructions from one person. If anyone else comes up to me and says, 'I've rewritten that link – let's try it in five minutes onstage', or 'read out this notice', or 'it's thingy's birthday and, while few people know thingy, my mates and I want you to tell this joke and sing a song,' I tell them they must clear it with my point of contact first. And even then, I might push back on things that are a) demeaning, b) add nothing to the event's congruity and focus, c) aren't really in my focus or d) involve me in any singing. There's nothing wrong with fun, but most facilitators would want to help guide how that might work and, indeed, what's appropriate and what is not. The chain of command is important in any aspect of event management and delivery and it'll save you (the producer) from all sorts of tricky situations that have the possibility of making you and the facilitator or MC look bad or silly. At all times, the facilitator needs to be seen to be in control.

Another thing – there's nothing worse than a facilitator or MC bounding back up to the lectern to introduce the next speaker or activity only to find that his/her notes have gone. They might have blown away, might have been gathered up by the previous speaker, tidied up by crew or stage managers, used to scribble down a note or stolen. The facilitator/MC must take his/her notes or script with him/her wherever he/she goes (yes, even there), and anyway *you* should ensure that you keep a copy (safely) just in case.

Facilitators will have certain ways of working with event technology so ensure that your production manager, or whoever is running the technical side of the show, is introduced to the facilitator and indeed all speakers both of the internal and external variety. Each person will have specific needs as to positioning, lectern usage, moving about, sound and so on. One of the roles of the facilitator or MC is to watch and control the timing. You must help the facilitator by making sure that you subtly remind any speaker how important it is to keep the event on track. Subtlety may need to go out of the window if a particular speaker has form! Also, make sure you double check with the speaker how long he or she has been allotted. Then make sure that the facilitator/MC knows of any changes to timings or coffee breaks and so on. Don't ever assume that people can read minds. Don't assume that anyone knows what you know.

Make sure the facilitator and you discuss with any speaker how you or your crew are going to signal the time remaining to them. Sometimes a large clock at the back of the auditorium is necessary, sometimes a traffic light system with green, amber and red indicating remaining time, sometimes a series of monitors onstage. Sometimes none of these work and rarely, but occasionally, a facilitator will be obliged to interrupt a speaker and (kindly) close his or her session (usually with much audience relief and some speaker embarrassment although the latter can, with care, be kept to a minimum).

You need a plan for how you're going to deal with the situation if things do run late. Do you get speakers, for example, to cut short their presentations in order to get everything back on track or do you just allow things to run and tighten timings for elements that you can control like breaks and lunch or activities and breakouts? Most facilitators will work with you here to get the event back on track and discussing 'what if' scenarios early on can go a long way towards solving potential timing problems.

CANCELLATIONS

When a producer or project manager learns about a speaker cancellation, they should immediately call the bureau or agent to discuss the back-up plan – even if it's hours before the due appearance. You *must* have something of a back-up plan although it might be vague out of necessity. In truth, there should be a contingency plan for *every* eventuality for *every* part of your event.

If it's a large event with more than one guest speaker, you may be able to arrange one of these to do double-duty in the case of a no-show. Or, if the agency/bureau knows that another speaker is geographically nearby, it may just be possible to ask him or her to make a detour to your event and save the day. That's very rare. Sometimes there simply isn't a solution and you and your client will need to think fast in order to close up the agenda or allow other activities or presenters a little more time. Whatever the case, you and your client need to know the bureau or agent's rules for cancellation, and you also need to know what that cancellation means financially.

Every project manager/producer has the same nightmare. He or she spends months planning and developing the perfect event, with an eagle's eye for every detail. Then at the last minute the keynote speaker backs out. While rare, this of course does happen from time to time. Because most professional speakers work in and with the event industry all the time, they understand and respect all the effort that goes into managing and delivering an event. So, they're likely only to pull out if the reasons are genuine and large. A bureau chief who I always think looks vaguely like Beethoven in his middle years, says, 'Most professional speakers have a network of industry friends, one of whom they may be able to recommend and who might be able to step in at the last minute if a problem occurs. Same goes with talent agencies of course. Another course of action could be to look at your event programme and see who could possibly be upgraded from say a breakout to a keynote speaker. Also your audience will undoubtedly be full of brilliant people. A few could make up a panel to go onstage and discuss some issues of the day, relevant of course to the event's proposition and content. You might, with your client, select two or three topic questions that are cutting-edge. Get your facilitator or MC to explain openly and honestly about how the speaker could not be there. Next, proclaim this to be a fantastic opportunity in which to share best practices on x, y or z. Then share the discussion topics, having each table or group elect a discussion leader. Every few minutes (or however long is deemed fair) the MC will encourage a new question be discussed. During the last part of the session, each table can report briefly to the room the best thoughts shared in their group.

Another thought from an excellent facilitator/moderator contact of mine is this: 'Turn the speaker-less event into a networking speed-dating bonanza by encouraging people to make more contacts. Extend a lunch period perhaps and, once seated, have everyone introduce themselves around their table and discuss a preset question or topic. If it's a buffet, make the best of the scenario as you can. Extemporize. When a buzzer goes or a horn blares, everyone has to move as directed to a new seat in the room.'

Actually, such ideas can work well. A main reason why people attend business events *is* for the networking opportunities (although actually, as you know, few attendees ever make proper use of such opportunities) and most event specialists admit that, no matter how much time they schedule for people to mingle, they don't mingle that well. Some not at all. So, make this open time powerful by facilitating introductions and connections.

Leadership is paramount to success in this situation. If you ensure that communication to delegates or attendees is confident and if you explain that the unexpected opportunity is a golden one and that the impact of that will be powerful, then people will follow. If the change to the programme is presented poorly, weakly or timidly, then the delegates will feel let down and gloom and dissent will settle in.

Some things occur that are clearly outside your control – such as the weather, flight connections, illness and emergencies. However, that doesn't mean you need to pick up the bill if your speaker cancels, so do ensure that you have clauses in your contracts with the bureau or agent or speaker that favour you and your client in these circumstances. If the speaker cannot make it for the allotted speech at the allotted time, for reasons that have nothing whatsoever to do with you, you or your client should receive your deposit and any payments back, and should not have to pay anything at all.

'A few years ago,' muses my cousin over dinner one evening, 'we had a late cancellation from a very, very big name politician and a great orator. We were stuck. However, the bureau suggested an alternative – a Russian conductor.' My cousin smiles. 'This was a banking conference for very senior executives and everyone was expecting this future presidential candidate but they got a Russian conductor. But the guy knew whom he was replacing and he was good. He got everyone playing Gershwin's *American in Paris*, or perhaps it was Tchaikovsky's *1812 Overture*. Anyway, whatever it was, the delegates played on glockenspiels, the conductor having explained the analogy of running a business and an orchestra. It worked really well and, while there was some disappointment, the event went well – to the point that these senior execs wanted to carry on playing. After his session, the conductor became depressed following a call with someone back in Vladivostock and his jaunty mood iced up a bit. He mentioned a woman who had ruined his life and had taken all his zithers and balalaikas. Then he hugged us all, my team and me, smiled tearfully and left full of Slavic melancholy. I liked him a lot and we were definitely in his debt. Then, as a bonus, we had a plenary conference phone call live in the next day's plenary from the speaker who hadn't turned up, so that was a bonus.'

SPEAKER EVALUATIONS

Speaker, or any, evaluation is a step that many producers and clients would like to overlook. However, a good speaker evaluation form (hardcopy, online or app) can be used as an important tool to measure the effectiveness of the event and specifics within it – such as specific sessions and speakers. Perhaps the biggest challenge associated with creating a speaker evaluation form is to format it so that it's easy to complete. That, of course, is important with any measurement or evaluation process. The next most important item that you should consider when developing a speaker evaluation form is the importance of keeping the form short. So try to:

► Provide clear, brief instructions at the top.

► List the session name and speaker on the form.

► Measure the effectiveness in a maximum of five options.

► Ask if the session objectives were met.

► Ask if the session was perceived as valuable (and why or in what sense).

► Ask an open-ended question for more information.

► Keep the form optionally anonymous.

► Ask if there's any interest in follow-up contact with the speaker or his/her materials.

Of course, feedback on evaluation forms will be subjective (and often sardonic and mean), but the kind of thing that can be asked might include:

▶ Please rate how well this session's learning objectives were met.

▶ What value did you receive from this session?

▶ What is the best idea you heard in this session that you could use? Tell us how.

▶ What did he or she do well?

▶ What could have been done differently?

▶ Was the topic on-message and useful? In what way?

As you can see, this isn't rocket science. Once the evaluation forms are collected, whether via an app, email attachment, website or hardcopy, you, or someone in your team or someone at the client end, should compile the results into a report that summarises all the event evaluation results. This includes information about speaker ratings in the various categories measured, as well as the comments themselves. Such reports, usually as part of a wider evaluation process, are used to measure how effectively a conference session met the needs of the audience and what might be improved in the future. A friend, a director of a research company based in Brussels adds, 'You have to be honest about all speakers – external or internal – and attendees have to be honest about what worked, what didn't, and should come up with solutions for improvement. There's absolutely no point (and less value) in just moaning without offering up some valid and constructive ideas.'

CHAPTER NINE
POWERPOINT AND OTHER AIDS

POWERPOINT? OMG!

The other day I was so cheerful – while preparing scrambled eggs and thinly cut, well-done, almost crispy toast (the way I like it) – that I whistled and then hummed. I whistled and hummed a bit from the end (Act IV) of *Carmen*. It's the part when cheers and hurrahs are heard from the bullring crowds and Carmen tries to enter, but José gets in her way. He asks her to come back to him, but she throws the ring at him that he gave to her ('Cette bague, autrefois') with a good continental sneer. He (naturally) stabs her as Escamillo is acclaimed in the arena and, to the strains of the chorus of the *Toreador Song*, which I always think is highly inappropriate (too jolly), she dies. Don José kneels in despair beside her. The spectators flock out of the arena and find José ('Ah! Carmen! Ma Carmen adorée!'), confessing his guilt over his lost true love.

My good lady wife asked me to be quiet on account of my whistling going through her teeth like a bullet. She said that it was like fingernails on a blackboard or watching too much PowerPoint. Ah, PowerPoint, I thought, then ate my eggs and toast, now with a gloom that deepened and darkened as the day wore on.

PowerPoint is a software package that is meant to enhance an oral presentation and to keep the audience focused on a particular subject. It operates like an old-fashioned slide show, but uses modern technology in the form of computers and digital projection rather than a slide projector of old. But, by all that's holy, it's overused and abused and I loathe it. When it comes to your event or the event that you're managing, do please try and get your speakers to use PowerPoint either not at all or with great caution. That probably won't work because most executives believe that, without PowerPoint, they can't function in the making of a presentation.

My favourite PowerPoint designer in the whole world sighs, 'You know, as do I, that very, very few executives will follow your advice.' He sighs again. 'Executives, on the whole,' he says wearily, 'treat their audiences – those comprising of staff – appallingly.' The execs don't prepare well, they don't practice at all and they regard rehearsals with disdain. U.S. presidents (or their speechwriters) spend weeks honing a State of the Union address. Some brilliant business and political leaders spend a very long time preparing all aspects of their presentations. If engagement counts, then presenters *need* to prepare presentations, and that includes understanding how PowerPoint can support, not replace.' A shadow falls across his face and he looks sadder still. I nod. In deference to the night, he puts his baseball cap backwards on his head and we head for pizza.

OK, SO LET'S DO POWERPOINT – IF YOU INSIST

Let's get straight to it. If you can advise your speakers, advise as follows. Get them to choose images rather than words to reinforce or underline what they're saying – big, clear, relevant images or images that are mysterious, but become clear through what you say. Good photographs or brilliant graphics, *not* clip art or a surfeit of arrows. Don't let them put an image in as a filler. Do get them to use a slide with one word on it rather than using an irrelevant or distracting picture – or a slide filled with tiny font text or oodles of diagrams that mean nothing to anyone beyond the front row.

Get your speakers to say 'so what?' to themselves as they practice or rehearse, *if* they rehearse. Should they not be able to answer the 'so what?' question, then that particular slide should be binned and probably the point that the speaker was going to make along with it. Insist, as far as you are able, that a slide should have no more than seven words on it, unless it's a quote and, if it's a quote, why not speak it rather than read it from a slide? Less on a slide is really more focus on the speaker. Tell your speakers that they aren't meant to read directly from the screen. I'm going to say it again – *never* allow your client presenters to read their slides word for word. You have to hope and assume that any guest speakers will know better too. Some do, some don't. And make sure that there aren't too many slides. The use of too many slides means that a presentation will be too long – guaranteed. The presenter will say, 'Oh, I can whizz through those in no time.' He or she can't. Most presenters haven't a clue how to gauge time and how to measure x number of slides against y amount of time. Help them. Be forceful.

The CEO of a new but already flourishing event agency is showing me the superb new offices. We talk about presentations and presenters and eventually hot the buffers with a chat about wretched PowerPoint. She says in some despair that, 'The biggest mistakes that people make with PowerPoint presentations are that there are too many words on each slide, there'll be no practice or rehearsal and no compromise on content. It's important that when producers guide client speakers you tell them that they should do any planning and thinking on paper, because as soon as they commit an idea to PowerPoint, they become attached to it.'

One of her seasoned producers agrees. 'Even if a speaker misses a slide or a topic as they're speaking – and it happens often – they should avoid fumbling to find the lost slide and they should simply move on. They should on no account apologise and fiddle with the clicker trying to find the missing slide. At no point should it be felt that the speaker isn't in charge. Not being in charge of your own PowerPoint is all too common. If speakers prepared properly, they could abandon the wretched PowerPoint – and the audience would cheer.' The producer's production assistant joins in, 'If the projectors stopped working and a speaker had to carry on speaking without PowerPoint, then the audience would cheer some more! Members of an audience want to hear what the speaker has to say, they want to learn about his/her views on the event's proposition, they want to be persuaded about something. PowerPoint by and large won't add value to that.'

ALL THAT JAZZ
PowerPoint comes with loads of features – jazzy graphics galore including wild displays and animations – but speakers must avoid the trap of trying to

use them all to show their proficiency in making a PowerPoint bright and cheery. Lots of flying text and flashing photos are to be avoided. Dreadful cartoons, speech balloons, multi-coloured arrows and monotonous musical files are to be avoided too. Tacky transitions that push up and wipe down are to be left alone. 'PowerPoint presentations,' says a learned communications adviser to a major software company, 'are built on templates. You can populate the slides and also embed elements, like videos.' He admits that, 'People do overuse the facilities and that just confuses or bores audiences.' Later I phone the marketing director of an agricultural machinery business. He's weary because he's just been to a three-day conference in Vienna. He sighs and grumbles, 'How many times do I have to try and read shrunken spread-sheets sized to fit a slide? Why do some executives have so many slides, so many slides that are impossible to read? And why must people hand out advance hard copies of their presentations? It's just foolish to think people will simply follow along when they can flip ahead and go cross-eyed on page 73 when the speaker is still on page five. And what is it about shades and shadows and serious subjects presented in a ridiculous rainbow of colours?' He sounds a little tearful and so we bid each other adieu.

Before getting all caught up in the wow features of PowerPoint, remember that the purpose of a presentation (*any* presentation) is to present information, to enthuse and to explain – not overwhelm the audience with a demonstration of software – unless you're a Microsoft salesperson. PowerPoint is only a tool and it's only a *supportive* tool. It should never ever lead. So, decide if your client's speaker presentation is meant to entertain, inform, persuade, sell, change minds or whatever. Is a light-hearted or a more formal approach most appropriate to the subject and your audience? An event designer says over afternoon tea, 'A producer has to try and ensure that the PowerPoint supports that purpose and then all concerned must be as frugal with its use as possible. Unfortunately, many presenters or their acolytes just won't listen and they'll revel in delivering the presentation the night before the event and it'll be too long, too messy and generally a right royal mess.'

My PowerPoint designer colleague says over a large Bellini (and after an argument with a waiter who disagrees that the cocktail originated in Venice or that the peach purée should be fresh), 'When you overload your audience with graphics, you push people to focus on the screen and not on the proposition. Any understanding is then diminished and often sunk because people are trying to make sense of the screen information, not the speaker's argument. Take away pointless and irrelevant words or pictures from a screen and you can increase the audience's ability to remember the information by a far higher percentage. What's more, they'll apply that information when the time comes much better.'

A brilliant presentation is so engaging that it makes anyone in an audience forget about the speaker and become absorbed in the message, which sounds negative but actually isn't. I can't stress enough that, as is the case with any design, all visual clutter must be cut. Most presentations are largely about delivering a clear message. Focus on this and this alone. Too many presentations fall short. These days, so much competes for delegates' attention. More than ever, what is said and *how* it's said, needs to be intentional and precise, carefully and cleverly expressed, interesting, engaging and on-message. Good oratory is rare and it's certainly not aided by 'powderpoinie' as one Brazilian colleague used to charmingly call it.

CLIENTS – DONTCHYA LOVE 'EM?

I once had a client who would insist on sending me her PowerPoint presentations via email. She would write cutesy little notes like, 'Hi. Hope you have nothing to do this afternoon!! Attached please find my teensy weensy PowerPoint presentation. Hope you like it!' That sort of thing happens all the time. Maybe it's what iCloud is for – the heaven for good little PowerPoint presentations – and the nasty ones go to iHades.

Do try and persuade your clients to seek professional PowerPoint design. They'll still insist upon too much stuff on a slide and the poor designer will grit his/her teeth, but one can only hope for a gradual change in PowerPoint behaviour. *You* know that PowerPoint isn't essential for any presentation and it's certainly not a must, even for financial speeches. Really, it's not. I repeat, the very best orators in the world of business and politics, in the worlds of education and learning, do not use PowerPoint or, if they do, then the use is imaginative and therefore sparse.

Client presenters and their acolytes have no real idea how long a presentation should be. And people sending presentations by email generally don't care or don't think about the presentation in terms of audience. They think about the presentation in terms of weight and self. A brilliant producer, who's produced huge and complicated corporate events around the world, each with aplomb and a generosity of spirit, says over a glass or two of Suffolk's finest bitter: 'Most event producers work to ensure that content is delivered through great planning and production, but they rarely get a full opportunity to contribute to the process of really establishing what is actually being communicated. Clients keep that to themselves or ignore it – mostly because they choose not to focus until the last minute. This also relates to what goes up on screen. If there's nothing but text on the screen, people will try to read and listen at the same time – and won't succeed in doing either very well. If the print is too small to read, they'll get irritated at being expected to do the impossible. Nor does it help when speakers say "as you can see", or the equally annoying "you probably won't be able to read this but …".'

My producer companion then says forcibly, 'Few corporate speakers are willing to open their mouths until they have their first slide safely in place. But all too often the slides are verbal crutches – a bit like metaphorical Zimmer frames – for the speaker, but not proposition support for the audience. To prepare a presentation requires careful planning, hard work and time. Many, many clients just don't see that – or the benefits of doing it properly. That's such a wasted opportunity.'

The person who emailed me her huge PowerPoint presentation didn't see the benefit of shortening it and I was patient and understanding in my 'argument'. I wanted to say something like, 'This highlights the biggest problem with slide-based presentations, which is that speakers mistakenly think that they can get far more information across than is actually possible in a presentation. At the heart of this is a widespread failure to appreciate that speaking and listening are fundamentally different from writing and reading.' But I didn't say that although I tried to persuade the lady to rehearse and sharpen what she wanted on screen. But she wasn't interested in changing anything; her subsequent presentation was appalling and her evaluation scores were very low. No one cared except the people in the audience who cared very much.

The trouble is that PowerPoint makes it so easy to put detailed written and numerical information on slides that it leads presenters into the mistaken belief that all the detail will be successfully transmitted through the air into the brains of the audience.

VISUAL AIDS AND ATTENTION GRABBERS

The End is the last track on *Abbey Road*. The lyrics are: 'In the end, the love you take is equal to the love you make.' It's essentially The Beatles' closing statement. It's the last lyric on the last album they recorded and starts at the close of the wonderful medley that finishes with *Carry That Weight*. The whole segued piece (for it is really one piece featuring several songs) catches the ear and the mind's eye. Every nuance enhances the previous nuances. Visual aids can be a great way of enhancing a presentation – when they're used sensibly and with a clear purpose. Speakers need to relate their visual aids to an audience and to the type of presentation being designed. Like PowerPoint, any visual aid is there to help your audience to better understand what a speaker is talking about – *not* replace it. They're also there to grab attention, to amuse and to make a proposition come alive.

If you need to give the audience more information to support your message, then you may want to suggest that you or your company or your client produces an app or a website attachment or a variety of methodologies whereby material can be sent to smartphones or email addresses. These pieces of information can and must be visually interesting and not just great chunks of text that nobody will read. Don't forget it's all about content meeting the audience's needs *not* the presenter's ego.

Cousin Maier sends me an email with some ideas of props that he's used in presentations. He begins with lemons. He is bold if sometimes plain weird. He maintains that a lemon is a great visual and tactile prop. A lemon can be used to reinforce many points and themes, including touch, colour, smell, humour, sharpness, simplicity and so on. Lemons are great props he says for passing round and getting people to touch, smell and feel what they may take for granted. So he says. I say – use wisely.

I'm at a party. 'What about a chef's hat?' asks a junior producer, daughter of a good friend. I look up with surprise. She explains, 'Preparation (of anything), mixing, blending (teams), selecting ingredients (identifying and choosing quality components, people, suppliers, methods). Her father, an accountant and beset with small imagination, says, 'What about an orange?' And then he too elucidates. 'You know, goodness, simplicity, it's what it says: clarity.' Unfortunately, there are many people at this social gathering and now the ideas come thick and fast: 'A globe,' says one, swaying slightly. 'You know,' she slurs, 'travel, global markets, partners, suppliers, transport, import, export, international law, exchange rates, time differences, cultures, ethnicity, people – really you can do mostly anything with a globe.' The key is to be careful. Use something that really supports a comment or an idea. Amusing or serious, a prop has to work so, if in any doubt, don't recommend it. However, a well-placed prop can be fun and can make a point come live.

You can use anything provided it has a real, solid relevance and purpose. I recall, in 1989, when the Berlin wall had just come down and a large travel firm wanted to emulate the wall analogy (you know the sort of thing: barriers, perseverance, change, power, teamwork). The conference set was a huge wall of junk comprising of competitor signage and materials, references to IT, everything that was stopping the company moving ahead. That was fine. But the very last speech was of the MD holding a fizzing stick of dynamite that he was supposed to chuck at the wall – and the wall would tumble down to a huge cacophony of sound and big images. Unfortunately his peroration went on far too long and his dynamite went out causing the audience to giggle a little and thereby making the ensuing wall tumble slightly less powerful than it should have been. Mind you, playing Pink Floyd very loud indeed was good and that drowned out any audience opportunity for bad commentary as they left the auditorium.

I've persuaded (and taught) some speakers to juggle. It creates a smile, particularly if it's a senior someone who wouldn't normally juggle. The analogy is clear – creativity, keeping tasks and priorities in the air, using different parts of the brain, fun, practice and dexterity. I've had a professional juggler spinning plates onstage to help reinforce a point. I've also used a very large framed picture or one that's been projected large onscreen to use as a prompt for information, storytelling, observation or attention to detail, and so on.

A great prop I once used was at the beginning of a management conference. There was nothing on stage except a simple lectern and a huge, but huge, leather-bound book. The CEO came on with no notes and no PowerPoint, having been well tutored and having taken the time to rehearse and practise. He walked to the lectern, opened the book and said, 'I want to tell you a story, a story about this business … Let's start at the beginning …' and then he opened the big book at a page where there was an amount of talcum powder. The powder that rose up looked like dust. The CEO then blew the powder. He looked at the page, pretending to read. Then he slammed the book, creating even more dust, the lighting state changed and the book and lectern disappeared. He said, 'Let me tell you in my own words what's happened and what's going to happen. As for the happy or unhappy ending, that's down to you.' It doesn't necessarily read well off the page and you may indeed squirm; however, the idea was simple, brilliantly executed (important) and brief. It caused a smile and created absolute focus.

Another device I used was at the end of a management conference speech on Halloween, where a senior director said, 'And there's as much chance of that happening', (I think something about change or growth), 'as there is of this old broomstick flying.' Then the old broomstick, leaning up against a chair on stage, flew from that spot high up in the air to the back of the auditorium. Brilliant! I did the same with snow on another occasion – simple, effective and cheap.

SOME TRICKS OF THE TRADE

It's hard to know how you will personally get on with speakers and clients at events in which you're involved, but there are some things you can do to encourage greater efficacy and power from the stage. The average attention span of an average audience listener is between five and ten minutes for any single unbroken subject. I don't really care what anyone else says. That's my view and it's been reinforced (in my experience) a hundred-fold. And that's just the older folk. The PlayStation, Twitter, Facebook and texting generations will have less tolerance than this, so content should be planned accordingly.

Suggest that a speaker breaks up the content so that no single item takes longer than a few minutes, and between each item try to inject something amusing, amazing, remarkable or spicy – a picture, a quote, a bit of audience interaction – anything to break it up and keep people attentive, but keep it relevant. Using a variety of media and movement will maintain maximum interest. The MD of a major London venue complex has something to say: 'Think of it like this – an audience can be stimulated via several senses – not just audio and visual (listening and watching).' A client acquaintance of his interrupts his flow (none too politely think I) by telling him none too kindly that his colleague didn't need a parentheses explanation for 'audio' and 'visual'. The MD takes little notice and steams on. 'Consider including content and activity which addresses the other senses too – touch certainly, taste maybe, smell perhaps – anything's possible if you use your imagination. The more senses you can stimulate the more an audience will remain attentive and engaged. Something magical and different, something engaging and exciting – all add to a story unfolding. I've had clients using machines that create the smell of baking bread or mown grass or – or anything. You can stimulate other things in your audience besides the usual 'senses'. You can use content and activities to stimulate feelings, emotions, memories and even physical movement. Simply asking the audience to stand up, or snap their fingers, or blink their eyes (assuming you give them a good reason for doing so) immediately stimulates physical awareness and involvement.' There's a pause for effect and breath, and then the conversation switches to discussing the merits and otherwise of London's City Airport.

Quotations are a wonderful and easy way to stimulate emotions and feelings and of course quotes can be used to illustrate and emphasise just about any point or concept you can imagine. Amusing quotes or funny stories can light up, inspire and touch audiences, but for goodness sake get your client speakers to acknowledge quotes. There's nothing to make a speaker look sillier than passing off a quote as his or her own or to somebody else. Stories are excellent at sustaining interest, provided they are relevant, on-message and short. Analogies and fables work too. Straw polls – via a series of hands-up votes or reactions to something or the use of an electronic voting system – create interest and energy. On the spot prizes for questions answered, or as a reward for coming up onstage for some reason, can work a treat – particularly if the awards are fun. Statistics are good too – if they're mind boggling or very powerful – and relevant. I once asked members in an audience to demonstrate their ringtones at the same time. I forget why but the effect was great.

CHAPTER TEN
DIGITAL AND FUTURE TIMES

GET WITH THE PROGRAMME

I had a boss once who would say things like, 'We're not on the same bus,' and 'Are we all on the same programme?' – with a frequency that made my colleagues and I nervous and her irritated. I had little idea what caused her wrath. She put the fear of any god you care to name into her direct reports because few of that team (us) understood her process-management-diagram psyche or her teeth-baring rages when one of her complicated MBA-driven processes ended up in a bedraggled mess. She once said to me, after a rant about something or other, 'We're not on the same page. *Ira furor brevis est.* That's Latin for …' 'I know what it means,' I cut in with well-placed rudeness (for I'd had enough of hers), 'Anger is a brief madness'. Creativity, design and client culture featured low on her 'pages' or 'buses' and certainly there was no room on page or bus for event measurement unless, that is, it involved vast quantities of more (irrelevant) process.

Anyway, one thing this manager had been most keen on (apart from brightly coloured diagrams that resembled Rorschach inkblot tests) was the advent of digital communication devices that would, she averred, change the event management and delivery world. I don't pretend that any of us much understood what the myriad of suppliers showed and told us as they trotted through their presentations, but there was more than just a glimmer of excitement in our eyes as we imagined the future of events.

In truth, digital applications for events are just a simpler and more engaging way of doing things that before were largely paper-based. Digital should mean convenience and fun. Soon almost every aspect of the non face-to-face part of an event will be digitally driven and, as my dear old boss foretold: the future is very much a digital one.

Let's start at the beginning. Choosing a venue with free Wi-Fi is almost a given these days and any venue that makes a charge should be challenged. At the very least there should be venue or hotel hotspots and certainly free Wi-Fi in every bedroom. If there's a cost involved, it really is well worth your while convincing your client that this is a 'must have' facility – because these days it just is. While smartphones make the Internet less relevant, plenty of people will still want access on their iPads or laptops. Internet connections also encourage social interaction during an event. One of these is Twitter.

You'll know what a hash tag is. For those who don't I explore definitions. 'Well,' says the excellent commercial director from a large advertising agency specialising in social media content, 'it's a tag that's embedded in a message posted on a Twitter micro-blogging service, consisting of a specific word of your choosing (or someone else's) within the message and prefixed with a hash sign. The tag denotes something specific and, if people know the tag, then they can follow all relevant messages relating to a topic. The hash tag symbol (#) was created organically by Twitter users as a way of categorising messages. Clicking on a hash tagged word in any message shows you all other Tweets in that category. Hash tagged words that become very popular are often termed "trending topics".'

Most event organisers and project managers have caught on to using Twitter hash tags to aggregate buzz about an event. It's cheap, easy and works. A very senior marketing agency acquaintance, who manages vast quantities of financial events throughout the world, says, 'Plenty of organisers forget to make clear to delegates what the official hash tag is – resulting in a variety of tags made up by attendees. That, of course, totally defeats the purpose of the hash tag to capture all the chatter in one spot.' He stops to pour coffee for us both and he offers me a small tray of silver-paper-wrapped biscuits. I shake my head then take one out of good manners of course. He continues, 'I'm impressed when event producers display the hash tag in a big font on event signage and, pre-event, on websites, emails and documentation. It's also a good idea to show the stream of comments live onsite during the event. This doesn't have to be in the auditorium, but could be directly via a smartphone app, onscreen in hotel room TVs or via monitors around the venue.'

Digital and social media is all around us; it's inescapable, it's growing at an outstanding rate and every one of us has felt its power directly or indirectly. Many of the world's recent social and political uprisings are said to have been started by Facebook or, in particular, Twitter. My senior marketing agency acquaintance has more to say as I help myself to another silver-paper-wrapped biscuit. 'As we begin to understand the importance of digital and social media, it's important to consider when and how we use it. We're not all going to plan Arab Springs. We tend to break down the digital communication plan into three stages – pre-event, that's setting the foundation; during the event, that's generating a buzz; and post-event, that's maintaining contact and measuring.' A colleague joins us and she has views on this. 'Firstly,' she says, 'it's crucial to establish your channels and create a content plan before formally announcing your event. Protect yourself (well, your client really) by registering relevant online properties early such as website domain names and social profiles. Ensure a presence on Facebook by creating a privatised event page. And Twitter is easy. Choose a twitter hash tag for your event to allow interactive discussion and to post any immediate event news – remembering to keep it short, sweet and unique. Creating a content plan will ensure you are never lost for words and the build-up to your event is always brimming with valuable information. That's the idea certainly. Include new announcements and keep the process interesting by releasing precious "insider information" such as behind-the- scenes features, competitions, incentives and useful facts and figures – material that keeps interest and the countdown to the event high.'

We're interrupted by two telephone calls, neither of them for me and I stare out at a misty, grey, cold and wet London vista. My father recently spoke of London trams and trolley buses and that wasn't such an age ago. My reverie is interrupted by another someone eager to contribute to the discussion on social media. He's a dapper gentleman who looks a little like the actor Sir Ian McKellen (one of my heroes). The dapper gent says, 'The event website, or a blog within the site,' he says speaking with a rather squeaky voice (nothing at all like the great actor's), 'should act as your central hub and the place to drive all traffic from any relevant social profiles, but it's important to get that URI out everywhere.' I must be looking more than a tad askance because he says none too gently, 'Short for Uniform Resource Identifier, the generic term for all types of names and addresses that refer to objects on the World Wide Web. Yes? World Wide Web?' A pause while we all nod, although the only one who seems to be ignorant of URIs is me. 'Well, fine then,' the smart gentleman says. 'A URL (Uniform or Universal Resource Locator, the address of a web page) is one kind of URI. Okay?' I nod. More coffee and then more really good advice from this chap. 'If the event's news is good enough to talk about, it'll be shared across the Internet with little effort on a producer's part. By the way, to use the information, the site will (or should) be password protected.'

KEEP GOING

Keep promoting that Twitter hash tag and facilitate real time feedback (and discussion) by encouraging attendees and other agreed parties to tweet. This way, the event's audience will feel even closer to the action and become an active participant. Turn passive spectators into active participants by sharing the discussion. This can be done by displaying live Twitter feeds prior to the event, as mentioned earlier and encouraging Facebook page check-ins. Websites such as 'Qik' and 'Ustream' can bring your event to the world with live online video.

Once the event is over, the discussion shouldn't grind to a halt. Maintain the momentum by blogging the highlights and encouraging user-generated content on your site. The content generated is an asset so be sure to archive it. Don't let your central hub get stale or lost; maintain audience engagement through your social platforms. You need to assess the event's outcomes to build upon its successes. That's a core objective and you need to get your client onboard with that at an early stage. If the objectives are precise then it'll be easier to establish what worked well and what didn't – with the help of Facebook insights, Google alerts, Twitter and trackable Bit.ly links. This can all form part of event evaluation. You can also garner feedback from all those involved in the event through, for example, Facebook polls, Facebook forums and Google Docs.

But, let me make an important point. Virtual information and presentations won't replace face-to-face communications – not for a very long time. But we shouldn't find fault with virtual technologies, because frankly some of them are pretty amazing. So, without being too 'born again' here, let's embrace the new to enhance the old rather than dismissing the new as a fad. Equally, we shouldn't regard the new as a panacea but as a very good set of tools which will only get better and, like all good tools, will make our event lives easier.

'What we need to be doing,' says my cousin, having no benefit of any alcohol, 'with or without the help of virtual technologies, is to work out how we build and maintain relationships with our audiences – how we facilitate communication and collaboration between individuals both through a single live day and an online presence; and how we use the unfettered enthusiasm of our audiences to create a profitable business model for the future.' Quite a little speech that, but it's true. Conferences and events are changing and will continue to change and *we* producers must change too in order to benefit audiences. Far too often in my hearing, the audience has come low down in the food chain when an event is discussed and debated.

With so much new technology at our fingertips and at reducing cost – mobile apps, matchmaking solutions, RFID (Radio Frequency Identification – a system that uses intelligent bar codes to track items in a store but also at a conference or indeed anywhere), and social networking platforms, for example – it's becoming more difficult for conference organisers and producers to keep attendees up-to-date on how to use the tools. Add in augmented reality – a live, direct or indirect view of a physical, real-world environment whose elements are augmented by computer-generated sensory input such as sound, video, graphics or Global Positioning System (GPS) data and add hybrid events (an event that combines a live conference, say, with a virtual online component) and then the solutions designed to streamline and enhance any event experience suddenly add a fabulous layer of complexity and amazing excitement.

At the moment all of these new communication tools and solutions come from different sources and suppliers, so there is no single source for how-to information for event project managers and producers. Similarly, using new and newish technology can provide a problem during the event. A producer who adores new ideas for giving his events edge and freshness enthuses, 'An on-site tech support desk – with representatives from the various technology suppliers or a tech savvy team that can point delegates to support resources is a way to assist attendees, but that's rare. Asking technology suppliers (as part of their contracts for service) to provide a video tutorial of their applications – which are then prominently displayed on the event website – is one way for organisers to collect the content and tutor users without the production costs. But that might confuse. Creating a hash tag exclusively for technology questions is a great way for the tech support team to communicate (by sending tweets and links) with event participants who have quick questions about technology. But, really, if any technology needs vast amounts of explanation, then it probably shouldn't be used. I would tend only to recommend devices and digital media with which the whole audience is already pretty comfortable.'

On a few events in which I've been involved recently, we engaged a technical support team (mobile concierges) to roam the conference during meal and coffee breaks with iPads, offering assistance and pointing delegates to additional resources. Also, sometimes the simplest way to provide instruction about technology tools is with freestanding signage that participants can read, touch or scan as in the case of QR codes. You'll have seen QR codes. Quick Response codes are a type of two-dimensional code first designed for the automotive industry to track vehicles as they were being constructed. More recently, the system has become popular outside of the motor industry due to its fast readability and comparatively large storage capacity. The code consists of black modules arranged in a square pattern on a white background. You scan it with say a smartphone and will see information, visuals or a video. A producer colleague and QR enthusiast adds, 'Even with all of the advanced ways to get information to attendees, the low-tech methods are still popular. With nearly everyone carrying a mobile phone, what could be easier than calling one number to get all the answers? Even if the person at the other end of the line doesn't have *all* the answers, they can point or transfer callers to other resources for help.'

MORE INFORMATION SHARING

I'm in the 'Village of Olives': that's how Bangkok translates. 'Bang' means village and 'kok' is an olive-like fruit, although Thais prefer to call their capital Krung Thep or 'City of Angels'.

I'm attending an industry conference on new thinking in corporate communications. Hmm I think, it's a long way to come for this, although a few of the sessions are excellent particularly those that relate to content and communication strategy. I catch up with some people I haven't seen for a long time. One is a technical whizz and we discuss what I call information sharing at corporate events. 'Although the iPad was meant to occupy the device category between the mobile phone and the laptop computer,' he says, 'its mobility and utility has enamoured users so much that analysts predict tablets will replace laptops in the next few years. They're already responsible for significantly reducing the sales of netbooks and laptops. Due to their widespread adoption, iPads and similar devices will also influence the design of mobile apps for events.' An editor acquaintance, one whose probity and sense I admire, agrees and later sends me an email on how iPad devices might be and are being used:

1. **Programme details – obvious.**

2. **Floor-plans, maps and directions – obvious.**

3. **Evaluation – obvious.**

4. **Videos – the ability to view archived and live streaming content will prompt developers to build more spaces for viewing video into apps – including session and speaker videos, video abstracts, product overviews and virtual exhibition 'booths'.**

5. Demonstrations – instead of complicated material on stage screens, speakers can use tablets to demonstrate products, showcase product videos and send electronic literature to delegates. This last is very exciting although it'll be commonplace very soon.

6. Records – smartphones and laptops make it easy to share event content and the photo and video capabilities of most tablets make it easy to display all sorts of content.

Much later I muse, not for the first time, about the use of technology and recall the time when video editing was reel to reel and cutting or making changes was a very long process. Editing now takes moments. We take telephony and constant information for granted. It's easy and that's a good thing. We can now develop (with actually ease and at lowish cost) technology for communications within corporate events. That's exciting – provided we only use devices that a) work, b) add value or c) save time and paper. What is most important is that your clients don't run away with the notion of using a gizmo without fully understanding cost and value to the audience.

A VIEW FROM SOHO

'Some technological devices are old, like voting systems, but underused in the engagement of audiences: others, like apps, are available now, but not necessarily used well in events yet.' Here speaks a friend who's been in the events industry for ever. He and I are sharing a jug of hot saké after an equally good Szechuan dinner in London's deepest Soho. Despite the cacophony of noise and clatter, the restaurant is friendly and somehow unobtrusive. I know that when I go out into the crisp winter night's air my head will spin but, for now, I'm aglow and listening with the attention warranted by an old captain of events. 'Marketers,' he says, 'are increasingly challenged, by breaking through the clutter, to create brand experiences and experiential events which solicit emotional responses from audiences to accomplish marketing and strategic objectives,' he says and then pauses a little. 'Tried and tested techniques for engaging audiences,' he continues, 'including interaction and storytelling, are still relevant. Storytelling is much underused and, after all, stand-up comedians tell stories. As *you* well know, the best speakers and rhetoricians use stories.'

This is all relevant. Communication is evolving. What attracts us and motivates us is constantly changing. The way we interact with each other, our communities and the companies with which we do business is increasingly complex. Or is it? It's probably much easier than it used to be, but we often make it complex. On the other hand, it could be said that constant 24/7 access via phones and the Internet make the pressure to deliver that much harder. In contrast some might say that this constancy delivers precision and accuracy, while others may firmly believe that communications and event development and management are both compounded, certainly helped, by technology. Technology is everywhere and can be either a distraction or a useful tool to help us drive great event experiences that last well beyond a single moment in time. Isn't that what we all want?

Well, I could say that the old salt and I talked all night in Chinatown, but we didn't, although we did spend time wondering why some clients ticked the 'done' box the very moment a corporate event was finished. Sooner or later we wended our dozy but cheerful ways home – him to Greenwich in south London, and me to Highgate in the north. But we had discussed some good technological ideas for events and here they are ...

APPS

My cousin says, 'Apps are growing like nobody's business. There are around a million now and counting. They're being used for every aspect of our lives and more and more appear on the market every week. Apple still has the biggest share of the app market to go with its iPhone or iPad, but owners of other makes of phones and tablets like Google Android and Microsoft's Windows Phone 7 are getting their share too. Now, with apps, phones can become guidebooks, floor plan explanations, event signage, exhibition guides and directories. There are apps to help entertain you and there are apps to help you be creative – and there are tools for musicians, film-makers and authors. Some apps can help you to check-in guests and some will send you a text or email when a certain guest or delegate arrives. Attendees can also schedule meetings through apps.' He pauses and stares at my untouched sandwich. 'Are you going to eat that?' And because he's faster at the table than am I, he grabs the sandwich and eats it.

AUGMENTED REALITY

It is said by several websites that there are around 690 million Facebook users worldwide. How does this compare with other ways of communicating? Myspace claims 63m, Twitter 175m, landline telephones have around 1.2bn users, Internet users amount to a cool 2.1bn or so, mobile phones 5.3bn and the global population is about 6.9bn. It is also reckoned that in a few years, augmented reality will be the norm for entertainment, doing business and maybe holding events – with user numbers up there in the billions. Commonplace augmented reality would be very exciting particularly because, in the drive for various careers, I have dawdled, walked or run along miles and miles of corporate corridors, have read, skimmed or ignored fields of memoranda, and have borne both the nonsense and wisdom shot at me by the great and the dreadful, the arrogant and the modest. I think that augmented reality would have been a great help.

Video games have been entertaining us for nearly thirty years and I can still remember playing *Pong* in pubs. Computer graphics have become much more sophisticated since then and game graphics are pushing the barriers of photorealism, much as movies are. Now, researchers and engineers are pulling graphics out of your TV screen or computer display and integrating them into real-world environments. This new technology, called augmented reality, blurs the line between what's real and what's computer-generated by enhancing all of our senses. Augmented reality is close to the real world. Both video games and smartphones are driving the development of augmented reality. Everyone from tourists, to soldiers, to someone looking for the closest bus stop, can now benefit from the ability to place computer-generated graphics in their field of vision.

Augmented reality is changing the way we view the world – or at least the way its users see the world. Picture yourself walking or driving down the street. With augmented-reality displays, which will eventually look much like a normal pair of glasses, informative graphics will appear in your field of view and audio will coincide with whatever you see. These enhancements will be refreshed continually to reflect the movements of your head. By the way and lest we forget, AR is not to be confused with virtual reality (VR), which is an entirely digital experience that mimics real-world situations and is more of a simulation science.

Augmented reality combines visual, three-dimensional environments with virtual information creating a hybrid world. There are already augmented reality applications for smartphones that add information to maps, landmarks, aircraft, people or, indeed, conference topics. The most compelling vision of augmented reality, however, is not from a mobile device, but a small computer that you can wear. With this in mind, it doesn't take much imagination to visualise uses in understanding attendee, product, brand, speaker and subject matter information instantaneously. It doesn't take much more imagination to consider that we will soon pick up audio cues delivered through headphones and see event information and environments via heads-up displays built into spectacles.

Don't act too surprised if, sometime soon, you meet someone who explains that their business card isn't just a card but an augmented reality business card. You can design your own now on certain websites – by adding a special marker to your card, which, once put in front of a webcam linked to the Internet, will show not only your contact details but also a video or sound clip. It's not just business cards. Fashion houses and retail outlets have tried them out too – little symbols that look like barcodes printed onto clothing, which, when viewed through a webcam (on a smartphone), come to life.

The IT head of a newly established marketing and event agency explains, as we walk by the Thames at Windsor with assorted friends and relations. 'The idea is straightforward enough. Take a real-life scene, or (better) a video of a scene, and add some sort of explanatory data to it so that you can better understand what's going on, or who the people in the scene are, or how to get to where you want to go. Sports coverage on TV has been doing it for years – slow-motion could be described as a sort of augmented reality, since it gives you the chance to examine what happened in a situation more carefully. Cricket, tennis, rugby, football and golf have all started to overlay analytic information on top of standard-speed replays. Would that ball have hit the stumps? What happened to make that player win the rally? How good or bad were the wingers in that rugby match? Let's examine the flights of those golf shots. And so on.' He looks at the fast-moving river for a moment and then continues. 'The arrival of powerful smartphones and computers with built-in video capabilities means that you don't have to wait for the AR effects as you do with TV. They can simply be overlaid onto real life. Apple's iPhone and other phones using Google's Android operating system are capable of overlaying information on top of a picture or video. Some apps, given a location – and using a smartphone's inbuilt compass to work out the direction you're pointing the phone – can give you a 'radar map' of, say, Wikipedia information, Flickr photos, Google searches and YouTube videos superimposed onto a picture you've taken of the scene. Or, more usefully maybe, other apps can offer an augmented reality application that will show you ratings and reviews of a restaurant before you walk in.' He pauses for a moment to watch the river again. 'Another app', he says, 'allows you to point your phone at a person and if it can find his or her details, it will pull them off the web and attach them – their Twitter username, Facebook page and other facts – and stick them, rather weirdly, into the air around their head (viewed through your phone, of course). It's taking social networking to the next level. Obviously in the field of events, AR technology has many uses – the simplest being bringing to animation or video life a photograph or brand logo. An advertiser could use AR in a client's delegate management system perhaps.' We look out across the river at small rowing boats and blobs of colour against the water as ducks skid across the surface of the Thames and children giggle.

IN AN EVENT ENVIRONMENT, WHAT OF AR?

I'm sitting in a room with no windows and an array of extraordinary equipment. There's no hum of machinery, but absolute dead silence even though I know the air conditioning is on. This is a research centre where new equipment and IT trials are set up and they are amazing! A professor from a well-known British university and her colleague, an American specialist, are showing me what's what in the AR world. The British professor says, 'We mostly see the immediate AR application within conferences and exhibitions for networking purposes. Registering attendees with face recognition is on the cards now and associating online social profiles with the delegate's virtual badge is an absolute reality.' Her colleague nods and adds, 'We can also think about associating a registered attendee with a particular contact need – person or object – and point the camera at the room to find the matching profile. And there are wider benefits for event logistics. Integrating the floor-plan into the application would make it easy to find our way in a crowded exhibition hall or conference where there are a myriad of breakouts. And we can do that now.'

I ask whether we could point the smartphone camera at a speaker during a conference session and be told about the speaker's published books, shared online presentations and track record. 'Yes,' says the American, 'And that's available now too. But it's not such a big deal in context. It's hard to believe that, not so many years ago, Facebook didn't exist. The surge in AR developments is a wave now and it'll become tidal. Interactive virtual events will become commonplace – where participants have their smartphone webcams on, giving the virtual event producer the opportunity to customise content based on the same information to each screen. Amazing stuff.' I share out peppermints and we all grin at each other. The zeal of these people is contagious. The American says, 'More and more event producers and companies know that augmented reality combines visual, three-dimensional environments with virtual information, creating a hybrid view of the real world and relevant data, and their collective minds are boggling at the opportunities.'

The ad agency head of technology, whom I'm visiting in Paris, adds, 'RFID means radio-frequency identification and is a technology that uses radio waves to transfer data from an electronic tag (the RFID) attached to an object, through a reader, for the purpose of identifying and tracking that object. The tag's information is stored electronically but many RFID tags don't use a battery. Instead, the tag uses the radio energy transmitted by the reader as its energy source.' 'Phew,' say I. My cousin gets it though. 'The RFID system design includes a method of discriminating several tags that might be within the range of the RFID reader. RFID systems can already be used to, say, track whether or not attendees are sitting in breakout sessions, but the power of RFID is more than that. Much more. Soon RFID systems will be used to understand audience attendance, to create surveys, to understand break-out session activity, to drive attendee networking and even tie into signage that can be customised for each attendee. Imagine customised one-to-one signage.'

'O, THAT A MAN MIGHT KNOW/THE END OF THIS DAY'S BUSINESS ERE IT COME!'

The quote above is from *Julius Caesar* (V.i). It's Brutus wishing that he could know what might happen today before it happens. But he also believes that it's enough to know that the day will end – and then the end will be known. The future trends and technologies that will shape event management and delivery are something of a mystery and many in the industry wish that they knew where those technologies might take us. My view errs on the side that thinks that not fully knowing is part of the excitement. At the last event that I attended on the future of events, and at which I also spoke, topics ranged from ticketing, registration, scanning and cashless payments to content delivery, production techniques, projection, 3D imagery, new ideas in stage creativity, experiential marketing techniques and more. But everything was connected to the development of new technology.

A senior someone from the shipping industry said at that conference over a coffee and ginger biscuit break, 'Technology continues to evolve quickly; the events industry, at all levels, needs to tell inventors and manufacturers what the industry needs – *not* wait until there's something on the market which you people then have to try and apply. Also, any new gizmos have to be cost-effective and, for exhibitions, somehow help generate new revenue, reduce costs and increase customer engagement points; and for corporate events new technology needs to help us to communicate better and reinforce learning. Most of us on the client side would accept that face-to-face events aren't going to disappear overnight, but we want to know how gadgetry can help, how it can support objectives.' A procurement executive reinforced the point. 'Blog posts and Twitter hash tags aren't substitutes for attending a conference. The distinct advantage conferences have (and will continue to have) is face-to-face contact. Social media tools take participants only so far – before, during or after an event. They don't replace the event. Then at some point, you want personal interaction. No one wants to just be a spectator … if something is fun, people want to be a part of it. If the event is good, the 'being there' part is exciting, memorable and important.'

My view on this is that conferences as we know them won't fade away. But I would venture that they will become more dynamic – mostly as a result of social media popularity, and also because those with corporate information to share want that immediacy and the immediacy that technology can assist or make possible. Events will certainly have to work harder and it will become less incumbent upon an attendee or delegate to simply accept what they're given. Senior executives on the client side responsible for corporate communications will have to sharpen up and those whose responsibility it is to design content will have to wake up too.

An American friend visiting London has a lot to say on the matter as well she might, since she runs one of the largest communication businesses in the world. 'I think,' she says confidently, 'in the future we'll see more opportunities for delegates to move around an event. This "one hour for a buffet lunch and network" idea will need to be but one opportunity for people to talk properly with each other and, if relevant, to talk with exhibitors or sponsors. Any way of encouraging proper networking will be a highlight.'

Producer acquaintances concur. One, just returned from climbing the Eiger agrees almost over-enthusiastically, but before I get his views I have to listen to stories about the climbing experience. 'How was the Eiger I hear you ask,' he booms, glowing with rude health. 'Well it's in Switzerland, 3970m high and set in the Bernese Alps,' he yells. Maybe his hearing has been affected. He continues, slightly modifying the decibels because people are looking. 'It's the easternmost peak of a ridge crest that extends across the Mönch to the … you aren't that interested are you?' I shake my head in sorrow. The subject shifts to the way events are going. His voice is almost at customary levels of restaurant conversation. 'In most events,' he says, 'our audiences just sit back on a comfy (or invariably uncomfortable) chair and, because the client insists on a plethora of speakers, audiences listen passively to presenter after presenter. There is no interaction, little engagement, no dialogue – just somebody shoving a pre-scripted or long-winded speech made up on the run to an audience that is disinterested. There's no easy way to talk or discuss anything with the presenter, no way to avoid pathetic attempts at teambuilding, no way to avoid watching an infinite series of boring slides, nor an easy and respectful way to counter or correct what the poor souls disagree with. Client audiences are showing more and more that they feel very frustrated and angry in those situations when they cannot learn, understand, engage, contribute and exchange. But,' he says now more brightly, 'some clients are encouraging engagement ideas and opportunities for a two-way conversation with the audience. Breakouts too are often looked at with a refreshed eye where they become a *genuine* opportunity for asking questions, sharing suggestions, bringing in new ideas and viewpoints into the discussion, but they need better facilitation. The tired old format of some vaguely disinterested HR manager running a syndicate session is boring and of no use. But the biggest change will come about because of technology.'

We break off for a bit because our lunch is served and then we're joined by a senior journalist from a major broadsheet newspaper. The conversation heads back towards how technology might support the event industry. My Eiger climbing friend says, 'Well, I think that media platforms will converge in new ways. Today, we can watch video on one TV set in our homes, pause the show and then resume watching on another set. Very soon we'll be able to do the same thing across devices, starting a show at home in the morning, resuming it on our mobile phone while commuting on the train, and watching the rest of the video at our desk when we arrive at the office. That'll affect how we view things before, during and after a conference and content will be managed accordingly. E-book readers have become much more affordable, and over the coming years e-book content is likely to soar beyond the text of paper books and newspapers. Conference delegates will be taking, sharing and reviewing notes with their e-book readers or readers that are combined with tablet technology. With GPS capability, these devices will become the primary outlets for hyperlocal electronic newspapers, which will be able to change the news stories they display as people carry their readers from district to district or country to country. But they'll also change corporate information on subjects depending on where you are in the world.'

The journalist adds, 'Face-to-face communications will become a highly coveted phenomenon. With so much connectivity driving fewer office-type work spaces and even more online entertainment, individuals will place much greater value on what once were routine encounters, like conferences and corporate events. Electronic connectivity will drive us to more readily connect with each other in person and much more of our communications will focus on announcing, reporting and interpreting these interpersonal events. I also think that e-mails will be replaced by social media posts that will be filtered down to the level of the individual user. Combining geo-locational capabilities with mobile social sites, individuals will no longer need to open e-mails. Messages and links (instead of attachments) will appear instantaneously on mobile and computer screens and recipients will speak their replies, which also will be posted instantly. That's bound to find a use in the corporate event market and it's the kind of supplementary engagement that event companies seek now particularly where delegates are in breakout sessions.' He pauses for a moment and then says, 'Everyone will have to learn how to speak clearly and precisely in a way that matters less with tweets, texts and e-mails. Or language will become simpler.'

CHAPTER ELEVEN

HELPING CLIENTS TO TELL STORIES

STORYTELLING: 'AN HONEST TALE SPEEDS BEST, BEING PLAINLY TOLD'.

Shakespeare. *Richard III* IV.iv. Wonderful. Whether you're training a client executive in the art of rhetoric or helping them with a presentation, one of the greatest tools in your (and indeed their) armoury is that of storytelling. Helping your client to prepare stories is useful for a wide variety of reasons – and the results can be outstanding, motivational, powerful, moving. It would be safe to say that all clients in most events have to get over a particular set of messages and one of the best ways that they can do this is through the structure of storytelling.

You know very well that client speakers are not alone in believing that speaking in public is scary. Some, of course, are sufficiently arrogant to consider themselves to be on par with the great Roman orators, but they're nowhere close even if their acolytes tell them how very wonderful they are. Giving a presentation is indeed worrying for many people. Presenting or speaking to an audience regularly tops the list in surveys of people's prime fears – more than heights, flying or torture by fire and brimstone.

There is an ancient Tamil text called *Thirukkural*. It's an arrangement of couplets authored by Thiruvalluvar – a poet who is said to have lived between the 2nd and 6th centuries AD. The *Thirukkural* expounds on various aspects of life and is one of the most important works in the Tamil language. You might dip into it from time to time because it's proper food for thought. It includes the following words in its aptly titled chapter, *Fearlessness in an*

Assembly: 'Many are ready to even die in battle, but few can face an assembly without nerves.' (Couplet 723). I've no idea how precise this translation is but, however poor, the intent is clear.

A colleague from way back, when we together produced (what we thought were) incredible events, particularly for the privatisation of many British companies under the eagle eye of Prime Minister Margaret Thatcher in the mid-to-late 1980s – has strong views about how event producers should help clients. He says with a gleam in his eye and strength in his voice, 'A common physical reaction to having to speak in public is a release of adrenaline and cortisol into our system, which is sometimes likened to drinking several cups of coffee.' In fact, we too are drinking (rather weak) coffee at Heathrow Airport's Terminal Five. My colleague continues, 'This sensational reaction to speaking in public is certainly not only felt by novices; even some of the great professional actors, politicians, senior business people and entertainers suffer with real physical sickness before taking the stage. Event producers and project managers very often take little notice of this in their myriad of preparations for a show, but they should, or at least someone should. Mind you, you do get some very silly executives who pretend that they need no help at all or that, because they've done a multitude of events, assume they're supremely brilliant at presentations. (Tell them what would happen if their audiences had any choice in attending events at which these executives speak.) For mere mortals, however, when faced with a seemingly terrifying experience, our primitive brains shut down normal functions as the 'fight or flight' impulse takes over. But, through patience and some decent coaching, producers can't necessarily quite get rid of a speaker's butterflies, but can get them flying in formation. Storytelling – and explaining how most situations and message communication can be made into stories – usually works wonders in coaching people to give good presentations.'

Cousin Maier rings after Sunday lunch and, once I've listened (at length) to his litany of ailments, we discuss the issue at hand, chapter and verse: 'Everyone has heard the advice about incorporating stories into a presentation to make a message easier to understand. But, if you're not a natural storyteller (and I don't count myself firmly in this camp, although others may say differently of course … ahem) then how exactly do you go about telling a story? Think back to some of the stories you and I heard as a child. No, not the Gazumweller Beast that aunt Irma frightened us with; I mean regular stories. A story has a recognisable beginning, middle, and end. A story has engaging characters. A story has action. A story has conflict – a problem, dilemma or challenge that needs to be solved. These same elements are what you have to work with in your business stories.'

THE STORY THAT YOUR SPEAKERS CAN CREATE

Any story within a presentation should underscore and amplify the business message your client presenters are communicating. Including a story that seems to have no relevance to the content and message of a presentation is just confusing for the audience and will make the speaker look somewhat silly. Material for stories is everywhere: family, work, travel to work, newspaper articles, the news, the weather, colleagues, famous people, infamous people, people on the bus, people from history, people from literature, literary people, politicians, comedians. Personal stories are always intriguing and can lend authenticity to a message or a proposition in a speech. If your client's presenters genuinely don't have any personal experiences that will work, an option is to interview them and illicit their stories. That can be like pulling teeth but persevere, or get your scriptwriter/ speech specialist involved in perseverance.

The best presentations are those that are driven by storytelling. Honestly. Read any great presidential speech, any great political speech, any great historical speech, any great business leader's speech – and each will be driven by a story or stories. Great orators tell stories with which their audiences can empathise and engage. Stories move, motivate and explain a notion, a proposition or an idea. Stories can explain why something has to be or has to happen or why change won't go away. Stories can make the unpleasant less unpleasant or the good better.

'The amount of detail in a story should be just enough to make it vivid, but not enough to make it rambling.' Speaking to me across a boardroom table is a director of a company that specialises in corporate storytelling and it, the company, helps businesses to plan via storytelling. 'Remember,' he says while working his way through a dish of biscuits, 'this is a story within a presentation, not a stand-alone tale a man or woman is telling around a camp fire in days of old when nights were cold. It's important for a presenter to ditch the backstory unless it's relevant to the audience's understanding. It's the characters – what they do and what that action means – that form the heart of any story. Give them life, give them colour, give them dialogue. Only provide background detail if it really helps with the point he or she is making. You'll notice that stand-up comedians give very little background. A few words and people in the audience totally understand the framework in which the story or joke is about to unfold. However, if you're telling a story, you obviously have to know your audience – like any comedian or any presenter. It's the reason jokes don't work or why stories fall flat – because the teller hasn't understood the audience.'

He makes eminent sense, of which there was more to come in his relaying of his storytelling views: 'Each story within a presentation should be only long enough to make a point. Strive for around two minutes, with an absolute maximum of three. Anything longer is likely to include extraneous details or side issues that don't move the story ahead and indeed can just confuse. Aim for a crisp rendition, leaving the audience so engaged that they want more. And there clever public speakers give their audiences more by coming back to their main story or a character in the story.'

A story well told will, without question, get the audience on a speaker's side even if the topic or message is tough. I meet up with a famous American writer of business fiction. He adds, 'Pacing and tone are the keys to grabbing and keeping an audience's attention. So, it's a good idea to vary sentence length to create anticipation – short, staccato sentences suggest action for instance. Speakers must learn when to pause for effect and to let the audience absorb what's been said. Speech should be slowed down and each word should be clearly articulated when a bit of drama is required, you know, like E.G. Bulwer-Lytton's *Paul Clifford*: "It was a dark and stormy night."'

It's vital that you tell your clients that they must rehearse their stories until they have the language and pacing in good order. Rehearsal once again is key. Not to the point where all meaning and style is wrung out of the thing so that what remains is pathetic, but enough so that the delivery is natural and interesting. The goal is to have the story crisp, relevant to the overall message of the presentation, and engaging. And the speaker needs to know the story by heart.

As a way of further honing your speakers' storytelling skills, suggest that your speakers read some of the classic short stories (O'Henry, Poe, Asimov, Flannery, Hemingway, Gallico, Huxley, Maupassant, Marquez and Dahl for starters) along with some fables and fairytales (Aesop, Anderson, Brothers Grimm, Kipling) and a few comedy scripts (Woody Allen maybe) for insight and inspiration. Legends too are a good source for structure.

ELEMENTS OF A STORY

A well-known children's author entertains me with tea and Kirschküchen. He's in the middle of writing a murder mystery series for TV. After the cake and multiple cups of black tea (a fusion he tells me comprises of sunflower blossoms and something else that I don't recall), he settles into a large leather settee that creaks and protests a little. He looks up at the ceiling, nearly spilling his tea and says, 'A story has a recognisable beginning and end. A story has characters, each with personality and foibles with which we can immediately identify. A story has action. A story has conflict. These same elements are what you have to work with in your business stories.' He continues, 'Presidential candidates across the decades, from Ronald Regan to Bill Clinton to George W. Bush, yes really, have honed the art of picking out stories to bolster a policy position in particularly human terms. Why? Because it *works*. Look hard to find an appropriate, compelling story that will strengthen your message and, by and large, it'll work for you. Tell a story that relates to your audience's experiences (even of watching a TV programme – a soap maybe) and they'll understand and they'll listen to what else of interest you have to say. Most stories have a happy ending, but not all. If yours doesn't, then that's OK, but be very sure that you can carry it off. It's important not to let an audience hang, not quite sure whether the tale is finished or not, or they may think that they've missed the point and that's absolutely no good.' He continues, 'It's not that hard to tell stories because we're all wired to *like* storytelling. There's power in stories, analogies, quotes, metaphors – and there's sheer force in what they impose on the hearts and minds (not to mention the memory) of the listener. And even in a large crowd of thousands of people, stories can create a bond, can create unity and a sense of shared experience and belonging. We all laugh, smile and chuckle and, importantly, later we all remember.'

We want to remember a story and its message for the right reason. There are many business and political speeches where stories meander and travel slowly up cul-de-sacs, while the audiences, in vain attempts to keep up, lose their way and inwardly collapse. A lesson, moral, objective – should be obvious to the audience. And relevance is key too. We like to hear stories about ourselves – which is why the most successful stand-up comedians are indeed successful.

A creative director (responsible for some of the world's best TV ads) says, 'The first time to tell a story shouldn't be when you're standing at a lectern addressing your audience. You need to know how the story works. Try stories on your friends, colleagues and anyone willing to listen. Get your presenters to develop a small bank of stories. Most people are exposed to good stories every day and the best ones are the most natural. You can use many different types of stories to liven up a presentation. A success story, for example, documents the triumph of people, actions or ideas. Think of the stories that you liked as a child. Most of them ended with the words "happily ever after". Those words are the sign of a success story. Delegates like to hear stories about how an idea or action worked out successfully. And personal stories – stories showing how a challenge was met, or how a challenge was overcome – they work. Any time you add a personal story, you get people's attention. People are much more interested in personal stories than they are in just plain facts.'

A famous orthodontist who makes many speeches to his profession says, while he's examining my teeth, 'A personal story is (fairly obviously) a tale about something that happened to the presenter, with his or her friends, colleagues or relatives. Open a bit wider. These are the stories that can't be made up, although they might be embellished to suit a point, or they might not actually be the presenter's, but someone else's. Open wider. Actually, other people's stories are a great source of material that shouldn't be overlooked, and sometimes they seem more amusing than first-person tales. A humorous story amuses an audience while making a point. Does that hurt? Parables are good and you don't need to be a preacher to tell one. I use parables if I want to make a point about business ethics. There we are. All done. Rinse please.'

STORY STRUCTURES

'This is neither the time and certainly not the place to discuss political story structures,' says the American political scriptwriter looking sharply to the left and then to the right. I wonder why he thinks it isn't, but he leans forward in his chair and whispers, 'You never know who's listening. But there are a number of types that I use.' He talks as if he's discussing handguns or nuclear weaponry. I wait while he finishes his sandwich. He wipes his mouth with a napkin and begins 'Christopher Booker's *The Seven Basic Plots* gives us a good understanding of the basic story plots. His first is Overcoming the Monster where the hero learns of some terrifying, all-powerful, great evil threatening the land, a country (or, of course, a business or indeed an industry) and sets out to destroy it. Examples would include *Beowulf, Jack and the Beanstalk* and *Dracula*. Then there's Rags to Riches where a hero or heroine, someone who has seemed to the world to be quite plain and ordinary, is shown to have been hiding a more exceptional self within. Again you can think of political or business examples. In the world of well-known stories, think *The Ugly Duckling, Jane Eyre* and Clark Kent of *Superman* fame. The hero or heroine is surrounded by dark forces that suppress and mock him or her. But the hero slowly blossoms into a mature figure who can stand up to anything, wins through any odds and ultimately gets riches, a kingdom and the perfect partner. The business analogies are evident.' He pauses and looks dreamily out of the window. Flurries of snow target the cars and the Manhattan sidewalk. It's getting dark.

'And then there's The Quest,' the political scriptwriter continues eventually, 'where, let's say, a heroine learns of a great secret, treasure or code that she desperately wants or needs to find. She sets out to find it, often with companions, and wins through – although the story will undeniably have twists and turns and all may almost be lost before success is finally won. Plus, the secret or treasure may not be exactly what the heroine had in mind. Examples of The Quest can be seen in *The Odyssey, The Aeneid, The Count of Monte Cristo, Journey to the Centre of the Earth* and *Raiders of the Lost Ark.*

Voyage and Return has a hero, let's say it's a guy, heading off into a magic land with crazy rules and mysterious environments. He ultimately triumphs over the madness and returns home far more grown up and wise than when he set out. Often the hero is accompanied by a band of followers (or acquaintances gathered on the way). They travel out of their familiar, safe surroundings into another world completely cut off from the first. While the new world is at first wonderful, there is a sense of increasing peril. After a dramatic escape, they return to the familiar world where they began, having sorted out whatever needed to be sorted out or now able to face up to and confound any barriers to success. *Alice in Wonderland, Castaway* and *The Time Machine* are obvious examples, but *Brideshead Revisited* and *Gone with the Wind* also embody this plotline.'

The political scriptwriter orders another sandwich. He says, 'Comedy usually sees a hero and heroine destined to be together, but a dark force prevents them; the story conspires to make the dark force eventually repent and suddenly the two protagonists are free to do what they want. This is part of a cascade of circumstances that shows everyone for who they really are during which time there is some chaos of misunderstanding. To universal relief, everyone and everything gets sorted out in the end, bringing about the happy ending. Shakespeare's comedies come to mind. Tragedy tends to be the other side of the Overcoming the Monster plot. The main character is a villain (monster, baddy, devil, deluded principal character, newspaper proprietor, whatever), but we get to watch him or her slowly spiral down into darkness before being finally defeated, freeing the land (business, industry) from their evil influence. This type of story shows a flawed character who's increasingly drawn into a fatal course of action, and led inevitably to disaster. *King Lear,*

Madame Bovary, *The Picture of Dorian Gray*, and *Bonnie and Clyde* are all tragic.' It's dark outside and the snow beats a silent pattern on the window.

'Finally, according to Booker, there's Rebirth. This is similar to the Tragedy plot, but the protagonist manages to realise their error before it's too late and does an about-turn to avoid defeat. There is usually a mounting sense of threat as a dark force approaches the hero until it emerges completely, holding the hero in its deadly grasp. Only after a time, when it seems that the dark force has triumphed, does the reversal take place. The hero is redeemed, usually through the life-giving power of love. Many fairy tales take this shape, as well as stories like *Silas Marner* and *It's a Wonderful Life.*'

'You've alluded to the business world,' I say. 'Tell me more.' 'Well,' says my very helpful political writer, 'in the context of the business world, Overcoming the Monster – where the hero must destroy something in order to restore balance to the world – this might relate to overcoming a takeover bid, fighting off debts, beating a malaise in the marketplace or beating a competitor to win a huge contract. A storyteller can take the role of the hero/heroine or the trusted accomplice who helps win the day. The storyteller can choose to narrate the tale in the first or third person. With Rags to Riches, this is where a modest, moral, downtrodden person (or business), achieves a happy ending when their natural talents are displayed to the world at large. In the real world this could, say, apply to anyone with an undeniably incredible talent who wants to break through and become successful – maybe about a business that has struggled from a small, inconspicuous start to a superb current status. Again the storyteller can play the protagonist or perhaps the adviser who counsels the right thing at the right time.'

Sandwich number two arrives and it's vast, like a small boat. The political writer again checks out who might be listening and then cuts the boat in three offering me one of the thirds. 'In the Quest genre,' he continues with mouth half full, 'the hero, often accompanied by sidekicks, travels in search of a priceless treasure and must defeat evil and overcome powerful odds. The tale ends when he gets both the treasure and the princess or prince. These stories can relate to any huge challenge that a business overcomes in its entrepreneurial journey. Overcoming business odds of any sort (internal or external challenges or change) is a common example. With Voyage and Return, normal protagonists are suddenly thrust into strange and alien worlds and must make their way back to normal life once more. That could be settling into a new world after a takeover or a merger. Or a good analogy might be around the subject of expansion into overseas markets or launching a new product or service – anything involving risk. If you think a little, an analogy for storytelling in a business or any environment is easy.' There's a short pause for sandwich consumption.

'The Comedy genre,' says the political writer, 'is not necessarily laugh-out-loud stuff, but has more validity in a Shakespearean way. The plot of a comedy involves some kind of confusion that must be resolved before the hero and heroine can be united in love.' He pauses as the waiter brings a tray of coffee and some cookies. Once the coffee has been poured, the political writer holds on to the bowl of cookies. He munches and speaks, 'In the real world, confusions in business happen every day. Out of that confusion can come a leader or hero, or it can be a group of people, or a division or the research department, or someone from low down the food chain who has suggested a brilliant, winning idea from which the whole business can benefit. The "love" element can equal success in a business scenario. You see – not difficult. With Tragedy, the stories tend to be about the consequences of human overreaching and egotism. *Julius Caesar, Romeo and Juliet*, and *Hamlet* are obvious examples in literature. Very often, good stories exist in tales about ruthless leaders, ruthless companies or ruthless climbers up the rungs of promotion with attendant tragedies on the way or at the end. Rebirth stories almost always have a threatening shadow that seems nearly victorious until a sequence of fortuitous (or even miraculous) events lead to redemption and the restoration of a happier world. The best example of this is *A Christmas Carol*. In the real world, it's pretty plain that some businesses or business leaders realise the error of their ways either too late or just in time. A common business line is the tale of someone doing something to sort out something that has become a serious detriment to their company, or by shining a spotlight on the problem they may have been ignoring, then spelling out the realities of what will happen if this doesn't get sorted.'

He looks askance at the empty biscuit plate. So do I. Undaunted though, he continues, his tongue having removed any vestiges of crumbs around his moustache. 'But just as Scrooge needed a big push to see exactly how it was he affected the world around him in a bad way, people in business sometimes need a push to realise that something has to change and that there's a better way of doing something. Ultimately, once the Rebirth story has been started, everything else becomes that much easier, because people are more open to long-lasting change.'

As I'm walking down a Manhattan street on my way back to my hotel, I think about storytelling and how some people can tell wonderful, rich, amusing, frightening, educational, intelligent, witty, good stories. And the ones that can make us cry and those that make us laugh.

EFFECTIVE STORYTELLING

I have just arrived for a meeting seriously underdressed, a mistake that I don't often make these days. However, I've been to the launch of a major new pizza chain and it was de rigueur to wear the right thing – in my case, pleated denim shorts, baseball cap, a T-shirt with the pizza chain's name emblazoned on the front, sunglasses hung from my neck on a fluorescent cable and bright new trainers. I know, I know. You don't have to say anything. The Director General of a British organisation representing senior management smiles a wintery smile at my garb, but we know each other sufficiently well for it not to matter overly much. In any case, I have a change of clothing and go off to effect a more appropriate look. With my garb now acceptable in the corridors of power, we settle down with fresh mint tea and he says, 'Effective storytelling can serve anyone in leadership who seeks to persuade others of their point of view. Opinion-based rhetoric is often more polarising than persuasive, while details and statistics often go in one ear and out of the other. But a careful blending of rhetoric and some facts, woven into the right story, can change minds.' I nod encouragingly and the DG carries on to his peroration. He says, 'Shaping an effective story, with a carefully considered point of view and of use to the audience, is a learned skill. You've got to know your message. When it comes to persuasion, audience members resist being told what to think, but are open to *why* they perhaps should think something. Preachers used this technique on Sundays in the USA during the 19th century. Good stories are tools of persuasion. Look at propaganda. It's mostly story-based and people in a certain frame of mind lap it up.'

I suppose that in business, leaders consider what they want others to do and why they want them to do it. That's a message. If they want to persuade people to adopt, say, safety standards, then a story can be told of what happened when someone didn't follow protocol. If they want to demonstrate the benefits of a new process, they might use a story to explain how an individual, anyone in the audience perhaps, would indeed benefit.

'Ah, but,' says cousin Maier, pointing skywards as if for some sort of biblical emphasis, 'as powerful as storytelling can be, it may not be appropriate for every occasion. Sometimes you need to get to the point. And the best way to relate your point of view, especially with a business case, is to do it quickly and concisely. In these situations, facts and figures can be a story in themselves.' He collapses back into his armchair as if the effort of these bon mots has been far, far too much. He receives a small cognac as if it is his right and continues, waving his glass around, 'Storytelling need not be reserved for formal occasions. I recall an executive telling me that he had a boss, one who mentored him, who had a story for every situation. Most especially this boss told stories as a form of coaching. He would relate whatever the situation called for – an admonishment, a pat on the back, or a challenge – to a story. As a result, the lessons stuck. The executive who told me this could recite verbatim stories his old boss had told him twenty years ago. What's more, the executive had integrated the technique (and some of the same stories) into his own leadership style.'

I argue with my dear cousin that this is all very well, but how a story is presented on stage is as important as the story itself. Luckily we have staying with us a Cambridge professor who gives many a lecture to business audiences on a variety of economic topics. He too decides that a robust helping of the Maier cognac is the order of the evening and, once fortified, provides the following: 'Dialogue should make use of different voices for different characters. Practice different voices as you would when telling a story to a child. I always like to briefly create the atmosphere or tension as the story progresses and I use gestures and facial expressions to add to the visualisation of the story. Dialogue slows a story's pace down, while narrating action speeds it up. Repetition and exaggeration have always been basic elements of storytelling but don't ever treat people in an audience as comprising of a bunch of idiots or a group of people whose levels of tolerance and patience are unlimited.'

Storytelling traditionally begins with a ritual that serves as a signal that the teller is suspending time and space as we know it and transporting the audience to a world somewhere else. However, a story can be about the here and now and set in the present environment. Either way, we listen because we want to know what happens.

The Cambridge professor finishes up nicely (much as he has my cognac), 'Once you get to the end of the story – stop! Don't ramble on. Leave the audience's thoughts lingering over it. Let them savour it and the words. Don't feel you have to explain everything, or tie together all loose ends. People are more than able, *much* more than able, to make quantum leaps in understanding plots. Let them go away thinking about what has been said and drawing their own meaning and conclusions from it. Provided that what you've said isn't ambiguous of course. If that's the case the wrong meanings or conclusions will be construed.'

STORIES FOR A CHANGE

Storytelling can play a crucial part in any change process, offering clients at most events the opportunity to distil experience, build understanding and create new possibilities for the future. You can encourage people to step back and ask themselves to consider situational stories – those describing the current position of something. During times of organisational change (a constant, of course) those responsible for directing such change will be better able to avoid stress in the process and make more positive interventions by applying storytelling techniques. By that I mean explaining what has been, what is and what will be, but doing so exactly as if one was telling a story. It could be in the third person and often works better that way. Says one producer, 'It's a bit like saying "I have a friend and he/she has a problem …".'

For any change process and activity to last, people need to believe and then 'do'. Action is paramount and any involvement must move people from being victims to becoming active participants and drivers of change. Storytelling can help achieve this by positioning problems and/or scenarios in a context with which everyone listening can identify.

A creative director says, 'I've used a variety of ideas in helping participants at an event to better understand a situation. Some ideas work with small groups or during breakouts or seminars. For example, I get a group to analyse a painting in which all sorts of detail can be gleaned by studying the detail – and then telling a story involving all or some of the detail. We can give people the opportunity to distil experience, build understanding and create new possibilities for the future. By encouraging people to step back and ask themselves "what's the story here?" you can quickly engage them in listening to and telling the story that is relevant to their company or business circumstances. It's a question of getting the emotion out of the way and involving logic and action into play.' We're walking along a Suffolk beach and the water is grey, as is the sky. Spray creates a misty picture. We're looking for stones with holes all the way through and for amber, not uncommon on this coastline. I pick up every orange stone thinking it to be amber. Amber, for that is my walking companion's name, carries on: 'There are three ways of telling stories in the context of events. There's the public story and that tends to be all about "we" and "us" – the organisation – all embracing. Then there's the less common private story that is prefaced with "I" and is obviously first person and probably, but not always, personal. Then there's the joined-up story whereby the public and the private are, well, joined up. That one tends to be a mix of "us" and "I" – it sets a sense of belonging and, most importantly, allows listeners to feel involved.'

Later, Amber and I are joined by a speechwriter for tea and buns at some old coastguard's cottages at Dunwich Heath that are now partly National Trust tearooms. The window overlooks a beautiful area of heathland conservation and the eroding cliffs of Minsmere Beach. The speechwriter, also old and eroding, consumes two buns and three cups of tea before pronouncing, 'People often feel trapped and helpless in change, sandwiched in-between those who have authority over them and those who are demanding better leadership – or just participation. This can leave people feeling negative and with a sense of helplessness – which can be construed as obstructive. Storytelling can be used as a way for an individual to express and transform an organisational tale from negative to positive. What it can mean is that a healthy discussion (story) ensues which contains elements of the worst situation (doom, gloom, fears), of control (who manages who and what), of role and of outcome (what success looks like).'

Stories are about collaboration and connection. Through stories we share passions, sadness, hardships and joys. We share meaning and purpose. Stories allow us to understand ourselves and others better. Tweets, texts and emails can involve storytelling but the best storytelling is through the spoken word and better still face-to-face. Stories are how we make meaning of life. Stories are how we explain how things work, how we make decisions, how we justify our actions, how we persuade others. Stories provide certainty or explain uncertainty. Stories trigger our imagination.

CHAPTER TWELVE

ANTICIPATION, LIGHTING AND SOUND

ANTICIPATION

This is without question the key to good production management and delivery. Try to visualise everything that will be happening during your event. Walk through the entire thing from start to finish in your head, including where and when delegates and performers will be moving. If anything looks like it might be wrong, or even has the potential of going wrong, then address it immediately and certainly before the event, because, so says cousin Maier in low spirits, 'it probably will go wrong if you don't.'

Allow ample time for set-up. I've mentioned this before and it's frequently where inexperience causes disaster. There are just too many small things that can go off-track if people have to work within a serious time frame. And stress isn't a great motivator. It's far better to be too early and wait around than to still be doing a sound check as guests enter the event space. However, with rehearsals, there's not ever (in my experience) a lot of time left over. However, I'm fully aware that set-up time is not always within your control and clients (and, from time to time, venues) do need some education. Also, additional venue time costs more money and that's understood by most clients. However, a balance of what can and should be achieved is the order of the day. More to the point, if the set-up time *is* limited, then the event should be considered with that limitation in mind – staging, technical provision, creativity, complexity and so on. Focusing on content and delivery within the construct of a tight get-in and set-up isn't a bad thing. Frustrating yes, but impossible no. Much better to achieve well and exceed expectations than struggle to meet them.

'In any event,' says a high street retail company director who's been involved in a number of fashion shows, exhibitions and corporate conferences, 'whatever the circumstances, keep onsite schedules of everything to do with the event very tight. Know what's going on everywhere, all of the time. This is where a producer or good project manager earns their money.' He goes on, 'Keep in touch with all schedules of set-up, event running order and the get-out. The latter's just as important because, invariably, the venue wants you out by a particular time and an over-run will cost in all sorts of ways. By this point the client won't be much interested, and certainly not in paying any extra money for defaults. Stick to the schedules and ensure that all people involved with the event are on the distribution list with relevant parts highlighted so that the right people read the right sections. This includes venue staff, performers, speakers, all technical people, and of course, your client.'

The high street retail company director talks again of 'anticipation'. He says, 'Know all the requirements and technical riders for performers and suppliers. This can include everything from stage plots and sound and lighting requirements, to dressing room riders that can be awesome. Remember that comedian who wanted cucumber sandwiches with the crusts cut off? And the singers who wanted only blue everything, including the changing room walls? Oh, and the Irish dancers who would only eat burgers and nothing else? Be aware of the excessive riders of some celebrity talent and try to negotiate out all except what is reasonable. Good luck with that. But it can be done. Oh yes, and ensure that there are dressing rooms of adequate size and privacy for performers, with mirrors (unless they stipulate no mirrors). Don't forget that some shows require quick-change areas close to the main stage where fast costume changes, say, are part of the act. Be prepared to pay extra to set these up properly.'

We are at an Oxfordshire stately home that used to be training centre of a bank. The grounds (400 acres) are green, with trees as far as the eye can see. We walk by the ha-ha ('a ditch with a wall on its inner side below ground level, forming a boundary to a park or garden without interrupting the view' or so it says it says on a sign) and down towards a lake. The sun has almost disappeared and the air is cold, but the sky has turned orange and it feels like snow is in the air. The high street retail company director carries on with his advice. 'Ensure that you have adequate and capable stage management in place to run the show,' he says. 'In addition, ensure that adequate communication equipment is available for the stage managers. The best kind is wireless headset equipment that enables you to talk and listen without anyone else hearing the conversation – and to move about the venue freely and still be in communication.'

He has to go off for a meeting in Oxford and I walk back to the large 18th century manor house, proud against the darkening sky. I think about rehearsing events and become a little disappointed at all the missed opportunities when clients refused any rehearsals or insisted on the bare minimum only. Their loss of course, but they never felt that way and that was the shame of it. But it is so important to rehearse your show. Ideally this should mean every time but, in truth, it won't happen like that, either because of time restraints or because your client thinks that anything that happens on stage happens by magic.

Even the smallest show can benefit from some kind of in-depth run-through. If the event is complex, plan for at least a pre-event talk-through with the key participants, including all relevant venue staff, performers, sound and lighting people and client. Have contingencies in place for any unavoidable changes. Know how to react and what you will do before they happen. This goes along with anticipation, but is the last (and unfortunately) very important step. Try to see through the rough spots and keep smiling.

LIGHTING

When it comes to the conference or event, a dull performance can dramatically affect the message for the worse. People need motivation and there is nothing like a dramatic show, used appropriately, to bring a message home. Lighting is a secret to that effect, certainly in creating a strong first impression and surprises (mental oohs and aahs) throughout the event.

Nothing affects people more than the properly placed and designed lighting effect that comes in at just the right moment. Done right, a polite applause can quickly become a rousing, standing ovation. Well, sometimes.

But, what are the secrets to great lighting? I speak to one of the top event lighting designers who's just returned from lighting a circus show in Las Vegas and who's tucking into egg and chips and strong tea in an east London café. 'A standing ovation you say?' he enquires as he dabs three huge, speared chips into tomato ketchup. 'The first thing is to collaborate with an experienced and competent lighting company, unless you work for an agency with its own department – but that's rare. And you'll want a really good lighting designer. Ask to see some evidence of their work, to see if what they do suits your needs. In some agencies this wouldn't be the project manager's job, but the production department's, but there's no reason why you can't have a view on who's right for your show.' He stops for a while, finishing off his lunch. 'Gosh,' he says, 'I've been dreaming of good old British chips all the while I was in the US.' I struggle to get him back to the topic of the power of lighting.

'If the light is off just a little, too bright or the wrong shade of blue for the stage,' this star of the lighting design profession continues, 'the opportunity to create a good first impression is gone. Events aren't static and neither should your lighting design be. Whether you are on stage in a play or giving the best of presentations, the technical aspects of the staged activity must be as good as the scripts or the quality of those speaking. If you fail to consider the lighting, you might never know why the big announcement fell on a silent crowd. Timing too is a key element in lighting – knowing when to shift from a soft blue to hard whites can make or break a big introduction or the appearance of a new product or person. Even more complex are the tone and colour values. Knowing how different colours interact with one another and with shapes on the stage is as important as understanding about the timing. A producer doesn't have to know all these things, but it doesn't hurt to know a bit, and if I were a producer I'd *want* to know. I'd *want* to go and see West End shows and loads of professional theatre, opera, ballet, exhibitions, and live television programmes, to see how they're lit.'

Movement and transition in lighting are other key elements in a show. Should the spot appear suddenly, or come in gently from a far roof corner? The primary purpose of event lighting is to make certain that the action and the presenters are visible. This seems obvious, but it is important that the designer has ensured that all areas of the stage and all people on that stage can be seen. Lighting isn't something you can understand in five minutes, but it is important to spend time with experts to understand what can be achieved. That'll help with the creative process for pitches and will always add value when you discuss event entrances and exits with your client.

EFFECTS

A producer friend is writing an article on event effects and 'tricks' and I've agreed to talk through collective thoughts. She says, 'I've tried a new idea and it works a treat. If you want to drop a ceiling in a large hall, then use weather balloons that can inflate safely up to 24 or more feet in diameter. Suspended from the ceiling, the (usually) white balloons take lighting effects well and also help with sound issues often found in larger spaces. You can get pale blue and pink ones too which can be good for gala dinner ceilings.'

Another producer, who's just been working in Mexico, matches that with an idea that she's used there and which she declares probably isn't new. 'To fill a large space in an interesting way, hang picture frames of different shapes, sizes and colours from the ceiling and around the walls. Lit well, you can instantly transform big spaces into works of art. Another idea along the same theme is a lift from the Harry Potter books and films where people seemingly fixed in a portrait or painting move via video within the frame and from one picture to another. Not difficult to do and creates a good and surprising point of interest during a dinner.'

A party planner turned corporate event project manager says, 'For tricky spaces with columns or other view obstructions (a certain industry awards ceremony comes to mind when my table guests and I had to seek out the stage through a dinosaur), use small, wireless personal monitors placed on table rounds so that each attendee or dinner guest has his or her own.'

The producer from Mexico is feeling left out and contributes with: 'We had to deliver a gala dinner with very little notice and it was the anniversary of a company's division for a thousand or so people. The brief asked for romance. For a place-setting showing some aspect of romance, we tied every napkin in a ribbon matching the table overlay and tucked in a single rose. We decorated each setting with a miniature silver picture frame. It went down a treat and the men liked it as much as the ladies.'

I've dressed conference and gala dinners with, for example, a collection of inexpensive old lamps, similar in style, easily adapted to create individual dinner table centerpieces. You can do the same sort of thing with any collection of things that match the theme – wild west objects for a cowboy theme, pirate pieces for a, ah, pirate theme and so on. There are companies that specialise in the hire of these things and, provided you don't go mad with a weird set of props that make no sense, this is a good way to make a room work.

Colour and design are very subjective. There are many stories about clients who shriek in horror when they see something that the producer thought had been agreed for months. It really is important that you ensure that your client knows exactly what's happening on stage or in a space at any time. Don't ever assume that what you think is clear actually is. If your client waves you away or claims that he or she has no time to listen, then insist.

Sets and backdrops can be as interesting as your imagination and budget allow. A good set designer is important and he or she has to have a clear understanding of what the event needs to achieve. All kinds of materials can be used from steel to starcloths (black or dark blue curtain material with little lights embedded that twinkle like stars), from backlit shapes to cut out images, from kabuki (silk) drops to creating cityscapes or countryside scenes, from creating a castle to a space where tricks abound – all possible and more. Making a car appear or disappear, making torrents of water fall but where nobody gets wet, making things fly and turn, making things move as if by magic. Stages that revolve, audiences who revolve around the stage, delegates sitting in boats in a flooded hall, a funfair revealed as a set 'collapses', interactive this and interactive that. Anything that you see at the theatre (*Les Misérables* and the hydraulic Paris barricades, *Spiderman* and people climbing vertical walls, a crashing chandelier in *Phantom of the Opera*, a flying car in *Chitty Chitty Bang Bang*) can be done on a corporate stage with space, time and, as I said, budget willing. More than anything though, it's all down to whether the idea is appropriate to the message and the event's purpose.

MUSIC

The use of music at events is a practice that is thousands of years old. These days, music may be used to build the energy of the audience, to motivate people or to celebrate an achievement. Sometimes it's used to create a sombre or thought-provoking mood. There are some 'standards' that get over-used, but perhaps still stand the test of time. Queen's *We Will Rock You* and *We Are the Champions* (and actually mostly anything by Queen) have become common fare for example (perhaps over-common), as have long-term standards like The Verve's *Bittersweet Symphony*. There are many others, and choosing the right piece for a specific moment requires as much thought as any other part of the show.

It's always hard because everyone has totally different views about music and songs – and a client will add complications by insisting on the CEOs favourite Lady Gaga number or the theme from *Spartacus*. Yes, that's happened. Spending a little time deciding on some great music for your conference is a worthwhile and easy way to add fun, enjoyment and another dimension to the experience. Don't just leave this up to the client (please don't) or to anyone else. By all means, ask around your team and sound designers who will have (literally) heard it all before, but you should have a good, solid view about what's needed.

These days an iPod, iPad or laptop can be easily patched into the main sound system, so choosing tracks is very easy even on a low budget. Here are some moments that music can be used to enhance the conference:

- ► Creating atmosphere when people enter the room in the morning, afternoon or evening.

- ► A signal that you have temporarily stopped for a comfort break or coffee, much like an interval in the theatre.

- ► A signal that they should come back into the room (something that's often forgotten, although a 'voice of God' announcement would do the job, but less well, unless the voice is akin to Alan Rickman's).

- ► Short 'stings' when people walk on stage – particularly appropriate and normal for an awards ceremony.

- ► Other short pieces of music that introduce a new section within the event.

- ► Quiet music to play when groups are discussing topics or when people are reflecting on something.

- ► Mood lifters, engagement pieces to raise the roof, announcement pieces.

- ► Celebratory pieces.

Someone who's been involved in many musicals and has designed sound for many a corporate event, suggests some excellent tracks to use. 'Have a listen to these,' he says giving me a neatly typed up list. Later, I dutifully run through said list and people in the flat below knock on my door wanting an invitation to the party.

Eye of the Tiger by Survivor.

Alive and Amplified by the Mooney Suzuki.

Stronger by Kanye West.

Harder Better Faster Stronger by Daft Punk.

One More Time by Daft Punk.

Holiday by Green Day.

Chariots of Fire by Vangelis (although I think that this is still very 1983 and overused).

Rocky theme instrumental *Gonna Fly Now* by Bill Conti (also very much of its period – 1977 – but still works).

Born to Run by Bruce Springsteen. (Did you know that this is from 1983?)

Get Ready For This by Crazy Frog.

Here I Go Again by Whitesnake.

Footloose by Kenny Loggins (not my choice, but I'm told it's good stuff).

Dreams by Van Halen.

Don't You (Forget About Me) by Simple Minds.

Olympic Fanfare by John Williams (worked in 1984 and this sort of thing will always work – it's like World Cup themes or any sports related music).

Almost by Bowling for Soup.

Closing Time by Semisonic.

100 Years by Five for Fighting.

This is the Time by Billy Joel.

Boulevard of Broken Dreams by Green Day (just brilliant if used well).

I Don't Like Mondays by Boomtown Rats (extraordinary to think that this is 1979!).

Eye of the Tiger by Survivor (I hated it in 1982 and still loathe it now, but some clients love it to bits).

Burn It To The Ground by Nickelback.

Boom Boom Pow by Black Eyed Peas.

Car Wash by Christina Aguilera with Missy Elliot.

Fire Burning by Sean Kingston.

Song 2 by Blur.

Written in the Stars by Tinie Tempah.

The (subjective) list goes on and includes classical pieces and even some operatic segments – something for everyone and every occasion – but it's pointless being prescriptive here. You'll create your own list and you'll know what works in which situations. Suffice to say, music is an extraordinarily powerful device. The same applies to sound effects – as appropriate obviously. I recall a scenario well when I was producing a management conference for a bank. Training was the overall theme and the whole stage was made to look like a huge ship with the CEO in the role of captain. A famous TV personality was to take the part of training officer and he was to arrive by helicopter. We were treated to the quiet thrumming of a helicopter getting closer and then louder and louder. Through quadraphonic speakers the whole room throbbed and the floor vibrated as a vast fan whisked the delegates' hair and hair-pieces. A life-size helicopter was lowered onto the 'deck' and the famous personality hopped out, lifted his flying helmet and was received to tumultuous applause. OK, it wasn't the best story in the corporate conference world, but it wasn't the worst either. I was pleased. Anyway, sound effects can work.

SOUND

'It could just be the way they normally sound,' the music director offered as we were listening to some musical rendition at a Belgian conference on event management. 'Maybe this is what they do when they're cross with the audience,' said the director of two West End musicals. It didn't sound much like a song, more like a German drinking number. Here was a case of appalling sound equipment where a willing audience couldn't understand anything.

I was recently at a poetry festival at a very prestigious and famous concert venue, where I've heard Dave Gilmour do his thing with brilliant sound. The poetry however was lost, either because the poets were a bit the worse for wear, were lousy deliverers of their own poems (sadly not unusual) or because the sound system and its set-up were useless. I've had to sit through school concerts where the sound was crackly or where a microphone was badly placed, rubbing continuously against a headmaster's beard or tie or the bosom of a bored guest sportswoman. I've heard sound quality debated by all sorts of experts with hysterical zeal and passion, and I've also attended (and, I like to think, produced) corporate events where the quality of sound has been fantastic. I like sitting high at the back of a raked-seating auditorium. I prefer it that way and actually I've never liked the 'stalls', where your view can be obstructed. An exalted perch with a downward eye-line is congenial. The acoustics are usually perfect too. Actors are trained to 'project to the back wall' and that's where you are, ideally placed to hear the words at conversational pitch. Sound quality in events is important and is an ingredient that is sometimes left to sort itself out.

In order to have the best event production, it is important to make sure your audio is excellent. Before you even start, you need to be aware of the capabilities of whatever system you're using. Not in detail, but the basics certainly. I talk to a sound designer who has a brilliant pedigree. 'One of the things that people forget,' he says, 'is that the acoustics of an empty or full room will be very different from each other. You also need to bear in mind any external noises – like aircraft about which you can do little and rattling crockery about which you can do something. Air conditioning can be a problem too but then so too can turning it off. But, with sense and an accommodating venue management team, most extraneous conference room noises can be managed.'

CHAPTER 13
ENTERTAINMENT

TEAM-BUILDING – CAUTION

Once, long ago, I was out in the Welsh mountains taking part in the company's teamwork away day. It was billed as entertainment and I have no idea why, but I was reminded of it just now (I still limp) and wanted to share a word or two about team-building 'entertainments'. Actually it was an away day lasting three days and it created resentment, grazed knees, minor concussion, terrible indigestion, stretched bladders and a limp. It also taught us not to rely on our colleagues, particularly in times of dire straits, of which there were then many. One of the organisers at the time said to me apropos of nothing whatsoever (so far as I could make out), 'Sir Thomas Beecham, the conductor, maintained that there was only one rule to life – try everything except incest and folk dancing.' For many years my faith in team-building activities was severely tested and I doubted the sanity of Sir Thomas Beecham.

Great teamwork makes things happen more than anything else in organisations. Empowering people is more about attitude and behaviour towards staff than about processes and tools. Teamwork is fostered by respecting, encouraging, enthusing, and caring for people – not exploiting or dictating to them. That's what most manuals and textbooks say and I suppose they're right. Anything that genuinely helps to bring mutual respect, compassion and humanity to work must be good. People working for each other in teams can be a powerful force – properly taught and properly channeled. But whatever is used to engage the team has to be valid, otherwise individuals won't take it seriously. Not just that – most people at work actually don't want to go out into the Welsh hills for some prescribed exhaustion and mud.

People are best motivated if you can involve them in designing and deciding the activities – ask them. Secondly, you will gain most organisational benefit if the activities are geared towards developing people's own potential – find out what they will enjoy doing and learning. Games can be trite or patronising for many people – they want activities that will help them learn and develop in areas that interest them.

A team specialist who's also a psychiatrist helps me out a little. 'If you're planning a whole day of team-building activities at a conference or an event, bear in mind that a whole day of 'games' is a waste of having everyone together for a whole day. Find ways to provide a mix of activities that appeal and help people achieve and learn – maybe build in exercises focusing on one or two real work challenges or opportunities, using a workshop approach.' He stares at me for a moment and I wonder what blob of shaving foam or jam from breakfast I have on my face. But he's just pondering and shortly goes on, 'Ensure that team-building activities and all corporate events comply with equality or discrimination policies and law in respect of gender, race, disability, and age. Age discrimination is a potential risk given certain groups and activities. Without attention to integration (that is, everyone being able to take part in some way), corporate team-building or planning events are, at best, a short-term boost to employee enthusiasm and positive morale. If they are planned and executed well, and if they are *relevant*, people feel good about themselves and about each other. But not if the whole thing is about muddy trainers and insects down your trousers. There aren't many employees or indeed any other audiences who would really enjoy a version of *I'm a Celebrity … Get Me Out of Here!*

Without being a party pooper, it's fair to say that team-building sessions can help event delegates become cynical about their organisations. This occurs when the team-building events are held outside of the context of the company's normal way of doing business. If you send people off to a team-building event, but all rewards in your company are based on individual goals and efforts, the team-building event will have no lasting impact. People will lose productive hours (and maybe days) around the water coolers complaining about the time and energy invested in the team-building or planning activities. Unhappiness, management criticism and employees complaining to and about each other sap energy, productivity and joy.

My cousin adds, 'Look, an event that's not followed up with meaningful activities in the workplace should not be held. They harm trust, motivation, employee morale and productivity. They don't solve the problems for which they were scheduled and held. This is particularly the case when a client says that he or she wants an activity or team-building something or other just to fill a vacant morning or afternoon. That's crazy. The event's objectives should rule content.'

A team-building expert from a management college says, 'You have to be careful. I facilitated a team-building and planning event recently in which a management team gathered to put together their annual priorities. The group did a good job; they were excited and felt a strong sense of direction. The next day, much to my disappointment and the team's lost morale, their manager pulled out a list of everything that had not made their priority list at the team-building event. He called this the "other" list and said that, even though these were not the priorities, they all had to be completed, too. Can you imagine the impact of telling them that all their work, thinking and prioritising really didn't matter?'

Team-building activities, properly thought-through, have the potential to get your client's delegates to adopt a strong sense of direction, workable plans and solutions, a powerful feeling of belonging with and on the team and clear, strategic customer-focused values. But they can achieve the exact opposite. Poorly planned and executed, created outside the context of the total organisation, team-building sessions can bring disillusionment, low morale and negative motivation. They can fail to deliver the results expected.

An ex-army major who has worked with several event companies and now grows acres and acres of tulips in Uganda says, 'There are a few main types of team-building ideas: communication exercises, problem-solving and decision-making exercises, adaptability and planning exercises, and exercises that focus on building trust. Despite what many clients think, the last isn't something that can occur through one afternoon's activity – trust takes time.

But, for corporate events, the idea is to perform various activities that are both fun and challenging – and that also build teamwork skills that can help improve employee performance and productivity at the office. Maybe. But I'm not sure. Entertainment you say? I really don't think so. Go carefully over those rocks now. I can see you have something of a limp.'

PLANNING ENTERTAINMENT

Planning entertainment for an event, be it a musical tour de force, a famous comedian, a circus act or a magician who can make a car appear from nowhere, can be frustrating and exhausting. The client wants one thing because their CEO wants it or because the client saw something at an event – totally, utterly different from this one – and it was terrific they say. Or the client can't make up its corporate mind despite the fact that you've made good recommendations that fit with the event's tone and message. You know that what the client wants won't work for the audience demographics. You've explained why. No difference. And then you spend days and weeks trying to cut a deal with an agent and ... well, so it goes, as Kurt Vonnegut asserted many times in the satire that is *Slaughterhouse-Five*. The number of decisions that you need to make in managing entertainment is only outstripped by the details you need to manage and, even if you have a team, much of the entertainment detail will be last minute and down to you.

Most types of events require some form of performance to amuse, engage, motivate and sometimes to give the attendees a boost or indeed a reward. Not only will entertainment allow your guests to enjoy themselves more fully, it can also make your event memorable and legacy memories are important in themselves, and also to reinforce messaging. Clearly, there will be some events like an AGM at which entertainment other than light background music might be inappropriate.

I talk quietly in a library to a director of studies at one of London's universities at which there is a burgeoning course in corporate communications. This lecturer has spent many years studying the effects of corporate event entertainment. 'There are many different types of event entertainment,' he says in a forced whisper. 'Your choice will largely depend on the type of event you're planning and, of course, your audience. One of the most popular types is live music. Few people dislike music, but choosing the right thing is hard. The key is selecting the right music for your attendees, not for your client. Like music, most people enjoy humour as long as it's matched properly to the audience and the event's main overall theme or purpose. Another option is to hire a mix of entertainers, but I've known events where the front rows of tables or seating are engaged, but the midway and rear sections of a room are totally disenfranchised – or drunk. So, the content and offering needs to be pitched absolutely right and must embrace and engage everyone.'

My cousin adds later over a beer, 'Planning entertainment is quite different from arranging a night out. People in the industry without much experience very often think it's the same. Propriety is the key word here. The last thing you need is for your show to be memorable for all the wrong reasons.'

GETTING SOME EXPERT HELP

If you're not sure of your ground, get some entertainment expertise – via an agency, agent or bureau. Having someone on your side (OK – for money, but still on your side) who's truly an expert in the multi-faceted world of corporate entertainment, is good practice. These experts understand that they can never know your client as well as do you, but they will take a good brief and will recommend what will work. Usually. You have to be a little careful that they don't simply recommend someone they want to place rather than someone who properly fits your brief and budget.

Whatever entertainment you do choose, it's important that you manage it with passion and enthusiasm, as this is bound to show through and must impress your client's attendees. The only limitation could be your budget and your imagination and, sometimes, your ability or your client's ability to take a risk.

ENTERTAINING ENTERTAINMENT

Entertainment is often part of the draw at events. If finding entertainment is on your to-do list as an event producer or project manager, you'll want to book the best and most relevant entertainment. Like much else, this is a very subjective area and you do need to know precisely what will appeal to the majority of the audience.

'The first step in booking entertainment for your event,' says an agent whose entertainers have worked the worldwide corporate circuit, 'is to consider message and proposition. What's the entertainment for? What does it have to do? Is it to allow people to relax, to let their collective hair down? Or is it to amuse and make them laugh? Or is it to help them focus? Will the entertainment entertain?' He now walks around his very large office twirling a set of keys. I get tired just watching pace and twirl.

He goes on and I have to confess that it's all good stuff. 'You could have murder mystery games or a big quiz. Corporate quizzes can be fully interactive with the use of wireless answering gadgets and giant projector screens with quiz rounds that are based more around fun than brain draining questions. Quizzes can be in the guise of TV game-shows but, as with anything, check that your not infringing copyright. Quizzes can also be a fun way of checking product knowledge. You can have Wii Olympics, sports demonstrations, sports personalities, live extracts from West End and Broadway shows – with the stars from those shows if you want, opera singers, percussionists who will get your audience drumming in harmony within minutes, dancers, aerobics instructors, real rock bands, tribute rock bands, Abba bands, singers from *X Factor*, singing waiters, *Stomp* style dancers, circus acts, *Cirque de Soleil* or similar acts, amazing magicians who can make a CEO disappear, close magic magicians who can make money appear, caricaturists, celebrity lookalikes … look I need to take this call. OK?' I stay for a while but the call is long and I feel like an interloper so I get up, wave in gratitude, he waves back apologetically and I leave.

My cousin says, 'The fashion at the moment is definitely activity involving cooking. Cookery is huge on television and for a corporate event it's ideal for mixed groups as it appeals to the broadest possible range of people. You need a good agent or bureau to help find the best act for your needs. You can get agencies that provide a complete service, supplying only the best and most established performers and services.' We're walking towards a theatre in the West End of London – to see the extraordinary Mark Rylance in the brilliant play *Jerusalem*. My cousin says, 'You can use illusionists and performers who combine magic, suggestion, psychology, misdirection and showmanship in order to seemingly predict and control human behaviour, as well as performing mind-bending feats of mentalism. You can get people to stun audiences.' Later we are part of a stunned audience. Rylance? Extraordinary and extraordinarily memorable. Entertainment and craft indeed.

CELEBRITIES

'You're a caution,' said the Peer of the Realm and we all smiled encouragingly. 'My son Bartholomew here,' he said with a rich, deep, baritone kind of voice, 'would be simply delighted to come along and shake hands with your people. Shall we say, ah, forty-five thousand?' That made our smiles vanish and his much wider. Bartholomew did nothing very much. Here we were at a stately home and, while the fee for the venue's usage was ridiculously low, the fee for a minor, minor royal was not. We were told in no uncertain terms that one could not be purchased without the other.

That was that and then was some years ago. Now, many celebrities – and they have to be pretty well known, from the worlds of TV, film, theatre, academia, business and politics – make a great deal of money from private bookings, speaking engagements, appearance fees and corporate performances. Many celebrities get paid just to show up at an event. Who can afford this luxury? You might be surprised. My cousin isn't. 'What kind of person buys a private performance from their favourite celebrity? Well, people who want an exceptional entertainment experience and where cost is no object, that's who. Business people, corporations, medical professionals, associations and even other celebrities and well-known personalities will buy A-list celebs for corporate events. OK, it doesn't happen at every event, but it happens. The twenty-first birthday party of a well-known retail store owner and you could be looking at a dozen or more top models and music stars and all that goes with these people – plus maybe a couple of very, very big names playing for a few hours. This is all about the experience rather than just an event and there's absolutely nothing wrong with that.'

My cousin flicks imagined fluff from a sleeve and then chooses Kalamarakia

Tursi (pickled squid) from the menu at the modest Greek restaurant. 'Of course,' he says, 'there are many reasons why people or companies would book a major celebrity to perform at one of their events and the reasons make sense. Large and medium-sized companies often want to book a national name or very big act for their annual conference for a number of reasons. Among them is to increase employee morale, raise turnover, boost productivity and increase overall loyalty to the company. When a company does this, the employees in turn feel like they are part of the family and are appreciated. That's the idea anyway and my experience has it that it works – but it does have to be the best celeb to fit with the company's ethic or style.' My cousin stops to address his squid and I my stifado (with rice and salad) to which I'm particularly partial. 'If the event is for customers,' says squid-satisfied relation, 'the entertainment provided by the presence of the big star serves to show how the company really appreciates the audience. So says the wisdom, but again my experience is that it works. Oh yes, it's key that the company book someone that *everyone* can enjoy. This can often be difficult, since everyone has different tastes. But there'll be a middle road demographic and that's where an entertainment company, bureau or agent can help you to narrow the choice. Are you going to eat all that?'

All celebrities have some sort of rider, or list of demands of things they believe they must have when making an appearance, performing or speaking. These usually include the typical things such as hotel accommodation, flights, dinners and other things you might expect, but the bigger the celebrity, the more demanding the rider might be. The celebrity will also most likely have an entourage of people who travel with them – personal assistants, bodyguards, friends, make-up artists and hairdressers. You will have to cover the cost of all this if these things are in the rider and little will be up for negotiation. One of the reasons celebs like corporate events is that they're not likely to be bombarded by the media.

SPONSORED AND DISCOUNTED CELEBS
Depending upon your event and your client, it might be possible to get sponsors to pay for various elements of the event. For example, if your client

is a retail business then it may be that some of their suppliers might be comfortable with the idea of sponsoring something – the gala dinner, menus, gifts, drinks or entertainment. This happens all the time with association conferences where the whole event is normally paid for by sponsorship.

Sponsorships are easier to obtain than one might expect – again of course depending on your event's objectives and purpose, but it will probably be down to you or your agency, or a specialist company, to create a sponsor package specific to the event's (and your client's) needs. Any sponsor will want to know that its money will equal relevant and quality exposure. Many event producers make the mistake of thinking that any company would consider sponsorship a privilege. Sponsorship is only very rarely a privilege. The sponsor will want a return and that return will undoubtedly relate to how many people the sponsor's brand can influence.

Paying for a celebrity might be a sponsorship opportunity – an appearance possibly at the awards gala dinner, or as a guest facilitator or at a special, surprise moment during the event. A bureau executive says, 'Contact the agent or talent company as early as possible. This can help in getting a discount because the entertainer/celeb can block off dates and not have to worry about filling them up later in the year. You may also want to ask if there is a discount if you book at certain times of the year. Also, try tying the event to a charity of the celebrity's choice or, if the celebrity already has a charity, offer to donate a certain amount to that charity. You could also find out if the celebrity is going to be in the area around the time the event is going on. Will he, she or they be on tour perhaps? It'll always be cheaper to get these people if they're already in the same city doing a show.'

CANCELLED CELEBS

Earlier on I commented on guest speakers cancelling. Cancellations and disappointments happen. You may have booked your favourite celebrity for your event and everything is set to go smoothly. However, at the last moment you find out that the celebrity is not going to show. Well, most celebrity contracts are structured in a way that favours the celebrity. The contracts have stipulations that give the celebrity the option to cancel your booking for a more favourable one or to refuse to perform if all requirements are not met. They do this to ensure that they are not missing any other opportunities when deciding to take on your engagement. So, it's imperative to work directly with an entertainment company, bureau or agency that knows how to negotiate the contracts and fees so that everyone's expectations are clear. Whatever the case, make sure you read the contracts thoroughly so that there are no surprises. If you have a legal department, take advice.

My bureau friend says, 'Why would celebs do corporates? Well, it's a lot less of a time commitment for them and therefore frees them up to take on other events. And there's a good chance that there'll be no media. If your event is a private one, then it could be a nice surprise for guests to meet and take pictures with their favorite celebrity. This is something the guests will talk about and remember for a long time. So, next time you want the star power of a celebrity, but perhaps don't want the enormous fees, consider an appearance or meet and greet, as they call it in Hollywood. Alternatively, at considerably less money, get a lookalike artist. Seriously, if the celeb doesn't have to speak and people don't have to be too close, then this may be an option. But don't use a lookalike if there is likely to be a backlash if the audience discover what you've done.'

THINKING ABOUT ENTERTAINMENT AND WHAT IT DOES

It isn't just the act or talent on stage or the high wire troupe that does it for audiences. There is also the atmosphere of occasion, perhaps the dressing up for a gala dinner or awards ceremony, the red carpet or the CEO talking, genuinely talking with interest, to people way down the ladder. Atmosphere of occasion is critical and, to create it, you will use the heady mix of table layouts, linen colours, lighting styles or effects, sound effects, props, music (both canned and live), the appearance of the space and ways to raise expectation or to create surprise. By now, you will know that you need around you some experts because *you* can't be an expert at everything. You can and must, of course, know about what lighting can do, what music to use and what it can achieve (and when), what set and staging devices work best (and when), but you will need a team, a part-time, freelance team undoubtedly, but still a team. Run that team well and you're more than half way there. However, the gut feel about how the event will work and the planning to make it good or better than good, lies with you. Always you. In any event, it's your job.

If you create the right atmosphere and setting for the inclusion of entertainment, whatever it is, then the audience will be onside (provided, I repeat, that what you have planned is fit for purpose, the audience's purpose, the event's purpose – and not yours or your client's). Having an audience onside is important for all parts of the event and that won't always be easy. A session may have something in it that's unpalatable or difficult to take on board. Something may have been said elsewhere about change which some will find hard to accept. A few (or indeed many) people might have felt disenfranchised by some aspect of a presentation. The entertainment can of course also disenfranchise, upset, annoy or bore. You know perfectly well that not everyone will like everything, and actually that's the way it is amongst viewers of cinema, theatre and TV, so don't beat yourself up. But the more you know about the audience, the better your judgements will be.

Your event may have some entertainment intermixed throughout the whole show, not just at the beginning or end or on the last evening. If that's the case, make sure that the entertainment is balanced and not only right for the audience, but right for the audience at *that particular time*. Mood is important. It may be inappropriate to have something that totally outshines anything else that happens in a day. Again make sure that the atmosphere and setting are right and, even if the entertainment after a presentation, say, is indeed a surprise, work hard, plan hard, and make that surprise work. If you create the right ambiance and atmosphere for any element of the event, no matter how small the entertainment or activity, people will feel that they are in a special place, no matter what the content. If that sounds a tad wishy-washy, it's actually not meant that way because it's perfectly true. If the audience is heavily engaged in a game-show type format led by a good TV presenter, people will become absorbed if the engagement and interaction are planned well. If that lookalike of David Beckham is presented in the right way with the right things happening round his entrance, as if he was the real thing, then it'll work and people will want to see him almost as much as the real thing. People will yell and shout praise for the Elvis up on stage because he's excellent, is wearing exactly the right garb, sounds exactly like him and because the ambiance is right, even though everyone knows that the real one is no longer singing *All Shook Up*. Even when everyone knows that the voiceover of a very famous actor, say Alan Rickman, Ian McKellen or someone from *Friends* or *EastEnders*, announces that 'dinner is served' is just that, a famous voiceover, people will be entranced and engaged that the famous voice is 'there' for them. The same goes for videos where the topflight and very famous leader of a business talks straight at the camera to the audience, as if he's in the room for them and as if they are the most important bunch of people that he's met for years. It's all about theatre and creating a show. It *is* a show and entertainment is the prime part of the show. Get the mix right, between the serious, the tough, the heady and the fun, the enjoyment that is spectacle, the humour or the music – and the whole smorgasbord of the event, all of it, will gel. It will. Most of all, *most of all*, the event and its content and message will be remembered long after the last balloon has popped and the last delegate has opened their own front door again.

CHAPTER 14
IT'S A WRAP

I could have done with a book like this one when I started out in the industry. Arrogant? No, I'm not at all, but there were very few back then who knew things that event specialists now take for granted. Few people could advise about venues, cities, countries, production techniques, content, delivery and so on. There were few who could offer insights. It was a burgeoning, new industry and I suppose that more than half the excitement and challenge was because of just that and making ideas come to life. Spectacle was still in its infancy; people were coming into the industry from the theatre, from design, from rock and roll to give fresh air to corporate shows. What I learned in the early days was that these individuals had great insights to impart, stories to tell, scenarios to relate – all helping to make people like me more adventurous and a bit daring.

During the course of my career I've learned extraordinary facts and theories from experts of all kinds telling me (and thousands of others) things I didn't know. One I keep recalling, and on which I've dined out many a time, is the fact that it takes seven million jasmine flowers to produce a kilogram of the concentrate used for scents. Other details that I've noted during my time standing/sitting at the back of an auditorium, wondering what the insurance risk would be if the lighting rig ever fell down, include the interesting fact that the word 'queue' is the only word in the English language that is still pronounced the same way when the last four letters are removed. 'Almost' is the longest word in the English language with all the letters in alphabetical order. 'Rhythm' is the longest English word without a vowel. In 1386, a pig in France was executed by public hanging for the murder of a child. Horatio Nelson was never able to find a cure for his sea-sickness. One quarter of the bones in your body are in your feet. The present world population of around six billion people is predicted to become 15 billion by 2080. Coca-Cola would be green if colouring weren't added to it. The average lead pencil will draw a line 35 miles long. I remember argued theories, fabulous and stimulating debates, world politicians giving some amazing speeches (and some dreadful ones), audiences being persuaded the business equivalent that white is black, audiences in floods of tears, people beside themselves with laughter, some audiences terribly offended, other audiences clamouring for more, audiences amazed and slack-mouthed with wonder, audiences asleep, audiences drunk with alcohol, power, happiness, audiences ready to walk out, audiences that did walk out, audiences that cursed me and one guy who spat at our guest speaker, another who hit a famous professor only to find himself floored when the professor karate-chopped him to huge applause, one who ran out of the room screaming, and people who just nodded, smiled and said thank you.

I remember two world-renowned politicians finishing each other's sentences. I remember the world famous movie actress whose beauty was and is fabulous. I recall artistes who were simply extraordinary, their craft astounding, I remember the voice-overs on films and videos of famous actors and actresses who would make a simple, single line live. I remember road shows, AGMs, EGMs where people threatened violence, management conferences where people were told that they'd more or less lost their jobs, the sales conference where someone received the keys to a brand new Rolls Royce (which then appeared on stage), another sales conference where a winner and his partner were given a holiday cottage to keep for ever, the management conference where a huge amount of money was raised for a charity and where the whole room stood for a fifteen minute ovation as the cheque was handed over to a child, the honouring of deserving and occasionally non-deserving sportsmen and sportswomen, the footballer who deliberately kicked the ball signed by a national team to a person who was having an operation the next day, the person who was meant to give a keynote speech but who forgot every word, threw down his notes and just stood and wept then gave a brilliant, brilliant twenty minute presentation from the heart, the famous politician who couldn't go on but then did, the car that wouldn't reveal itself, the revolve that didn't work, the lights that failed at the wrong moment, the fireworks that took five seconds to kick in on New Year's eve in front of a televisual audience of millions, the star who only arrived with a nanosecond to spare and the shows that worked beautifully, that made organisations change and that made people think differently.

Most of all, I remember loving events and trying new things, and honing things that I've tried before. Sounds trite but it's true. I have huge respect for the good technicians and designers, for the amazing writers and creative directors in our industry. I get frustrated by those who are bad. I admire those who can transform rooms and create atmospheres that are perfect. I admire those who take an idea and run with it, and make it better. Clients have been the opportunity givers and I won't have a wrong word said about any of them.

Event management and delivery is linked to everything else a client wants to do or achieve in the name of communications. I hope that this book has given you food for thought in how communications can work better, tighter, livelier and how everyone can enjoy the process. When I meet people who delight in communications and events the sun shines. Honestly. It's such a refreshing industry in which to work and, really, while some things are hard, the results are rewarding. Ultimately, what's important is that the attendees (the consumers, the delegates) have a positive experience that leaves them feeling good about something, or leaves them understanding something better, or leaves them having learned a new something. That's your job really – to make these things happen. To make people laugh, cry, be better informed, engaged, entertained, and so on. That's the job and I like it. So, I think, do you.

Event management and delivery in the corporate world is a career that offers excitement and, sometimes, a degree of glamour in return for hard work, a large amount of energy, flexibility, and a very high level of organisational skills. To succeed you need to be good at managing people and getting the best from them. You need to be patient and yet decisive, firm and yet fair.

You need to have imagination and you need to be able to understand client needs and cultures.

Above all, you must be a hard worker, who is prepared to put in extra hours to ensure that the job and all the component parts get delivered within budget and on time. This work requires perfection, so you must be willing to pay attention to every detail. You also need to be capable of handling last minute problems despite all of your superb preparation, co-ordination and arrangements.

You can't be shy and retiring in the management of corporate events and neither can you be arrogant. You will in your time need to step up to the plate and manage difficult clients and clients who rightly expect the best. You will need to talk to famous personalities and their agents and a vast number of professionals who will know a great deal about their skill area but who will expect to be guided and led by you. You will need to be creative and explain ideas. You will need to sell your idea to your clients. You will need to be a superb listener. Good networking skills, client management, business analytics, time management, ability to take on challenges, problem-solving skills and adjusting to rapidly changing situations are some other qualities essential for this role, but I reckon that the ability to (really) listen and to (properly) understand are the most important requirements.

I hope that these insights and points of view about an exciting, growing and vibrant industry have been helpful. The idea was to give you a taste of how the industry works and some of the factors that I think are very important, interesting and fun. Producing an event is time-consuming and testing. It's hard and it requires nerves of steel and a great sense of humour. It requires the interpersonal skills of a diplomat and the organisational abilities of, well, a superb producer or project manager – and the best ones are exciting people to be around. I wouldn't have missed meeting any of the ones I now know. Maybe you're one of them. Or maybe you will be. I hope so.

Charlotte Brontë (1816–1855), wrote, 'Life is so constructed, that the event does not, cannot, will not, match the expectation.' In the context of corporate events I like to think that she was wrong. Believe that please. It's important.

I'm also reminded of what my son, Ben, wrote about his eight-year-old experience of witnessing the set up and rehearsals of a big corporate event. He wrote that it was 'full of glittering potential.' And he was right because all corporate events *are* full of glittering potential. It's down to you to make that potential become a reality.

GUILDFORD **college**

Learning Resource Centre

Please return on or before the last date shown.

N̴ newals if any items are overdue.